PREPARE FOR REVIVAL!

PREPARE
FOR
REVIVAL!

Richard Sipley

Guardian
B O O K S

Belleville, Ontario, Canada

PREPARE FOR REVIVAL!

Copyright © 2002, Richard Sipley

ISBN: 1-55306-336-8

Guardian Books is an imprint of *Essence Publishing,* a Christian Book Publisher dedicated to furthering the work of Christ through the written word. For more information, contact:

44 Moira Street West, Belleville, Ontario, Canada K8P 1S3.
Phone: 1-800-238-6376. Fax: (613) 962-3055.
E-mail: info@essencegroup.com
Internet: www.essencegroup.com

Printed in Canada
by

Guardian
B O O K S

F 502 71898

Table of Contents

Preface

Why write a book on revival? First, because I am convinced that revival is the only thorough answer to our North American dilemma. Second, because I, like Elihu, a friend of Job, am full of matter and will burst if I do not speak (Job 32:18–20)! How can I know what I know and be silent? The Western Church is wallowing around in cultural adaptation, ear- tickling entertainment, pop psychology and a philosophy of sinner appeasement, trying to attract the ungodly into their midst. The result is an epidemic of broken pastors and disillusioned church members. All we need to heal us is the manifest presence of God! Like the vision of the Temple in the Book of Ezekiel, the glory has departed. Our answer has been to call more committee meetings, rather than prayer meetings, and to bring worldly filth into the Temple, rather than cleansing it!

We have said we are rich and have need of nothing, and do not know that we are wretched, miserable, poor, blind and naked (Rev. 3:17). Daily our society becomes more alienated from God, more degraded morally, and more filled with violence. We are on a collision course with the judgement of Almighty God. Hell has enlarged itself without measure to receive the lost about us, and the Church seems impotent to lift one finger to change it.

Meanwhile, where is the Lord God of Elijah? His arm is not shortened that He cannot save—neither is His ear heavy that He cannot hear, but our sins have separated between us and our God that He will not hear! What shall we do? I cannot give you three easy steps to revival. Only the sovereign God can bring revival! Nevertheless, I can tell you what the Word of God says on the subject, and what other believers before us have done to set the stage spiritually for God to work in revival power. We must come to believe in the necessity and possibility of revival, and then take the steps necessary to *Prepare For Revival*. If we do these things, we are encouraged by God to expect that He will do what only He can do, and pour out His Holy Spirit upon us in great revival power.

That is what this book is about. First, to encourage us to believe in revival for our day. Second, to help us understand the steps we must take to obey God in this matter. These are steps toward revival. If your heart is hungry for God—read on!

—Richard Sipley

BELIEVING
IN
REVIVAL

CHAPTER ONE

My Personal Journey

When the Lord turned again the captivity ofZion,
we were like them that dream.
Then was our mouth filled with laughter,
and our tongue with singing: then said they
among the heathen, The LORD hath done great things for them.
The LORD hath done great things for us; whereof we are glad.
Turn again our captivity O LORD as streams in the south.
They that sow in tears shall reap in joy.
He that goeth forth and weepeth, bearing precious seed,
shall doubtless come again with rejoicing,
bringing his sheaths with him.

~ Psalm 126, KJV

I will never forget how, as a young teen, I first became interested in revival. It happened on a Wednesday night, in a church where my father was the pastor. That evening was destined to mark my life.

I was a Christian, raised in a family where we all went to prayer meeting. Our home was right across the street from the church. About five minutes before time to start, I came out the front door of our house and started across the street toward the church. That was when I noticed something very strange. The church parking lot, and every street around the church, was filled with cars. I am sure you will believe me when I say that this was very, very unusual for prayer meeting night! Full of wonder, I went inside. There, I received my second surprise. The church was packed! This was obviously no normal prayer meeting crowd. I managed to find a seat at the back, and waited with mounting excitement to see what would happen next.

We sang a few gospel songs, had a word of prayer, and then my father introduced a man I had never heard of, by the name of Armin Gesswein. My father said that Mr. Gesswein had just returned from the revival in Norway, that he and his family were going to make their home in our community, and that he had agreed to speak at our prayer meeting.

As Mr. Gesswein came forward, there was a deep silence in the church. The air seemed charged with some kind of electric current. He did not go to the pulpit, but stood at the front with one foot resting on the first pew. He did not preach, but started talking in a quiet voice. As far as I could tell, this man did not know how to act in church—he was doing everything wrong. I do not remember what he said. I believe he told us about what God had been doing in Norway. All I know is that the impact on that crowd was tremendous, as if God had walked into that room and laid bare the hearts of everyone present! Soon, people throughout the room were weeping and praying. They began going to each other, confessing sin, asking forgiveness and praising God. Two men at the front, who I knew had been bitter enemies, stood with their arms around each other. What a night! The place was full of the glory of God! As a teenage boy, I sat and wept in God's holy presence. That night, there was born in me a hunger for revival that has never left.

What was it about that meeting that had such a profound effect on me? I believe it was the unusual sense of God's presence, and the unusual demonstration of His love, grace, and power. I had a tiny glimpse of the glory of God that left me yearning for more. Something is so utterly appealing about God's manifest presence that it draws the human heart as nothing else in the universe can.

By the time I was eighteen, I was in Bible College. I was twenty-one when I accepted my first position, as pastor of a small church in New Hampshire. While there, I married my lovely friend, Anita Ragland, and changed her name to mine. The years went by quickly, with congregations and responsibilities increasing in size. Throughout those years, we saw God work and manifest His presence and power in many ways. The year of 1968 found us moving to the Brown Street Alliance Church, an old church with a great history and fine reputation, in Akron, Ohio. God blessed the ministry there, the congregation grew, and the church was soon looking for ways to expand. In 1969, the church celebrated its seventy-fifth anniversary. Then came 1971—the year of the Canadian Revival! But wait, I am getting ahead of my story.

During those twenty-three years of ministry, I had never lost my interest in revival. Indeed, that interest had increased with the years. My library, by this time, contained many books on the subject which I had read with great hunger. I had often preached about revival, and even fasted and prayed, made restitution, and did what I could to try to bring it about. I made many mistakes, but God knew my desire was real, and He often blessed my efforts in spite of my ignorance. Nevertheless, I knew that what was happening in my ministry was a drop in the bucket by comparison to the need in the world around me. Other ministries, no matter how large or successful, all failed to keep pace with the growing godlessness of the masses. It seemed increasingly clear to me that the only answer to the needs of Western society was a great revival, of proportions I had read about from history.

I was senior pastor of a fine church, where conversions were a regular occurrence, missionary giving was high, church growth was pushing us into a building program, and the people loved and supported us. In spite of all that, I still prayed that God would allow me to be part of a true revival which would manifest His presence and demonstrate His power. I had heard about the revival at Asbury College, and wished I had been there. At that time, the news began to filter down into the States a powerful moving of God in Saskatoon, Saskatchewan, on the prairies of western Canada. My heart leaped within me! What should I do?

My first reaction was simple. I would fly up there, get in the middle of the revival, and see what God would do. God had other plans.

The more I attempted to make plans to go, the more difficult it became. I was blocked at every turn by church and family responsibilities. Then I heard that the seven-week crusade in Saskatoon had ended, and I had to set that plan aside. By this time, however, greatly excited by the thought of revival, I began to pray and preach about it with renewed vigor.

The beginning of that year, the Christian and Missionary Alliance planned an Evangelism Conference, for all of the United States and Canada, to be held in Chicago. I had registered and made all necessary plans to go. It was to run from Thursday evening through Saturday noon. I arrived Thursday afternoon, checked into my hotel, had supper, and went to the opening rally without any great enthusiasm. You may wonder at that, but the reason was two-fold. First, our church was already engaged in a strong evangelism program, with regular conversions. Second, and most important, my heart and mind were so filled with hunger for revival, that I could think of little else.

The service began, with about three thousand pastors and church leaders in the congregation. Following normal preliminaries, the chairman announced that two couples from the revival under way in Canada were present to share with us. One of those couples was Reverend and Mrs. Orthner. He was a District Superintendent from the part of Canada where the Canadian Revival had begun.

Mrs. Orthner came to the pulpit first. As soon as I saw her face and heard her voice, my heart leaped within me. I said to myself, "That's it! That is what I want!" Tears were running down my face. When it was Mr. Orthner's turn, he said, "For the first time in my life, I can say I really *know* I am filled with the Holy Spirit!" I looked around me and saw others weeping. Some had their heads bowed, while their bodies shook with deep sobs. Soon, the entire auditorium had become a prayer room. Everywhere, people were engaged in prayer, confessions, restitution and reconciliation. God had entered the room, and our hearts were filled with His glory.

Whatever else had been planned for that service never took place. I found myself crying and laughing all together. God began a new work in my life—forever spoiling me for "church as usual." The next day, the Evangelism Conference proceeded as planned, but I think all of our hearts were somewhat preoccupied with the glory still shining within.

I arrived home from the conference on Saturday evening. The next morning, I shared with our congregation what had happened at the Thursday evening service, along with some of the things I had heard about the Canadian Revival. I invited people to come forward if their hearts were hungry. I must have brought some of the glory with me, for they responded immediately, filling the altar area and the front of the church. I believe Ralph Sutera is right when he says, "The fame of revival spreads the flame of revival." There was a wonderful time of praying, weeping and confessing, but somehow I knew this was not what I was praying for.

A few weeks later, Rev. Orthner was in the area and agreed to speak in our Sunday morning service. The church was full. Anticipation was running high. Nevertheless, when I gave an invitation, nothing happened. Not a person moved! I dismissed the meeting with a heavy heart, and went home to dinner. We had Mr. Orthner at our home for the noon meal. I poured out my disappointment to him. He just smiled, and said quietly, "Let God be God." I could not have imagined what God had in store for us the following week.

It was Monday evening, and our assistant pastor was in his office counseling a young couple in the church. Mary had many problems, which were reflected in their marriage, and sometimes in bizarre behaviour on her part. Late in the session, the pastor asked, "Do you remember a time in your life when you personally invited Jesus Christ to come into your life and be your Saviour?" Mary had grown up in an evangelical Christian home, professed to be a Christian, and was involved in Christian ministries in our church. Mary thought for a minute and replied, "No, not really." As pastor Keith waited for Mary's answer, the Holy Spirit said to him, "And what about you?" As Keith proceeded to lead Mary to Christ, the Holy Spirit challenged him with every word he said to her. He did not know what to say to God. Keith had grown up in a good Christian home, graduated from

Nyack College, spent one year as an assistant pastor in another church, graduated from Conservative Baptist Theological Seminary in Denver, and served with us for two years. All this time, he sincerely thought of himself as a born-again Christian. For his conversion, Keith pointed back to a time when, as a five-year-old, he had attended a Good News Club and responded to an invitation. A large group of children had been prayed with together, but in the white light of the Holy Spirit, Keith knew he had never truly received Christ. He said nothing about this to Mary or her husband, but went home to spend a sleepless night as God dealt with him. About ten o'clock that night, rejoicing in her new-found salvation, Mary phoned me.

Tuesday morning about ten, my secretary said, "Pastor, Keith would like to see you, if you have time." I agreed. Keith came into my office, sat down and said, "Pastor, I know this is going to shock you, but I don't think *I'm* saved!" I will admit I was a little surprised. But shocked? No. Finally, God was beginning to move among us in unusual, supernatural power. Much more was yet to come. We knelt together, and with many tears, my assistant pastor received Jesus Christ as his personal Saviour and Lord.

Late Wednesday afternoon, there came a knock on my office door. When I said, "Come in," a woman entered whom I did not know. She sat down and burst into tears. When she finally could control herself, she said that I probably did not remember her, but that I had visited her home about a year ago with a church visitation team, and had presented the gospel to her and her husband, who was an alcoholic. She confessed that neither of them had been interested at the time. She told me how she had later left her husband, because of his drinking problem, and had gone to live with her parents in West Virginia. Then she amazed me by saying, "This morning God awakened me at five o'clock and told me to go back to Akron, Ohio, and to come and see you and get saved!" She asked her sixteen-year-old son to drive for her. They had been travelling all day, and had just arrived before she knocked on my office door. I explained the gospel to her, she prayed to receive Christ, and went on her way rejoicing.

That evening, at our midweek prayer service, a young woman suddenly rose to her feet and began to confess her sins. She wept, prayed, and sat down again. God was powerfully at work, I knew, but I was not as certain about how to make room for the Holy Spirit. Keith shared his recent experience with the Youth Group, and three teens gave their hearts to the Lord.

By the time the Sunday morning service got started, the church was full and the atmosphere was alive with expectancy. I asked Keith if he would like to share with the congregation what had happened in his life. He was anxious to do so. While he talked, the church was intensely quiet. When he finished, I invited Mary to come and also tell us about her recent conversion. This she gladly did. At this point, there had been no preaching. When Mary was through, I said quietly, "Is there anyone else who would like to share?" At that moment, it seemed as if God entered our sanctuary! "But," you say, "God was already there, for God is everywhere." Yes, you are right. But this was different. God is not manifested the same everywhere. That place was *full* of God! His holiness, His love, His power, and His grace were all around us, flowing through us in a way that cannot be explained.

Immediately, a young woman stood up in the congregation, weeping, and began to pray, confessing her sins publicly, asking God's forgiveness, surrendering her life to Him, and finally rejoicing in God's grace. As she sat down, someone else stood up and began to do exactly the same kind of thing. Then, another person followed that one, and another after that, in a seemingly endless stream. Within minutes, the entire church was filled with quiet weeping and a soft murmur of prayer.

When a young man came walking swiftly down the center aisle, and fell on his knees at the altar, sobbing. I asked if anyone else would like to come. Immediately, the whole front of the church filled with weeping, praying people. Soon, the platform was filled—then, the prayer room and the front pews. I did not know what to do, so I did nothing. I stood there, basking in God's glory, laughing and crying all together. God was completely in control of what was happening.

After about an hour had gone by, someone came to the pulpit where I was standing, and requested permission to share with the congregation what God was doing in their life. I agreed. Quickly, a line formed, and the testimonies began. It was a most unusual scene! People were weeping, praying and confessing all over the sanctuary. At the same time, people were standing at the pulpit, sharing with us what God was doing. Yet, all was orderly. Finally, close to one-thirty, I interrupted what was happening and dismissed the service. I would not do that today, but then I did not know any better. I suggested we all spend the afternoon in heart-searching and prayer, and come back for the evening service.

In the middle of the afternoon, I received a telephone call from a member of a neighbouring church who had heard we had experienced some revival that morning. Would I come to their church that night, the caller asked, and share with them? Their service began one hour before ours, so I agreed. I told them what had happened to us, and gave an invitation. People started to come forward in large numbers, weeping and praying. I left them at that point, returning to my own church for our evening service. We sang a few songs and had an opening prayer. Then I asked if anyone would like to share. Instantly, the morning service continued as if it had never been interrupted. How kind God is to our ignorance! That day saw a number of miracles. One of our godly women said, "I have seen God do more in this one day, than in the whole last nine years put together." This revival continued throughout the next two weeks and the following two Sundays, with only a slow abatement of its intensity. I am confident that over ninety percent of our congregation met God in some special way during that time.

One of those was Pat Jarrett. Pat, a young man in our congregation, had a wife and two children, a good job, a new home, and a hot temper. Pat had attended Nyack College in order to play basketball. He lacked twenty hours of graduating. He was deeply involved in athletic activities, and had developed a severe and painful case of arthritis in most of the major joints of his body. Pat had sat in my congregation for four years, taking careful notes of all my sermons on 4" x 6" file cards, but Pat was not truly born again. On the Sunday morning that revival came to Brown Street, Pat came hurrying down the side aisle, rushed into the prayer room, and was soundly converted. The following Sunday morning, we had a communion service. In that church, we used the entire time for the communion service. The revival was still in full progress, with people meeting God no matter what form of service was used. As we prepared to partake of the broken bread together, I invited those who wished to trust God for the healing of their bodies to stand, and remain standing, while we prayed together. Pat stood. He said, later, that as I began to pray, it felt like a warm liquid began flowing at the top of his head and went down through his entire body, going out at his feet. God instantly healed every joint and bone in his body. More than twenty-five years have passed, and he has never suffered with that problem since.

Pat was saved and healed, but God was not finished. On the third Sunday morning of the revival, God spoke to Pat again, and he found himself at the altar of the church, struggling with the call of God to professional Christian ministry. As we talked and prayed together, he gave everything to God; wife, family, job and new house. Today, Pat Jarrett is an ordained minister of the Christian and Missionary Alliance.

Report of what happened at Brown Street Church generated hunger in the hearts of other Christians. The experience of God's presence and His working in our midst also made the people of our church hungry for more. I shared with the Akron Evangelical Minister's Association what God had done among us. Some of these good men of God became interested in the idea of bringing the Sutera Brothers to Akron for a United Crusade. The Brown Street Baptist Church was located about five blocks from our church. They became leaders with us in planning for a Sutera Crusade. Enthusiasm kept increasing, until by the time the crusade was launched, there were sixteen churches cooperating. The Baptist church building and ours were about the same size. The question arose as to where we would hold the meetings. Our church board decided they could be held in the Baptist church building if they wanted them there. When I reported that to the Baptist pastor, he laughed with joy, and replied that his board had just voted that the meetings could be in the Alliance church building. He said, "The revival has already started!" I heartily agreed.

The Suteras gave us a date in 1974, but with the understanding that the date would need to be flexible, due to the fact that many of their crusades were being extended beyond the times planned. We agreed to that. We printed handbills, organized prayer meetings, and began to preach and pray to get our people ready for God to visit us. God moved in power in the crusade before ours, and a three-week meeting was extended to five weeks. We threw all our handbills in the trash, and printed some new ones with our hearts full of excitement.

As we approached the time for the meetings, and more churches became involved, we realized that neither of our churches would be large enough for the crowds. We obtained the use of a church building twice the size of ours. Then, as the excitement increased, we reserved another back-up church building twice the size of *that* one. It was good we did—the opening night of the crusade, the church sanctuary was packed to suffocation, with people standing around the back.

What a night that was! Old Dr. Brock, who wrote, "Beyond The Sunset," was the song leader. After a short time of singing, Ralph introduced two couples from another city who had experienced changed lives in one of their crusades. They gave their testimonies. Then Ralph said, "I believe there are many people here tonight who are ready to meet God now. There is no reason they should have to wait. If you want to meet God, just get up out of your seat and go to the prayer room now." Immediately, sixty people went to the prayer room! I went also to act as a counselor, and was thrilled to see the room full of broken people. Everywhere, they were weeping and seeking God. The sense of God's presence was intense. His glory filled the room. While we prayed with these people, the service continued in the sanctuary.

By the time we were finished, a second invitation had been given, and about fifty more people came for prayer. That first night, there was a great afterglow meeting, led by Henry and Freida Teichrob, who were traveling with the Suteras at that time. We used that building three nights, and then held the rest of the three-week crusade in the larger building.

Those were wonderful days and nights! At that time, there was a saying among those working in the prayer room, that "it is like heaven working with the Suteras, because there is no night there." It was true. Many times, we finally went to bed in the early hours of the morning. Nevertheless, God sustained us. Many blessings followed the crusade. One of the most striking was the increase in giving. Within two weeks, after the close of the meetings, both our church and the Brown Street Baptist church registered a forty-percent increase in regular church offerings. There was a new atmosphere at board meetings, due to the fact that every member of our board had been on their knees in the prayer room doing personal business with God.

As the meetings came to a close, I realized that it would be very important for me to do some careful follow-up teaching from the pulpit, so that our congregation would know how to apply their new steps with God in their daily lives. These sermons were eagerly received by our people. Soon afterward, the Canadian Revival Fellowship began to sell these sermons on cassette tapes. It wasn't long before I was invited to preach these same sermons in some of the weekend Family Conferences sponsored by the Canadian Revival Fellowship. Most of the people who attended these conferences had been in revival crusades somewhere, and were hungry for instruction on how to live this new, Spirit-filled life. On the Suteras' recommendation, I began to be invited to come in after their crusades, and do follow-up preaching. Soon, I was doing this after most of their crusades. I was a regular speaker at the Flames of Freedom Rally in Rives Junction, Michigan, for six consecutive years. During this time, I was still a busy pastor of a growing church in Akron, Ohio. These were wonderful, busy years.

The Canadian Revival Fellowship Office was located in Regina, Saskatchewan, Canada. Every year, the Fellowship sponsored a weekend rally in Regina, at the Hillsdale Alliance Church, which had experienced a powerful revival in 1971 through the Sutera ministry. In 1975, I was invited to be the main speaker at this rally. It was a great weekend, with a blizzard, a packed church, and the blessing of God. Two years later, when their pastor left, I was invited to come as pastor of the Hillsdale Alliance Church. Thus began almost fifteen years of exciting ministry.

During that time, God allowed me the privilege of seeing a church grow from 450 to 1,000. From a staff of two, we built a pastoral team of eight. This great missionary church sent me to preach on nine of our mission fields, and gave me the freedom to preach in many conferences, crusades and retreats across Canada and the United States. I became a Board Member of the Canadian Revival Fellowship, and continued being involved in revival ministries of all kinds. During those years, I saw God work in wonderful power and grace, both in the church of which I was pastor, and in other places. At the same time, I was well aware that the world around me was deteriorating rapidly.

In both the United States and Canada, the culture was shifting away from Christian values to a pagan, amoral view of life. In education, business, and government, North America was turning away from the God of the Bible. The revival I had experienced was for the most part limited to the people of God. It had not spilled over into the world in any significant way. Many fine Christians, in and out of government, were taking strong places of leadership in movements for reform. I myself spoke out boldly, in the pulpit and on radio talk shows, against the immoral drift of our society.

I have agreed with and supported all honest efforts to stem the tide of wickedness. Nevertheless, in my heart I know that these efforts—no matter how good and right—are not in themselves the answer. All the facts of history and the truth of Scripture tell us that reform does not bring revival—on the contrary, it is revival that always brings about true reform. Jesus said, "Make a tree good and its fruit will be good" (Matt. 12:33). I have become absolutely convinced that the only hope for North America is the true conversion of millions of people at the grassroots of our society. I am further convinced that church ministries as we know them today will not bring this about. I believe in those ministries, and have participated in them most of my life. They are right. They are biblical. They must be continued. But they are not enough! North America must experience a widespread revival like the great revivals of history! Nothing else will suffice. What shall we do? That is what this book is all about. I believe God gave us the church revivals of the last twenty-five years to teach us, and to get us ready for the great revival He now wants to bring. And that brings me to this point in my personal journey.

Recently, God began to speak to me about a radical change in my life. He made it clear that it was time for me to stop being a full-time pastor and give myself to His Church at large. As I have travelled, preached and listened, my heart has become increasingly burdened with the conviction that revival is the only answer.

How can that happen? Is it simply a matter of God's sovereignty in such a way that we can do nothing to produce it? I don't think so. I am convinced, with Charles Finney, that God has committed Himself to His children with promises that cannot fail. They are there to encourage us to "trust and obey." The laws by which God governs the physical world do not prevent His sovereignty, and yet, they are reliable and effective. Surely the laws by which God governs the spiritual world are every bit as reliable, and do not prevent His sovereignty. It is true that revival is a work of God. That is why the prophet prays, "Will YOU not revive us again, that your people may rejoice in YOU?" (Ps. 85:6). Nevertheless, there are things we can do besides praying, which will make it possible for God to do what He surely wants to do in bringing revival to His people, and salvation to the lost masses for whom Christ died.

What, then, shall we do? That is the purpose of this book: to set forth a series of steps that can be taken by an individual or group, that will move them toward that position before God, where He will pour out His Holy Spirit upon them in genuine revival. By putting these steps in a book, it is my hope that many individuals and groups will sincerely take these steps. If that should happen, and the fire should light other fires, then indeed, we could see in our day the great revival that is needed to advance the Kingdom of God, and save North America from judgment and destruction.

The steps in this book are steps *toward* personal and corporate revival. They are steps God will help us to take, if we are serious about seeking Him. The revival may come quietly and slowly, like new life in the springtime, or it may come as a rushing, mighty wind. That is not our responsibility. That is God's work, and must be left to His sovereign wisdom, love and power. Our responsibility is to begin taking the steps ordained by God for our part. As we go on, step by step, we will arrive at the experience of a revived life, Church or nation, to the glory of God and the change of our world.

Now, let us consider the steps which God has ordained, and which will naturally tend to bring about the conditions in which God is likely to revive a person, group or work. But before we do that, I believe it is important to do something else. We need to lay a firm foundation upon which to take these steps. The person or group entering this process needs to be convinced and inspired for the sometimes painful journey that lies before them. In order to do this, I will appeal to Scripture, Christian doctrine, history and testimony. I have already shared with you my own testimony. Let us turn, now, to the infallible Word of God.

CHAPTER TWO

The Foundation of Scripture

Revival! What does it mean? A friend of mine told me that a certain church was going to have a revival the following week, beginning on Sunday. I asked, "Can you guarantee it?" Of course, he did not mean what he said. He meant that this church was going to conduct a series of special meetings. They hoped some Christians would make a new step with God, and some non-Christians would be converted. If a *true* revival was to take place during that meeting, it would have surprised everyone. Such a glorious happening was most unlikely.

The word "revival" has been so misused that, in some areas of North America, it is almost impossible to explain it in a way that the listener would understand. In the southern United States, when I was a pastor there, almost every series of special meetings held in churches was called a revival. These meetings were, for the most part, soul-winning crusades. Their number-one purpose was the conversion of unbelievers. Though these attempts were commendable, they were *not* revivals. They did not begin with revival, nor did they produce a true revival. The advertisements for these meetings would read as follows: "REVIVAL—MARCH 1–10, Every Night At 7:30." If revival is a work of God—and it is—it is ridiculous to think that any human organization could schedule God's working to certain dates and times that are convenient. Of course, that is impossible!

Psalm 71:20 says, "You who have shown me many troubles and distresses will *revive* me again" (NASB). In Psalm 85:6, the writer prays for God to restore His people, and he says, "Will You not Yourself *revive* us again, that Your people may rejoice in You?" (NASB). In Habakkuk 3:2, the writer prays for the work of God in these words:

> LORD, I have heard the report about You, and I fear. O LORD, **revive** Your work in the midst of the years, In the midst of the years make it known; in wrath remember mercy (NASB).

In the first prayer, the writer prays about God reviving him personally. In the second prayer, he prays about God reviving His people corporately. In the third passage, he prays about God reviving His work in general. But in all three cases, the divinely-inspired writer prays for God to do the work of revival. Revival **is** a work of God— not a series of special meetings designed by man. On the other hand, as God's conditions are met, He may indeed decide to move in mighty revival power in the midst of a series of meetings designed by humble, obedient Christians for that very purpose. However, we must not confuse the meetings with the revival.

There is something for man to do, and there is something man cannot do. The purpose of this book is to help hungry-hearted Christians understand this matter, so they will do what they can do. Then God will surely do what only He can do—and we may experience the greatest revival yet seen in human history.

But again we ask, what does the word "revival" mean? To get a truly Christian definition, we must turn to the Scriptures for an answer. The actual word is used only twice in most translations of the New Testament, in Romans 7:9 and 14:9. In both cases, the very obvious meaning is "for something dead to become alive." In the KJV Old Testament, some form of the word "revive" or "revival" is found fourteen times. In each case, it comes from a root word pronounced "khaw-yah," which *Strong's Notes* defines as follows: "The word means to live, have life, remain alive, sustain life, live prosperously, live forever, be quickened, be alive, be restored to life or health." The word translated as "quicken" in the KJV comes from exactly the same word in the Old Testament, and is translated "revive" in the New American Standard translation. This word appears twelve times in the Old Testament and once in the New Testament, where it clearly means to give life or bring to life a physical body. REVIVAL IS NEW LIFE!

What kind of life is God talking about? In John 10:10, Jesus said, "I came that they may have life and have it abundantly." In John 14:6, Jesus said, "I AM ... THE LIFE." Again, in I John 1:2, we read, "The life was manifested, and we have seen and testify and proclaim" it. In the same Book, in chapter 5, verse 12, God says, "He who has the Son has the life; he who does not have the Son of God does not have the life."

From these and many other Scriptures, we conclude that revival, in the biblical sense, is a renewal of the life of God—or, more accurately, a new or fuller manifestation of the presence of God Himself in a life, a church, a city or a nation. Dr. Albert B. Simpson put it this way:

> *"Once it was the blessing, now it is the LORD.*
> *Once it was the feeling, now it is HIS word.*
> *Once the gift I wanted, now the GIVER own.*
> *Once I sought for healing, now HIMSELF alone."*

- **In the biblical sense, a revival is a new or fuller manifestation of the presence of God Himself in a life, a church, a city, or a nation.**

- **But how shall we know, in practical terms, if such a revival has taken place?**

- When the manifestation of the life of God is adequately expressed in the renewal of a person or a group, God will be glorified, and God's people will be restored to biblical standards of experience and practice. If the restoration is thorough and permanent, this will result in the conversion of the ungodly around them. If this process affects large numbers of people of both classes, the society of which both are a part will, to some degree, be reformed.

- Such have been those great works of God among men in the past, that have been known as the "Great Revivals." Just such a great revival is needed in North America today!

Since revival is a work of God, and is in fact a manifestation of the presence of God, is there anything man can do to help bring it about? All Christians do not agree on the answer to this question—but I am convinced, from both Scripture and history, that there is much God's people can do. One of the greatest revivalists of North America was Charles Finney. On this point he said,

> Revival is the result of the right use of the appropriate means. The means which God has enjoined for the production of a revival, doubtless have a natural tendency to produce a revival. Otherwise God would not have enjoined them. But means will not produce a revival, we all know, without the blessing of God. No more will grain, when it is sown, produce a crop without the blessing of God. It is impossible for us to say that there is not as direct an influence or agency from God to produce a crop of grain, as there is to produce a revival. What are the laws of nature according to which it is supposed that grain yields a crop? They are nothing but the constituted manner of the operations of God. In the Bible, the Word of God is compared to grain, and preaching is compared to sowing the seed, and the results to the springing up and growth of the crop. A revival is as naturally a result of the use of the appropriate means, as a crop is of the use of its

appropriate means ... And I fully believe that, could facts be known, it would be found that when the appointed means have been rightly used, spiritual blessings have been obtained with greater uniformity than temporal ones.[1]

In other words, God has set in motion certain spiritual laws which are as reliable as physical laws. Those spiritual laws have a natural tendency to produce revival. They are tied to the person, nature and character of God Himself. Cooperation with those laws does not automatically produce those spiritual results. What it does do is bring about a situation in which God is morally free to do what He already wants to do, and manifest Himself in such a way as to produce the revival that He longs to produce for the blessing of His people and the salvation of the lost. Moving in this direction is a process. There are steps for us to take. As we take those steps, individually and collectively, we will find that God is faithful. He will keep His promises. He has said,

Sow for yourselves righteousness, reap the fruit of unfailing love, and break up your unplowed ground; for it is time to seek the LORD, until he comes and showers righteousness on you (Hos. 10:12).

If the Bible teaches that revival is possible and desirable, that should settle the matter for the Christian. Let us examine some Scriptural evidence together.

The Book of Judges is a 115-year history of declension and revival. It begins in Judges 2:7–12,14,16,18,19, with a remarkable explanation of why revivals are necessary:

The people served the LORD throughout the lifetime of Joshua and of the elders who outlived him and who had seen all the great things the LORD had done for Israel. Joshua son of Nun, the servant of the LORD, died at the age of a hundred and ten ... After that whole generation had been gathered to their fathers, another generation grew up, who knew neither the LORD nor what he had done for Israel. Then the Israelites did evil in the eyes of the LORD and served the Baals. They forsook the LORD, the God of their fathers, who had brought them out of Egypt. They followed and worshiped various gods of the peoples around them. They provoked the LORD to anger ... In his anger against Israel the LORD handed them over to raiders who plundered them. He sold them to their enemies all around, whom they were no longer able to resist. Then the LORD raised up judges who saved them out of the hands of these raiders ... Whenever the LORD raised up a judge for them, he was with the judge and saved them out of the hands of their enemies as long as the judge lived; for the LORD had compassion on them as they groaned under those who oppressed and afflicted them. But when the judge died, the people returned to ways even more corrupt than those of their fathers.

Revivals are necessary because every generation must come to know the Lord for itself. God is a personal God, and will not accept anything less than a personal relationship with every human being. Indeed, God's nature and character are such that He could not do anything else and remain who He is. Man's nature and character, in his natural state, are such that, without a first-hand experience of God, he will quickly drift from the standards and teachings of his fathers. His children will drift even farther. As this drift continues, the separation line between God's people and the people of the world will gradually fade, until it can no longer be seen. The influence for righteousness which God's children exerted on the culture of the world around them will become less and less effective. As a result, the ungodly will become more bold in their sin, and gradually, that whole generation and their society will slide deeper and deeper into evil, until they are in danger of God's judgment. Those who claim to be children of God will no longer be able to stand before their enemies. Eventually, they will be utterly scorned, and finally, be openly and violently persecuted by the world around them.

Finally, when God's people become desperate, they begin to seriously seek the face of God in repentance and prayer. When God sees that they are ready, He then raises up leaders through whom He reveals Himself in such holiness and power, that their generation is confronted with the reality of the Living God. God's people humble themselves, and turn from their wicked ways. The Holy Spirit is poured out in fresh and overwhelming power upon God's people. They are now able to stand against their enemies. They confront the world with such commitment and power that the world is defeated, and thousands turn to the True and Living God. God's people are then revived, and the work of God is revived in the world. Once again, the influence of God's people is felt, and the society of which they are a part is restored to a new standard of decency and righteousness. These conditions will be maintained through the lives of that generation and their children. Their grandchildren however, will begin to drift. Their great-grandchildren will drift even farther, and soon, the whole cycle will repeat itself like a vast spiral. This is the picture that is painted in the Book of Judges. It is also the picture painted by Church history. One example from the Book of Judges will suffice to illustrate this cycle of declension and revival. Please consider with me the revival under the leadership of Gideon. The account covers chapters 6–8. Note especially Judges 6:1,6–16,25,26; and 8:22,23,28,32–35.

The account of Gideon's calling and ministry in revival is classic. The children of Israel had drifted far from God, and were living like the people of the world around them. Gideon seems to have had a knowledge of God, but not the power. He was living in fear and defeat. First, God sent a prophet to confront the people of Israel, and remind them of God's infallible Word and His supernatural working in the past. Then God chose and revived His leader, Gideon. Next, God used that revived person to demonstrate His power, and bring revival to Israel. Israel continued in this state of blessing and victory for forty years. However, when Gideon died, they quickly drifted back into sin, worldliness and idolatry. And so, the cycle was repeated.

This piece of Bible history incorporates many principles that generally accompany revival:

1. God's choice of a "nobody" to be His leader.

2. That leader's experience of renewed faith, cleansing from all idols, and yielding his life to death in his separation from and confrontation with the Godless world around him.

3. God's insistence on demonstrating His power first through a small group of committed people.

4. The gathering in of the larger body of His people.

5. Finally, the defeat of the world and the triumph, or reviving, of God's work in the world.

That is the story of Gideon—and that, in some measure, is the story of every great revival in history.

It is not the purpose of this book to consider every revival delineated in the Bible. My purpose in this chapter is to lay a scriptural foundation for our faith and instruction. To do this, I will consider the subject under three headings:

1. *Personal Revival;*

2. *Group Revival; and,*

3. *The Revival Of God's Work.*

First, let us consider:

PERSONAL REVIVAL

In Isaiah 57:15, we read,

> *For thus says the high and exalted One Who lives forever, whose name is Holy, "I dwell on a high and holy place, And also with the contrite and lowly of spirit in order to revive the spirit of the lowly And to* **revive** *the heart of the contrite"* (NASB, author's emphasis).

This is a very exciting promise—that the exalted God of eternity will come to the person who humbles himself and is truly contrite in heart, and will minister to him in personal revival, and will take up residence in his life. This is the manifestation of the presence of God Himself in personal revival in an individual life.

When we turn to the Psalms, we find the same truth reiterated again and again. Psalm 71 is the prayer of an elderly believer for God's blessing on his life in his old age. In Verses 17 and 18, we hear the writer pray that God will use him to show God's power to the next generation before he dies, in these words:

> Since my youth, O God, you have taught me, and to this day I declare your marvelous deeds. Even when I am old and gray, do not forsake me, O God, till I declare your power to the next generation, your might to all who are to come.

Then, in Verses 20 and 21, we have these great words of assurance,

> You who have shown me many troubles and distresses Will **revive** me again, And will bring me up again from the depths of the earth. May You increase my greatness And turn to comfort me (NASB, author's emphasis).

Here then, is the very thing we are talking about: a new generation who have not seen God's great power, and who have drifted. An aged believer who has experienced God's power in the past, but who needs to be personally revived so that he can minister that power in revival to the next generation before he passes off the scene. And God gives him the assurance that He will do just that!

Psalm 119 is the great psalm on the Word of God. It is to be expected that it will be full of the subject of revival, and so it is. Again, it is personal revival. I will quote from the NASB for this psalm, because it is more accurate in using the word "revive." In verse 25, we read, "My soul cleaves to the dust; **revive** me according to Your word." In verse 37, he prays, "Turn away my eyes from looking at vanity, and **revive** me in Your ways." His prayer continues in verse 40 with the words, "Behold I long for Your precepts; **revive** me through Your righteousness." In verse 88, he appeals to God's lovingkindness by praying, "**Revive** me according to Your lovingkindness, so I may keep the testimony of Your mouth." Again, he is in trouble, and prays in verse 107, "I am exceedingly afflicted; **revive** me, O LORD, according to Your word." In verse 149, he appeals to God's love and God's word as he prays, "Hear my voice according to Your lovingkindness; **Revive** me, O LORD, according to Your ordinances." Verses 154, 156, and 159 repeat some of the same themes in these words—"Plead my cause and redeem me; **revive** me according to Your word." "Great are Your mercies, O LORD; **Revive** me according to Your ordinances." "Consider how I love Your precepts; **Revive** me, O Lord, according to Your lovingkindness."

All of these passages are prayers and statements of faith concerning personal revival. The writer prays for personal revival on the foundation of God's Word. He also appeals to God's righteousness, lovingkindness and mercies. He argues that personal revival will lift up his soul, turn him from vanity, help him to walk in God's ways, keep God's testimonies, and deliver him from affliction. He reminds God, in Verses 145–148, that he has cried to God with all his heart, that he rose up before dawn, and that he prayed and meditated on God's word in the night watches in his desire for personal revival. He closes the psalm with a humble confession and the knowledge that revival is a work of God as he says, "I have gone astray like a lost sheep; SEEK YOUR SERVANT, for I do not forget Your commandments."

Jacob, Moses and Isaiah are other striking examples of personal revival in the Old Testament. Jacob, as you remember, had stolen his brother Esau's birthright and blessing. His name, which *Strong's Definitions* translates as "heel grabber" or "supplanter" described his character. After Jacob fled from his brother's wrath, he settled with his uncle, Laban. There, he continued to deceive and be deceived. In spite of all this, Jacob's heart hungered for God. When he was leaving home, an encounter with God moved Jacob to make a personal commitment to God—a kind of conversion. From that time on, Jacob served the Lord, but with many defeats and failures. Finally, it was time for Jacob to return home and face his brother. Many years had passed, and Jacob was now a wealthy man. As he neared home, the news came that Esau was coming to meet him with an army of four hundred men. Jacob was "greatly afraid and distressed" (Gen. 32:7, NASB). That night, Jacob went alone to pray, and wrestled all night with God. He held on to God, insisting on the blessing of God which he knew he needed on his life. God asked him, "What is your name?" He answered, "Jacob." "Yes Lord," he confessed, "I am JACOB, a deceiver, a supplanter and trickster." The Lord then touched him in his hip and crippled him. The cross did its work, and Jacob was changed. Then God said, "Your name shall no longer be Jacob, but Israel; for you have striven with God and with men and have prevailed" (Gen. 32:28,30, NASB). "So Jacob named the place Peniel, for he said, 'I have seen God face to face, yet my life has been preserved." The next day, his brother Esau received Jacob with tears and a warm embrace, because Jacob was now to be by God's power a "Prince" with God and with men. This is truly a thrilling account of a great personal revival.

Next, let us look at Moses. Miraculously saved from death as an infant, he was then raised to the highest position of privilege and power that the world could offer—the grandson of the Pharaoh of Egypt. "And Moses was educated in all the learning of the Egyptians, and he was a man of power in words and deeds" (Acts 7:22, NASB). It is very possible that the throne of Egypt could eventually have been his. Moses, however, was a Jew; his people were slaves in Egypt. When he was forty, he made a life-changing choice. We read about his decision in Hebrews 11:24–27:

> By faith Moses, when he had grown up, refused to be known as the son of Pharaoh's daughter. He chose to be mistreated along with the people of God, rather than to enjoy the pleasures of sin for a short time. He regarded disgrace for the sake of Christ as of greater value than the treasures of Egypt, because he was looking ahead to his reward. By faith he left Egypt, not fearing the king's anger; he persevered because he saw him who is invisible.

This is the account of a genuine conversion. Then Moses started out to bring revival to his people, but utterly failed because he did so in his own strength and wisdom, rather than in the power of God. Totally defeated, Moses fled for his life, and spent the next forty years on the backside of the desert. Then, one day, Moses had another life-changing experience. He met God in the burning bush. When God called Moses to go back to Egypt and bring revival to His people, he argued with God and struggled against the call, for he now considered himself incapable of doing anything for God. The cross had done its work well. With self dead, Moses was ready to go in the wisdom and power of God. By the time that struggle with God ended, Moses had experienced a personal revival that permanently changed his life, and made him the man God could use to lead an entire nation out of bondage.

Finally, we come to Isaiah, whose personal revival experience is recorded in his own words in Isaiah 6:1–9. Here was a man of noble birth and position, a friend of kings, already serving the Lord in the Temple. His hopes and faith for the work of God and the people of God were, however, too much dependent on another man, King Uzziah. When that earthly crutch was removed, Isaiah had a meeting with God that changed his life and ministry. Here, again, is that unusual manifestation of the presence of God and His holiness that makes us acutely aware of our sin and need. In the searing light of God's presence, Isaiah experienced personal revival. He was cleansed, called, and sent. The cross of Christ, represented by the altar and its sacrifice, did a deep work in Isaiah so that he was a servant of the heavenly King, rather than a servant of an earthly king. This is the kind of personal revival needed in every one of our lives, if we are to be of any use to God in the great revival He is preparing to bring in our day.

The New Testament also has accounts of personal revival. One is the spiritual journey of Simon Peter. Early in the ministry of Jesus, Peter became one of His most devoted disciples. Indeed, he was one of the inner circle of three. In Matthew 16:15, Jesus asked His disciples who they thought He was. Peter responded with the strong confession, "You are the Christ, the Son of the Living God!" Christ commended him with the words,

> *Blessed are you Simon son of Jonah, for this was not revealed to you by man, but by my Father in heaven. And I tell you that you are Peter, and on this rock I will build my church, and the gates of Hades will not overcome it.*

Peter was no pretender or empty professor, but a true lover and follower of Jesus Christ! Nevertheless, some spiritual problems in Peter's life would cause him to experience dismal failure and defeat. In the same chapter, we find Christ explaining to His disciples how He would be put to death and rise again the third day. Peter's response and the Lord's correction are recorded in Verses 22–26.

It becomes clear that a person can be a true disciple of Christ, but still be fleshly and worldly in his viewpoint. This will rob him of Christian victory until he takes his self-life to the cross and gives up his life in identification with Christ in His death, burial and resurrection. Peter could not see this, and did not see it until after his tragic denial of Christ. Christ saw Peter's problem, and warned him again on the night of the Passover supper, in Matthew 26:31–35. Peter declared, "Even if I have to die with you, I will never disown you." And all the other disciples said the same. Later, in the garden, Jesus chided Peter for not praying—saying "the spirit is willing, but the flesh is weak." Still, Peter was not listening. Finally, while Jesus was on trial, Peter was out in the courtyard by the fire. Accosted by three different people and accused of being a follower of Jesus, all three times Peter denied it. The last time, he:

> *began to call down curses on himself and he swore to them, "I don't know the man!" Immediately a rooster crowed. Then Peter remembered the word Jesus had spoken ... And he went outside and wept bitterly* (Matt. 26:74,75).

Peter was in desperate need of a personal revival, which is what the Lord had planned for him. After His resurrection, Jesus told the women, "Go tell my disciples and Peter." Then, during the fish fry on the shore of the lake of Tiberias, three times the Lord asked Peter if he loved Him more than the fishing business. Peter's heart was truly broken. He said, "Lord, you know all things; you know that I love you." Then recommissioned by Jesus, Peter was on the way back, but would not be fully revived until he was gloriously filled with the Holy Spirit. Jesus had told Peter that when he was revived, he would be used of God to revive his brethren. This prophecy came true, as God poured out His Spirit through Peter's sermons and miracles. Thousands of people were saved, and the work of God was revived with such impact on the world that the ungodly cried out, "They that have turned the world upside-down have come here also!"

John Mark was another person who experienced personal revival. The New Testament tells us he was a nephew of the godly Barnabas. It seems that the all-night prayer meeting that brought the Apostle Peter out of prison was held in Mark's mother's home. Mark had, as his examples and mentors, some of the most godly men and women who have ever lived. Outwardly, his Christian growth and testimony must have been outstanding, for the Apostle Paul and Mark's uncle Barnabas decided to take Mark with them on their first great missionary journey. Mark quickly found that the wonderful atmosphere of the Christian gatherings at home were a far cry from the dangers and deprivations of missionary labours. In Lystra, he saw Paul stoned and his bloodied body left for dead. Shortly after that, while they were ministering in Pamphylia, Mark deserted Paul and Barnabas and went home. I doubt there is any question about the reality of Mark's Christian faith. His problem was the same as Peter's. He had not yet taken self to the cross and given up his life.

This is the problem with average Christians today. They have never dealt with the self-life! Many who pray for revival do not understand that revival will mean their death. Both Peter and Mark tried to live the Christian life in the strength of the flesh, rather than the power of God. Both had to become desperate through failure before they would exchange the self-life for the Christ life.

When Paul and Barnabas planned their next missionary journey, Paul was adamant that Mark could not go. Nevertheless, his uncle Barnabas took him. This indicates to me that Mark had gone through a deep repentance and a life that was thoroughly revived. Indeed, it must be so—for, a number of years later, we find Paul writing to Timothy and saying, "Get Mark and bring him with you, because he is helpful to me in my ministry" (II Tim. 4:11). The final outcome of this revived life is the divinely-inspired Gospel of Mark.

Every kind of revival always begins with an individual who seeks the face of God and is personally revived. From there, the revival may influence a few, or become world-changing—but it must start with one person. Maybe that person is you. Maybe that person is me. How dreadful it is if neither one of us is willing to pay the price God requires of us! On the other hand, what immeasurable joy awaits us if we respond to God, and He uses us to turn many to righteousness. We will shine as the stars forever and ever! But, let us move on to the subject of:

GROUP REVIVAL

Many personal revivals eventually produce some kind of group revival. In Psalm 80, the writer prays for God to revive His people. Three times, he says, "Restore us, O God; make your face shine upon us, that we may be saved" (3,7,19). Then, in Verses 14–18, he prays,

> *Return to us, O God Almighty! Look down from heaven and see! Watch over this vine, the root your right hand has planted ... Your vine is cut down, it is burned with fire; at your rebuke your people perish. Let your hand rest on the man at your right hand, the son of man you have raised up for yourself. Then we will not turn away from you;* REVIVE US, *and we will call upon your name.*(Emphasis by the author.)

Psalm 85 is one of the most remarkable prayers for revival in the Bible. It is the revival of God's people for which the writer pleads, but he also recognizes that such a work of God will affect the land in which God's people dwell. In Verses 1–3, he prays in faith as if God had already answered his prayer:

> *You showed favor to your land, O LORD; you restored the fortunes of Jacob. You forgave the iniquity of your people and covered all their sins. You set aside all your wrath, and turned from your fierce anger.*

Then in Verses 4–7, he begins to pray in earnest for God to do what he is anticipating.

Restore us again, O God our Savior, and put away your displeasure toward us. Will you be angry with us forever? Will you prolong your anger through all generations? **Will You not revive us again,** *that your people may rejoice in you? Show us your unfailing love, O* LORD, *and grant us your salvation.* (Emphasis by the author.)

Now he pauses in his prayer to hear God's response.

I will listen to what God the LORD *will say; he promises peace to his people, his saints—but let them not return to folly. Surely his salvation is near those who fear him, that his glory may dwell in our land.*

Next, in Verses 10 and 11, he describes what happens spiritually in a revival:

Love and faithfulness meet together; righteousness and peace kiss each other. Faithfulness springs forth from the earth, and righteousness looks down from heaven.

Finally, he ends his prayer with the assurance that God has heard and will answer his prayer. "The Lord will indeed give what is good, and our land will yield its harvest. Righteousness goes before him, and prepares the way for his steps."

One of the most important group revivals in Scripture is the revival at Pentecost. It is a striking illustration of a revival within a revival. The larger revival is the revival of God's work in the world which began with the ministry of John the Baptist and continued with the ministry of Jesus Christ, the ministry of the Apostles, and the early Church. The group revival at Pentecost launched the third aspect of the larger revival. In its beginning, it included 120 people—a group about the size of many small churches.

Christ's crucifixion brought the itinerant revival ministry of Jesus and His disciples to a grinding halt. Even after the resurrection, there is no indication of a return to that ministry. For forty days, Jesus appeared periodically to His disciples, but did not preach to crowds.

Indeed, even though He had given the disciples the Great Commission, He specifically told them to "stay in the city until you have been clothed with power from on high" (Luke 24:49). After Jesus' ascension, the disciples still were not involved in any public ministries as far as we know. What were they doing? They were waiting on God in prayer for the outpouring of His Holy Spirit upon them as Jesus had said (Acts 1:13,14). It also appears that they were getting right with one another, for we read in Acts 2:1 that they were "all of one accord in one place." Then came the answer to their prayers: a powerful group revival that literally changed the world. Acts 2:2–4 tells us the wonderful story of how the lives of these 120 men and women were transformed, resulting in the conversion of thousands among the masses. That group revival was the final thrust of a great revival of God's work in the world. It continued and spread until the whole course of human history was radically changed. Who knows which group revival, or revivals, will be used of God in our day to bring about just such a revival of God's work, and will be the means of saving our own civilization from judgment and destruction? This brings us to our next kind of revival—

THE REVIVAL OF GOD'S WORK

The classic Scripture passage for this is found in Habakkuk 3:1–4,13a:

> *A prayer of Habakkuk the prophet ... LORD, I have heard the report about You and I fear. O LORD, **revive Your work** in the midst of the years, In the midst of the years make it known; In wrath remember mercy. God comes from Teman, And the Holy One from Mount Paran. His splendor covers the heavens, And the earth is full of His praise. His radiance is like the sunlight; He has rays flashing from His hand, And there is the hiding of His power. You went forth for the salvation of Your people* (NASB, emphasis by the author).

In this passage the prophet is praying concerning "erring ones." He has heard what God has done in the past and is afraid of what

God's judgment could mean in the present. He knows that God's wrath is justified. He is pleading for mercy. He is aware of the fact that that mercy can only be realized through revival. That will mean that God must make Himself known in a way that He is not manifest in the present. God answers his prayer. A new, powerful manifestation reveals God's glory, God's holiness, God's brightness, God's hand and God's power. The result is salvation for the people, praise to God, and the revival of God's work in general in the world. That is a perfect picture of what needs to happen in our day. Our Western civilization is certainly under God's wrath and is headed for righteous judgment. Our only hope is a revival of the magnitude outlined above. I believe God is calling for thousands of intercessors who will come before Him and plead for mercy, like Habakkuk, until God answers with a great revival of His work in our world.

A historic account of the revival of the work of God in the world is the great revival under the leadership of Ezra and Nehemiah—which also involved the ministry of Zerubbabel, Joshua the High Priest, and the prophets Haggai and Zechariah. This revival covered a period of about eighty-one years. The greater part of the population of Judah was taken captive following its conquest by Babylon. Israel had long ago been deported to the land of Assyria, and never really returned. In Jerusalem, the walls of the city were broken down, and the Temple was destroyed. The priesthood was dispersed, and formal worship of Jehovah had ceased. Here and there in Israel, Judah, Assyria, and Babylon, true Israelites continued to worship Jehovah privately or in small groups. Nevertheless, it seemed as if the work of God in the world had been crushed, never to rise again.

There were, however, two bright spots in this spiritual darkness. First, the Word of God, through Jeremiah, had promised that this captivity would only last seventy years. We find this prophecy in Jeremiah 25:11, 29:10–14.

The second bright spot was the light of God shining in the hearts and lives of individuals who believed the Word of God. These earnest believers were ready to give themselves to earnest, believing prayer, and to whatever action was necessary to bring about this revival. As they sought the face of God, miracles began to happen. God moved on the hearts of pagan rulers so that they opened the doors for Jews to return to their land and rebuild both the Temple and the walls of Jerusalem. This physical rebuilding was only a small indication of the spiritual rebuilding that needed to take place, in order for true worship of Jehovah to be re-established and the work of God to be revived in the world. The repentance that was necessary is clearly seen in the prayer of Ezra, in Ezra 9:

> *"O my God, I am too ashamed and disgraced to lift up my face to you, my God, because our sins are higher than our heads and our guilt has reached to the heavens. From the days of our fore-fathers until now, our guilt has been great. Because of our sins, we and our kings and our priests have been subjected to the sword and captivity, to pillage and humiliation at the hand of foreign kings, as it is today.*

> *"But now, for a brief moment, the LORD our God has been gracious in leaving us a remnant and giving us a firm place in his sanctuary, and so our God gives light to our eyes and a little relief in our bondage. Though we are slaves, our God has not deserted us in our bondage. He has shown us kindness in the sight of the kings of Persia: He has granted us new life to rebuild the house of our God and repair its ruins, and he has given us a wall of protection in Judah and Jerusalem.*

> *"But now, O our God, what can we say after this? For we have disregarded the commands you gave through your servants the prophets when you said: 'The land you are entering to possess is a land polluted by the corruption of its peoples. By their detestable practices they have filled it with their impurity from one end to the other. Therefore, do not give your daughters in marriage to their sons or take their daughters for your sons. Do not seek a treaty of friendship with them at any time, that you may be strong and eat the good things of the land and leave it to your children as an everlasting inheritance.*

"What has happened to us is a result of our evil deeds and our great guilt, and yet, our God, you have punished us less than our sins have deserved and have given us a remnant like this.

"Shall we again break your commands and intermarry with the peoples who commit such detestable practices? Would you not be angry enough with us to destroy us, leaving us no remnant or survivor?

"O LORD, God of Israel, you are righteous! We are left this day as a remnant. Here we are before you in our guilt, though because of it not one of us can stand in your presence." While Ezra was praying and confessing, weeping and throwing himself down before the house of God, a large crowd of Israelites— men, women and children—gathered around him. They too wept bitterly (Ezra 9:6–15; 10:1).

This is the kind of prayer needed today from God's leaders! There followed a great repentance on the part of the people and another step forward in this great revival. The final outcome was that the Temple was built, the wall was repaired, the worship of Jehovah was re-established, and the work of God was truly revived in the world.

The great revival under the leadership of John the Baptist, Jesus Christ, and the Apostles came at a time when it seemed that the true work of God in the world had almost ceased to exist. The prelude to this revival, a historical period often called "The Four Hundred Silent Years," extends from the ministry of the prophet Malachi to the birth of John the Baptist. The reason it is called "silent" is because, throughout that time, there was no genuine prophet of God, and no legitimate "Word" from God. The one who seemed to be silent was God. After the revival of God's work under the leadership of Ezra and Nehemiah, the work of God prospered in the world for a number of years. Both the Persian and Greek rulers treated the Jews kindly, and the Jews had godly leaders who re-established the true worship of Jehovah in Jerusalem.

As time passed, however, the generations that followed drifted farther and farther from real godliness, and became more and more involved in religious formalism and politics. World power passed from the Persians to the Greeks, and from the Greeks to the Romans. The Jewish state became independent for a time under the rebellion and rule of the Maccabees and the Hasmonaean dynasty. Soon, Rome conquered that part of the world, and the Jews were again occupied and ruled over by a foreign power. Through most of this period, the Jewish high priest—appointed by foreign, pagan rulers—soon came to be not only the religious leader, but often the political ruler as well. This brought corruption of all kinds into the religious life of God's people. It also brought internal conflict, as various religious and political parties fought for control.

By the time John the Baptist came on the scene, four major movements were struggling for control and leadership among the Jewish people. First, there were the Herodians—Jews of influence and standing, who supported the Herodian rule and its connections with the Roman government. Totally opposed to them were the Zealots, whose intense patriotism brought them into sharp conflict with the Herodians and the Romans. Then the Sadducees, wealthy Jerusalem aristocrats, were religious liberals who were more Greek than Jewish in their philosophy and lifestyle. Finally, there were the Pharisees, who were orthodox in their Jewish faith and highly legalistic in teaching and practice.

The Temple in Jerusalem, at that time, had been built by Herod the Great. It boasted a complete priesthood and total program of rituals, sacrifices and public worship. It was the center of Jewish religious life, but was filled with corruption and was spiritually bankrupt. Here were those who outwardly were the people of God—yet, they had not had any word from God for almost four hundred years, they were ruled by pagans and their puppets, and their highest religious leader was appointed by Rome. Their place of worship had become a place of empty, orthodox ritual, and as Jesus said, "a den of thieves." They had a form of godliness, but denied the power. It looked as if the work of God in the world was dead.

Nevertheless, here and there were a few godly Jews who worshiped the Lord in spirit and in truth. Indeed, there were those who prayed continually for God to revive His work, and some waited expectantly for the Messiah himself to come. Two of these were the prophetess Anna and the Spirit-filled Bible scholar, Simeon. Any careful Bible scholar of that day could have known, from a study of the prophetic Scriptures, that it was about time for the Christ to appear. Here is a repeated pattern: a world where the work of God has almost ceased; promises from God's Word as to what He is willing to do; a few earnest believers who weep and pray for revival—and then the miracles begin. God comes on the scene with a new manifestation of Himself. Some of God's people are revived. Then the fire spreads. More and more are caught up in the blaze. Finally, it spills over into the world and the work of God is revived. This is exactly the picture before us—let us look at the details.

A priest named Zechariah, and his wife, Elizabeth, were both "upright in the sight of God, observing all the Lord's commandments and regulations blamelessly. But they had no children, because Elizabeth was barren; and they were both well along in years" (Luke 1:6,7).

These are the kind of people God generally chooses to begin a revival. So, while Zechariah was praying in the Temple, God sent an angel to tell him that his prayers had been heard, and God would miraculously give them a son who would be used of God to spearhead the revival of God's work. In Luke 1:15–17, we read:

> *He will be great in the sight of the Lord ... and he will be filled*
> *with the Holy Spirit ... Many of the people of Israel will he bring*
> *back to the Lord their God. And he will go on before the Lord,*
> *in the spirit and power of Elijah, to turn the hearts of the fathers*
> *to their children and the disobedient to the wisdom of the righ-*
> *teous—to make ready a people prepared for the Lord.*

The result was the birth of a baby boy who would become John the Baptist. Then, Luke 1, verse 80 tells us, "And the child grew and became strong in spirit; and he lived in the desert until he appeared publicly to Israel."

The miracles continued. When Elizabeth was six months pregnant with John, the same angel who appeared to Zechariah appeared to Elizabeth's young cousin, Mary. Again, God chose a young woman who was full of grace and had found favour with him. The startling message to her was that she would give birth to the Messiah, who would be God in human flesh, and would be the Saviour of the world! At that point, the Holy Spirit came upon Mary, and she miraculously conceived the one who would be called Jesus. Soon after, Mary went to visit Elizabeth, where she found those of kindred spirit and the small group of the revived could strengthen one another in faith, prayer and praise. The birth of Jesus was attended by more manifestations of God's presence, and the two second cousins grew up in a circle of godly people who clung to God's promises and expected the revival to come. Now, the stage was set; we read, in Luke 3:2,3,

> *The word of God came to John son of Zechariah in the desert. He went into all the country around the Jordan, preaching a baptism of repentance for the forgiveness of sins.*

What was the response?

> *People went out to him from Jerusalem and all Judea and the whole region of the Jordan. Confessing their sins, they were baptized by him in the Jordan River ... he saw many of the Pharisees and Sadducees coming to where he was baptizing* (Matt. 3:5–7).

> *The people were waiting expectantly and were all wondering in their hearts if John might possibly be the Christ. John answered them all, "I baptize you with water. But one more powerful than I will come, the thongs of whose sandals I am not worthy to untie. He will baptize you with the Holy Spirit and with fire. His winnowing fork is in his hand to clear his threshing floor and to gather the wheat into his barn, but he will burn up the chaff with unquenchable fire." And with many other words John exhorted the people and preached the good news to them* (Luke 3:7–18).

This first wave of a revival of God's work in the world would so change human thought and practice that the world would never be the same again. The Spirit-anointed preaching of John the Baptist reached all segments of society, and even attacked the immorality of the king himself. It cut right across the hypocrisy of the day, which claimed to believe the Scriptures, and carried on an outward form of godliness, but actually lived by the crooked philosophies of the world. That message insisted on genuine repentance. It offered the forgiveness of sins, proclaimed death to sin and the world, and a new life lived unto God through the public ritual of water baptism. It pointed to Christ as God's lamb and sin-bearer, and promised the fullness of the Holy Spirit as a gracious baptism from God's Son, Jesus the Christ.

In one form or another, that message has been preached by every revivalist in human history! The crowds that came to hear included almost the entire population of that part of the world. Many lives were changed, and the attitude of the common man and woman toward spiritual matters was profoundly affected. This general change of attitude was necessary to prepare the people for the next wave which would be led by Jesus and the Apostles.

This new ministry was launched right in the middle of John's great mass meetings. In Matthew 3:13–17, we read,

> *Then Jesus came from Galilee to the Jordan to be baptized by John. But John tried to deter him saying, "I need to be baptized by you, and do you come to me?" Jesus replied, "Let it be so now; it is proper for us to do this to fulfill all righteousness." Then John consented. As soon as Jesus was baptized he went up out of the water. At that moment heaven was opened, and he saw the Spirit of God descending like a dove and lighting on him. And a voice from heaven said, "This is my Son, whom I love; with him I am well pleased."*

Further developments are recorded in John's Gospel:

> *The next day John saw Jesus coming toward him and said, "Look, the Lamb of God who takes away the sin of the world! This is the one I meant when I said, 'A man who comes after me has surpassed me because he was before me.' I myself did not know him, but the reason I came baptizing with water was that he might be revealed*

to Israel." Then John gave this testimony, "I saw the Spirit come down from heaven as a dove and remain on him. I would not have known him, except that the one who sent me to baptize with water told me, 'The man on whom you see the Spirit come down and remain is he who will baptize with the Holy Spirit.' I have seen and I testify that this is the Son of God." The next day John was there again with two of his disciples. When he saw Jesus passing by, he said, "Look, the Lamb of God." When the two disciples heard him say this, they followed Jesus (John 1:29–37).

With these two disciples, the shift began from John the Baptist to Jesus. Others soon followed, and those becoming disciples of Jesus increased rapidly. Jesus was led by the Holy Spirit into the wilderness for His great encounter with the devil, and upon His return began His itinerant preaching ministry. The transfer of revival ministry leadership to Jesus is described graphically in John 3:22–30:

After this Jesus and his disciples went out into the Judean countryside, where he spent some time with them, and baptized. Now John was also baptizing near Salim, because there was plenty of water, and people were constantly coming to be baptized ... They came to John and said to him, "Rabbi, that man who was with you on the other side of the Jordan—the one you testified about—well, he is baptizing, and everyone is going to him." To this John replied, "A man can receive only what is given him from heaven. You yourselves can testify that I said, 'I am not the Christ but am sent ahead of him.' The bride belongs to the bridegroom. The friend who attends the bridegroom waits and listens for him, and is full of joy when he hears the bridegroom's voice. That joy is mine, and it is now complete. He must become greater; I must become less."

Not long afterward, John was arrested and was finally executed because of his stand against the immorality of King Herod. Many more of John's disciples became followers of Jesus, and His ministry grew rapidly. We read in John 4:1,

The Pharisees heard that Jesus was gaining and baptizing more disciples than John, although in fact it was not Jesus who baptized, but his disciples.

Jesus was now preaching to the masses, as John had, and the revival movement was growing, rather than declining with John's death. We see this even more clearly in Matthew 4:23–25:

Jesus went throughout Galilee, teaching in their synagogues, preaching the good news of the kingdom, and healing every disease and sickness among the people. News about him spread all over Syria, and people brought to him all who were ill with various diseases, those suffering severe pain, the demonized, the epileptics and the paralytics, and he healed them. LARGE CROWDS from Galilee, the Decapolis, Jerusalem, Judea and the region across the Jordan followed him.

This mass movement of repentance, forgiveness, healing and deliverance from evil spirits continued to grow, until some of the crowds were between fifteen and twenty thousand—in Matthew 14:21, for instance, when Jesus multiplied the bread and fish, "the number of those who ate was about five thousand men, besides women and children." In most such crowds of that day, there would have been more women and children than men. Therefore, it is safe to conclude that this crowd was above fifteen thousand.

The teaching of Jesus was even more confrontational than John's. His entire ministry was a direct challenge to the religion and lifestyle of those who claimed to be the children of God. Speaking directly to the Jewish religious leaders of that day, he said,

You hypocrites! Isaiah was right when he prophesied about you: "These people honor me with their lips, but their hearts are far from me. They worship me in vain; their teachings are but rules taught by men… " Woe to you, teachers of the law and Pharisees, you hypocrites! You shut the kingdom of heaven in men's faces. You yourselves do not enter in, nor will you let those enter who are trying to. Woe to you teachers of the law and Pharisees, you hypocrites! You travel over land and sea to win a single convert, and when he becomes one, you make him twice as much a son of hell as you are... Woe to you teachers of the law and Pharisees, you hypocrites! You clean the outside of the cup and dish, but inside they are full of greed and self-indulgence. Blind Pharisee! First clean the inside of the cup and dish, and then the outside also will be clean. Woe to you teachers of the law and Pharisees, you hypocrites! You are like whitewashed tombs, which look beautiful on the outside but on the inside are full of dead men's bones and everything unclean. In the same way, on the outside you appear to people as righteous but on the inside you are full of hypocrisy and wickedness... You snakes! You brood of vipers! How will you escape being condemned to hell? (Matt. 15:7–9; 23:13–15; 25–28, 33).

Naturally, these words were not received kindly. Fear and resentment quickly turned to hatred, and these religious hypocrites began to plot Jesus' destruction.

As the Jesus movement increased in size and power, Jesus took time to call and train twelve disciples who would be the nucleus of this revival when He was gone. By this time, the revival of God's work in the world was becoming so strong that it threatened the very existence of the dead orthodoxy that had prevailed on every side. This all came to a head in John 11:47–50,53 as follows:

Then the chief priests and the Pharisees called a meeting of the Sanhedrin. "What are we accomplishing?" they asked. "Here is this man performing many miraculous signs. If we let him go on like this, everyone will believe in him, and then the Romans will come and take away both our place and our nation." Then one of them, named Caiaphas, who was high priest that year, spoke up, "You know nothing at all! You do not realize that it is better for you that one man die for the people than that the whole nation perish." So from that day on they plotted to take his life.

This, of course, finally led to Jesus' betrayal, false trial, crucifixion, resurrection, ascension and pouring out of the Holy Spirit at Pentecost.

After Jesus' death, the disciples were totally defeated. It appeared that the revival movement had ceased. For a time, even after the resurrection and ascension of Jesus, there was no preaching or carrying forward of the mass movement which had been growing through the ministries of John the Baptist and Jesus. This was, however, only a temporary pause. Some of those whose lives had been radically changed began to meet together for heart-searching prayer. As they repented deeply and sought God with all their hearts, God responded on the day of Pentecost.

The third stage, or wave, of the revival was on its way when 120 people received a mighty infilling of the Holy Spirit. Quickly, the tremendous working of the Holy Spirit spilled over into the unsaved masses. On the very first day, about three thousand conversions took place! This revival continued to explode until the number of male converts alone numbered 5,000. The religious leaders had done away with Jesus, only to find that dozens of Spirit-filled believers took His place—teaching His truths and performing the same miracles.

Soon the crowds of believers were larger than any that had followed John the Baptist or Jesus. "Then the high priest and all his associates, who were members of the party of the Sadducees, were filled with jealousy" (Acts 5:17). There followed an intense persecution of these Christians, which only served to scatter them over the world. Everywhere they went, the revival went with them. This revival was so powerful that we read, in Acts 19:10, "This went on for two years, so that all the Jews and Greeks who lived in the province of Asia heard the Word of the Lord." Without any of our present-day travel or communications technology, the Word of God was heard by an entire province in two years! A vast missionary enterprise was launched, so that the gospel was preached and the Church of Jesus Christ was firmly planted in all of the Roman empire, and parts of India, Africa and Spain. This is always one of the results of the revival of God's work in the world. With explosive power, this revival continued and expanded for 300 years—during which the entire New

Testament was written, copied, and parts of it were distributed to various parts of the world.

This chapter is far from an exhaustive, scriptural study of the subject of revival. It may suffice, however, to make the point that the Bible lays a solid foundation for the study of revival. In fact, its biographical and historical parts are almost entirely accounts of personal revival, group revival and the revival of God's work in the world. I trust that everyone who reads these words will find his own heart burning with the prayer, "Do it again Lord! Do it again!"

CHAPTER THREE

The Foundation of Doctrine

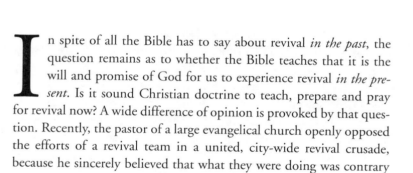

In spite of all the Bible has to say about revival *in the past*, the question remains as to whether the Bible teaches that it is the will and promise of God for us to experience revival *in the present*. Is it sound Christian doctrine to teach, prepare and pray for revival now? A wide difference of opinion is provoked by that question. Recently, the pastor of a large evangelical church openly opposed the efforts of a revival team in a united, city-wide revival crusade, because he sincerely believed that what they were doing was contrary to sound doctrine. I disagree with him. Who is right? We will consider this question under two headings: Negative Voices and Positive Voices.

NEGATIVE VOICES

In the revival of God's work in the world, in which Jesus was the very heart, He faced these negative voices. This was His response:

> *Do you not say, 'Four months more and then harvest?' I tell you, open your eyes and look at the fields! They are ripe for harvest.*

Even now the reaper draws his wages, even now he harvests the crop for eternal life, so that the sower and the reaper may be glad together (John 4:35,36).

When Jesus was told by some that He could not expect great movements of God among men in his day, He argued that when the fields are ripe, you can expect a harvest. He urged them to open their eyes, saying, "Even **now** the revival is starting!" Our answer is the same to the negative voices of our day. But let us see what they are.

1. The Voice of Liberals

It is no surprise that liberals in the Church are against revivals. They say that revivals are just emotional binges, mass hysteria, and religious fanaticism engineered by clever men and women who take advantage of the problems of ignorant people, in order to bring them under their control. Unfortunately, there have been some false prophets who have done exactly that.

Nevertheless, by and large, that has not been the case and is not the main reason liberals take this position. The real reason is that liberals deny the inspiration of the Scriptures, deny the deity of Christ, deny the blood atonement, deny the new birth, deny heaven and hell, and deny the supernatural salvation of the individual by grace through faith. They preach, instead, the redemption of society by human means. No wonder then, that liberals are against revivals! The Apostle John said some strong words about this group:

Many deceivers who do not acknowledge Jesus Christ ... have gone out into the world. Any such person is the deceiver and the antichrist ... Anyone who ... does not continue in the teaching of Christ does not have God (II John 7,9).

The Spirit clearly says that in later times some will abandon the faith and follow deceiving spirits and things taught by demons. Such teachings come through hypocritical liars, whose consciences have been seared as with a hot iron (I Tim. 4:1,2).

2. Worldly Christians

Sometimes raised against revival are the voices of worldly Christians, because revival calls Christians to a life of holiness and separation from the world. Revival convicts God's children of sin and calls them to repent, deny self, and take up the cross and follow Jesus. Many Christians who hold places of leadership in the Church are also involved in much that is worldly. They do not want to give up the world, and therefore fear revival. God's response to this is found in I John 2:15–17:

> Do not love the world or anything in the world. If anyone loves the world, the love of the Father is not in him. For everything in the world—the cravings of sinful man, the lust of his eyes and the boastings of what he has and does—comes not from the Father but from the world. The world and its desires pass away, but the man who does the will of God lives forever.

In the Welsh revival of 1904, one of the most common prayers expressed by those responding to God was, "What have I to do anymore with idols?" Revival takes the idols from the lives of worldly Christians.

3. Lukewarm Christians

Christians who seldom pray or read their Bibles, who never witness for Christ, who are not really concerned about the lost, who do not expect God to perform miracles today, who are critical, contentious, unbelieving, and unloving, are lukewarm and on the slippery slope of backsliding. These Christians may oppose revival because they do not sense need for it. They are satisfied with conditions as they are. But to those people Christ says,

> I know your deeds, that you are neither cold nor hot. I wish you were either one or the other! So, because you are lukewarm ... I am about to spit you out of my mouth. You say, "I am rich; I have acquired wealth and do not need a thing." But you do not realize that you are wretched, pitiful, poor, blind and naked. I coun-

sel you to buy from me gold refined in the fire, so you can become rich; and white clothes to wear, so you can cover your shameful nakedness; and salve to put on your eyes, so you can see. Those whom I love I rebuke and discipline. So be in earnest, and repent. Here I am! I stand at the door and knock. If anyone hears my voice and opens the door, I will come in and fellowship with him and he with me (Rev. 3:15–20).

4. Jealous Christians

There are Christians in the Church who have been considered important, and who have had influence, but who are not really godly leaders. When revival comes, these people often sit on the sidelines wanting their former importance and control in the church, while the main body— under the leadership of others who are under God's anointing—goes forward with God. Jealousy prompts criticism and opposition toward the revival. Every flaw is pointed out, and jealous Christians argue that these imperfections prove the revival is more harm than good. The Apostle John mentions these people in III John 9,10 when he says,

I wrote to the church, but Diotrephes, who loves to be first, will have nothing to do with us. So if I come, I will call attention to what he is doing, gossiping maliciously about us. Not satisfied with that, he refuses to welcome brothers. He also stops those who want to do so and puts them out of the church.

5. Conservative Christians

Conservative Christians become dignified, proud or fearful through nature, training, or culture. In a true revival, as God breaks through false reserve and dishonesty, there is deep conviction for sin, and godly sorrow. The resulting brokenness, tears, public confession and restitution offends and sometimes frightens these Christians. They are shocked at what they consider a public display or an emotional outburst. Sometimes, they are afraid that God might produce similar reactions in them. These dear people would rather have their personal lives kept private, and their church gatherings to be conducted without emotion. God's Word has the following to say to these Christians:

> *There is nothing concealed that will not be disclosed, or hidden that will not be made known. What you have said in the dark will be heard in the daylight, and what you have whispered in the ear in the inner rooms will be proclaimed from the roofs* (Luke 12:2,3).

> *This is the message we have heard from him and declare to you: God is light; in him there is no darkness at all. If we claim to have fellowship with him and yet walk in darkness, we lie and do not live by the truth. But if we walk in the light, as he is in the light, we have fellowship with one another, and the blood of Jesus, his Son, purifies us from all sin. If we claim to be without sin, we deceive ourselves and the truth is not in us. If we confess our sins, he is faithful and just and will forgive us our sins and purify us from all unrighteousness* (I John 1:5–9).

"For God did not give us a spirit of timidity, but a spirit of power, of love and of self discipline" (II Tim. 1:7).

6. Ultradispensationalists

I believe it is obvious to any careful student of the Scriptures that God has used different methods of dealing with mankind at different times in human history. These periods of history have been generally known as "dispensations." Because this is true, there are those who have divided the Bible along dispensational lines. They assign certain parts of the Bible to certain periods and groups of people. In this process, they go farther than God goes. They teach that only small portions of the Bible are for us today. They would have us believe that the promises of the Old Testament and the Book of Acts do not apply to us. They tell us that we are in the "LAST DAYS," that the great apostasy is already begun, and that we cannot expect any more great revivals. These teachers are more harmful than the liberals, because they are earnest Christians, believe the Bible, and influence many of God's people. What does God say?

WHAT IS THE "LAST DAYS," ACCORDING TO GOD'S WORD?

Proposition: The "Last Days" is the period from the baptism of Christ to the return of Christ in power to reign on earth.

This is made clear in Hebrews 1:1–3:

> *In the past God spoke to our forefathers through the prophets at many times and in various ways, but in these last days he has spoken to us by his Son, whom he appointed heir of all things, and through whom he made the universe. The Son is the radiance of God's glory and the exact representation of his being, sustaining all things by his powerful word. After he had provided purification for sins, he sat down at the right hand of the Majesty in heaven.*

The "last days" include the ministry of Jesus Christ. Along with referring to the prophetic ministry of Jesus as God spoke through Him here on earth, Hebrews 1:1–3 mentions His atoning work on the cross and includes the Church age, since the writer asserts that Christ ascended and is seated at the right hand of God. Because of the context, the last days mentioned here may even include the future reign of Christ—verse eight, in reference to Christ, goes on to say, "Your throne, O God, will last for ever and ever." The last days, according to this passage, covers a broad span of history rather than a short period of time right before the return of Christ.

One of the most striking passages on this subject is Acts 2:15–21. The setting is the "day of Pentecost." The Holy Spirit has come upon the 120 in the "upper room"—they are witnessing with power to people who are accusing them of being drunk. Peter responds:

> *These men are not drunk, as you suppose. It's only nine in the morning! No, this is what was spoken by the prophet Joel: 'In*

the last days, God says, I will pour out my Spirit on all people. Your sons and daughters will prophesy, your young men will see visions, your old men will dream dreams. Even on my servants, both men and women, I will pour out my Spirit in those days, and they will prophesy. I will show wonders in the heaven above and signs on the earth below, blood and fire and billows of smoke. The sun will be turned to darkness and the moon to blood before the coming of the great and glorious day of the Lord. And everyone who calls on the name of the Lord will be saved' (emphasis by the author).

What was happening right then, Peter says, was a fulfillment of the prophecy made by Joel. He states clearly, "this is that."

The whole passage is about the last days! In other words, the pouring out of the Holy Spirit at Pentecost, the proclamation of the Word of God by all classes of believers, and even the events leading up to the glorious day of the Lord (the return of Christ), are all included in the last days! From this Scripture, it seems clear that the entire Church age is part of the last days.

Let us go next to the Epistles. I Timothy 4:1–3, another passage that talks about the last days, describes certain doctrinal errors that will be taught during that period of time. As we examine these false doctrines, we see immediately that they not only exist today, but have been in the Church from the earliest times. The Roman Church taught these doctrines during the "Dark Ages."

It would be easy, as we look at the account in II Timothy 3:1–5 of the terrible, degenerate human behaviour that will prevail in the last days, to say "See? That exactly describes the day in which we live!" I would answer, "You're right!" But, I would also hasten to add, the same passage exactly describes the prevailing behaviour in many different places at many different times in history. That lifestyle is not unique to our day—nor is it unique to some particular time just preceding the return of Christ. Anyone who thinks so is obviously ignorant of history.

There is another description of the last days in II Peter 3:3,4.

First of all, you must understand that in the last days scoffers will come, scoffing and following their own evil desires. They will say, "Where is this 'coming' he promised? Ever since our fathers died, everything goes on as it has since the beginning of creation."

That this cannot refer to a particular time immediately preceding the return of Christ is obvious, since the fact is, during a long period of Church history, most theologians believed that Christ would only return after the Church had converted the entire world. Not only did scoffers not expect Christ to return in their day, but most Christians would have agreed with them. That period of history has come and gone, and Christ has not returned. The "last days," therefore, does not refer exclusively to a time just before the return of Christ.

Let me cite one more passage on this thought. It is I John 2:18:

Dear children, this is the last hour; and as you have heard that the antichrist is coming, even now many antichrists have come. This is how we know it is the last hour.

This writer is not only talking about the last days, but he is talking about "**the last hour!**" He concludes by saying that the time in which he was living was already the last hour. This ought to make it clear that the period of the last days covers at least the whole Church age.

From these Scriptures, we conclude that the last days is a long period of history that covers the ministry of Jesus Christ and the entire Church age until the glorious return of Christ to earth. This means that the last days is not a short period immediately preceding the return of Christ, a period often called the "Laodicean Period," in which the Church will be only lukewarm, and no great revivals can be expected.

Dr. John R. Rice, a Baptist evangelist of the generation before mine, wrote a book entitled *We Can Have Revival Now*. I want to include two brief quotes from his book on this subject. He said:

From a consideration of all the passages which speak about the last days in the New Testament, it is quite clear that the term in the Bible never means just the few years preceding

62

Christ's coming. And it is quite clear that God has not set off the last few years before Christ's coming to be different from the rest of the age. God has not even intimated in the Scriptures that before Christ comes there would be a special period of time when men would be harder, when revivals would be impossible or more difficult ... I hope every honest reader will shake out of his mind the wicked defeatism which often accompanies the thought of the last days. The term "the last days" means this whole gospel age. It is an age of the pouring out of the Holy Ghost. It is an age of the conversion of multitudes. It is an age when "whosoever shall call on the name of the Lord shall be saved." The fullness of the Spirit, the power to win souls, is for all flesh, servants and handmaidens, old men and young men, sons and daughters—all who will pay God's price for fullness of power. What a wonderful gospel age in which we live! How our unbelief, our defeatism, our selfish alibis for our powerlessness and fruitlessness have grieved God! These last days are the blessed days of revival, the one period in all the world when revival is easiest, when the power of God is promised in the greatest fullness, when the gospel is offered most freely to every creature! Let us take advantage of our heritage, and enter into the power promised and the fruitage promised![1]

7. Certain Teachers of Prophecy

The teaching of prophetic truth is of great importance—especially that which focuses on the return of our Lord Jesus Christ. If such teaching stresses the need to occupy until Christ comes, to preach this gospel of the Kingdom as a witness among all nations, and to call out a people for His name and glory, then such teaching is indeed fulfilling its God-given purpose. If prophetic teaching is preoccupied, however, with interpreting present world events and painting a picture of a defeated Church desperately hanging on by its fingernails—a picture in which there is no longer any place for earthshaking revivals—

such teaching has missed the whole point of prophecy and becomes an enemy of the cause of Christ. That kind of teaching may become a hiding place for those who do not want to pay the price for revival. It can easily draw off the time, energy and spiritual passion of those who otherwise might be involved in the greatest revival the world has ever seen. This kind of prophetic teaching is all the more dangerous, because those who are both leaders and followers are, for the most part, true Christians who love the Lord Jesus Christ, and think they are doing God service.

Any prophetic teaching which weakens our faith in God's ability to work in our day, and draws off our commitment to win the lost and build the Kingdom of God, needs to be examined very carefully and put in proper perspective as it relates to the important issues surrounding the return of Christ. All truly biblical teaching on the return of Christ must emphasize the outpouring of the Holy Spirit and the evangelization of the lost—or it misses the point! All prophetic teaching that is negative to revival is, in some way, in error.

If we go back to the great revival in the Book of Acts, we find some very important statements on this issue. In Acts 2:14–21, the period of history under discussion covers the cataclysmic events spoken of in other prophetic Scriptures concerning the time immediately preceding the return of Christ. Verses 19 and 20 mention "wonders in the heaven above and signs in the earth below, blood and fire and billows of smoke. The sun will be turned to darkness and the moon to blood before the coming of the great and glorious day of the Lord." These two verses' context makes it clear that we are to expect the outpouring of the Holy Spirit and the salvation of the lost as modeled by Pentecost, from that time right up until the glorious return of Christ!

Another passage strongly supporting this truth is Acts 3:19–21. The healing of a blind man had attracted a large crowd, and Peter took advantage of the situation to preach the gospel. The times of refreshing that are talked about here are to be expected right up until the return of Christ, which will precipitate the restoration of all things. Again, the prophetic Scriptures are appealed to as support for this position.

These are some of the negative voices that despair of revival. What has been said here ought to give every sincere Christian on the negative side of this issue real reason to examine his position very carefully in the light of God's Word. Let us turn now to the positive voices concerning the doctrinal foundation for revival.

POSITIVE VOICES

As we study the Bible and draw from it our basic Christian beliefs, we organize those beliefs in an orderly manner, and call the propositions which result from this process our Christian doctrine. A more academic term would be biblical theology. Let us ask ourselves a very important question: does the main body of this system of belief support the conviction that we can experience both personal and corporate revival in our day? If it does, it would be necessary to have very specific, clear doctrinal teaching to the contrary in order to discount this position! It is my sincere conviction that the main body of systematic Christian doctrine held by most evangelical Christians does indeed support the position that we can experience personal and corporate revival in our day. It would be impossible, in a book of this size, to examine all basic Christian doctrine thoroughly to test this question. I do believe, however, that we can look at major doctrines in a general way, and get a satisfying answer to our question. That is what I intend to do. As I proceed, I will list the doctrine and then make some remarks about each one as it relates to this proposition.

1. The Attributes of God

As we study God Himself, aspects of His being should convince us that God, under the right conditions, revives individuals and groups as He has in the past. God is immutable (that is, He never changes)—what God has been, He is now, and always will be. In Malachi 3:6, God declares, "I am the LORD, I change not!" In Hebrews 13:8, we read, "Jesus Christ the same, yesterday, today and forever." Again, in Joshua 1:5, God said, "As I was... so I will be." The history of God's dealings with men in the past is filled with instances in which God revived both individuals and groups. Since God does not change, there is every reason to believe that He would do the same thing today.

Another outstanding characteristic is that "God is love" (I John 4:7–12). All around us, society is deteriorating and drifting deeper and deeper into sin. The result is human pain and destruction—both now and for eternity—on a massive scale. In the past, great revivals have brought salvation to thousands of individuals and to society in general. If God is a God of love, He must be deeply moved by this situation. Why, then, would He not be willing to do the same things for us that He has done for others? Indeed, God's Word says, in Acts 10:34, "God is no respecter of persons!" The fact that God is love is one of the strongest possible arguments for expecting Him to gladly revive us again, if we will only meet the necessary conditions as others have done.

Other attributes of God are His omnipotence—that is, His infinite power—and His omniscience—His infinite knowledge and wisdom. The question then arises: does God have the knowledge, wisdom, and power to produce a great revival in our day? Has God become old, tired, and a little senile?

Some people seem to think that our world is too much for God. God, they say, cannot do today what He has done in the past. Only a little thought would reveal how foolish such an idea is. The unquestionable knowledge, wisdom, and power of God make it possible, and even likely, that He will revive His work in our day. Then, there is God's faithfulness. God has given promises throughout His Word that He will hear prayer, forgive sin, and restore His people. God is a God of truth, and God cannot lie! One outstanding promise concerning revival is found in II Chronicles 7:14. God says,

> *If my people, who are called by my name, will humble themselves and pray and seek my face and turn from their wicked ways, then will I hear from heaven and will forgive their sin, and will heal their land.*

Now, I am fully aware of the historic setting of this promise. Some will say, "that does not apply to us." My friends, it applies to God!

That is what He is like. He is faithful. He is unchanging. He loves us today. He is wise and He is all-powerful. He can—and He will—revive His work in our world!

2. The Doctrine of Christology

This includes the person and work of Christ. Why did Christ come into the world? He came to "seek and to save what was lost" (Luke 19:10). Paul said, "I am not ashamed of the gospel, because it is the power of God for the salvation of everyone who believes" (Rom. 1:16). In everything Jesus did and said, He showed Himself to be the Saviour. His whole life, including His death, was given to saving and restoring both individuals and groups. Jesus was, Himself, the center of an ever-widening revival. It is impossible to study His life, death, and resurrection without thinking that He would be passionately concerned for the people of our generation.

Jesus Christ is, without question, the only hope for our present human tragedy! How is it possible that God would pay the price He paid to give His Son to the world, and somehow withhold Him from the great masses of our day? People need the Lord! All of our present efforts to reach our world—as good and right as they are—are not enough. Only a revival of historic proportions will suffice. Christ is all they need.

Will God withhold the one thing that will set the Church ablaze with love and power? Will God refuse the one thing that will grip our youth and send them around the world? Will God say no to the one thing that will open the pockets of Christians and provide money to evangelize the world? Will God refuse the one thing that will set Christians praying until they tear down the strongholds of Satan and build the Kingdom of God? I say NO! The love of Christ constrains us to believe that He will revive His work today! Romans 8:32 states, "He who did not spare his own Son, but gave him up for us all—how will he not also, along with him, graciously give us all things?" I believe that includes revival!

Then what shall we say to the great work of redemption which Jesus Christ has provided through His death, burial and resurrection?

Has the blood of Jesus Christ lost its power? Are the sins of present human beings too much for the cleansing of that blood? Isaiah said, "Though your sins are like scarlet, they shall be as white as snow; though they are red as crimson, they shall be as wool" (Isaiah 1:18).

The Word of God tells us that Jesus conquered sin, death, and Satan through Calvary. It also states that in Christ we have all we need for both life and godliness. There is no reason to think that the wickedness of our day is too difficult for Jesus Christ to deal with. I believe the gospel of Jesus Christ is the power of God unto salvation in our day, the same as in the time of Peter and Paul!

3. The Doctrine of the Holy Spirit

All evangelical Christians believe in the mighty power of the Holy Spirit of God to do the work of God in the world. All Christians I know believe the Holy Spirit is here, in the Church and the world today. In both Scripture and history, revivals were wrought by God through the powerful working of the Holy Spirit. This was true in revivals under John the Baptist, Jesus Christ, and the Apostles. Jesus said, "How much more will your Father in heaven give the Holy Spirit to those who ask him!" (Luke 11:13). Peter said, "We are witnesses of these things, and so is the Holy Spirit, whom God has given to those who obey him" (Acts 5:32). At Pentecost, Peter said that what was happening was the fulfillment of Joel's prophecy about the "last days." We have already shown that we are now living in that time period. God said it was to be a time in human history when the Holy Spirit would be poured out on all kinds of human beings, with the result that whoever called upon the Lord would be saved. God also said, a little later, that these times of refreshing would come again and again, until the return of Christ. The time in which all these statements were made was a time of great revival. The great revival under the leadership of Jesus was a ministry of the Holy Spirit. As Jesus began His ministry, He stood in the synagogue in Nazareth, and read from Isaiah 61:1,2. This incident is found in Luke 4:18,19,21 as follows:

"The Spirit of the Lord is on me, because he has anointed me to preach good news to the poor. He has sent me to proclaim free-dom for the prisoners and recovery of sight for the blind, to release the oppressed, to proclaim the year of the Lord's favor." Then he ... said, "Today, this Scripture is fulfilled in your hearing."

Peter said, in Acts 10:38,

God anointed Jesus of Nazareth with the Holy Spirit and power, and ... he went around doing good and healing all who were under the power of the Devil, because God was with him.

Acts 1:7 recounts how, as Jesus was preparing to return to heaven, He promised this same power to His followers:

But you will receive power, when the Holy Spirit comes on you; and you will be my witnesses in Jerusalem, and in all Judea and Samaria, and to the ends of the earth.

Shortly before his death, Jesus told His disciples,

I tell you the truth, anyone who has faith in me will do what I have been doing. He will do even greater things than these, because I am going to the Father (John 14:12).

Jesus was talking about the power the disciples would share because He would send the Spirit of truth, the Holy Spirit, upon them to fill and empower them to build His Kingdom.

This same Holy Spirit is in us today! Nothing in Scripture indicates that the Holy Spirit has changed in His person or work. Therefore, it is an almost inescapable conclusion that we may expect the Holy Spirit to work in the same way today, and to produce the greatest revival yet seen on earth.

4. The Doctrine of the Inspired Word of God—the Bible

One of the great doctrines of the Christian faith is the doctrine of a God-inspired, infallible Scripture. We who are evangelicals take our stand on the Scriptures and declare that the Bible is our only rule of faith and practice. We believe that the Bible is different than other books in that it is inspired by God and is alive and powerful in a sense that no other book is or can be. In Hebrews 4:12,13 we read,

> *For the word of God is living and active. Sharper than any double-edged sword, it penetrates even to dividing soul and spirit, joints and marrow; it judges the thoughts and attitudes of the heart. Nothing in all creation is hidden from God's sight. Everything is uncovered and laid bare before the eyes of him to whom we must give account.*

Again, in Jeremiah 23:28,29 God says,

> *"Let the prophet who has a dream tell his dream, but let the one who has my word speak it faithfully. For what has straw to do with grain?" declares the Lord. "Is not my word like fire," declares the Lord, "and like a hammer that breaks a rock in pieces?"*

Do we evangelicals really believe what we *say* we believe about the Bible? If God's Word has the power these verses clearly state it has, why should we doubt its adequacy to bring revival to our generation? Can God's truth still refute and defeat the Devil's lies? Can God's Word still break the hardest hearts, and bring healing to the deepest human wounds? Do we believe the Bible has adequate answers for the ills and woes of our period of history? All great revivals of the past have been based on the truth and power of the Word of God. What we believe about the Scriptures is the strongest possible argument for expecting that the proper use of this unchanging Word will again bring revival in our day!

5. The Doctrine of Future Events

This includes the return of Christ, Judgement, Hell and Heaven. All true evangelicals believe that human beings will exist after death in a conscious, unending state. Even now, all who have died—though separated from their bodies—are in a self-conscious condition in either heaven or hell, comfort or torment. Christ will return to earth, all human beings will be judged, and everyone will enter into either eternal punishment and death, or eternal life and joy. To think nothing more can be done is so terrible as to drive a thoughtful person to despair! If I believed I am living in a day when for some reason God will no longer work in mighty power, and therefore, there is no hope for the masses of people around me, I do not know how I could stand it! I would not be able to preach. I could only stand and wring my hands in anguish, and weep uncontrollably over the fact that God had decided that there was nothing I could do but tell Christians to hang on and hope for Jesus to come.

What wicked nonsense! God Himself declared that He would destroy the intolerably wicked city empire of Nineveh in forty days. Nevertheless, when the great revivalist, Jonah, preached that message under the anointing of the Holy Spirit, that city repented. God then saved their souls, changed their society, and spared their city. The awful and glorious doctrines that have to do with man's eternal condition demand the possibility of a great revival, right up until the last moment before the final judgement falls!

6. The Doctrine of the Church

In Matthew 16:18, Jesus said, "I will build my church, and the gates of hell will not prevail against it." The Book of Acts is a historical account of the beginning of that great work. Though Christ used obedient men as His agents in the building project, it is unquestionable that Christ Himself was building the Church as He said. The building of the Church, in those days, included great revivals. Those great revivals were undoubtedly the work of the ascended Christ through His Spirit-filled body.

That same body is here now and the same Holy Spirit dwells within it. The same Lord Jesus Christ, the Head of that body, is seated in heaven at the right hand of God—still carrying on the building of His Church. The gates of hell (which I take to be the powers of darkness) are still raging against the Church. Who shall prevail—Christ or Satan? Do we indeed believe that the powers of the world, the flesh, and the devil have become so strong that Christ, our Head, can no more prevail against them? All the great advances of the Church recounted in the Book of Acts were precipitated by revivals. Each time, a new beachhead was established and the Church advanced in great strides.

As I will demonstrate in the next chapter, throughout the history of the Church, Christ overwhelmed the forces of evil and swept thousands into the Kingdom of God through no less than revival. Today, all the Church's best methods don't even begin to stem the tide of wickedness or evangelize the world. Why, then, would we think that the Head of the Church, our Lord Jesus Christ, would abandon His most successful method of establishing His Church?

The biblical doctrine of the Church, as set forth in the New Testament, leaves us no room but to believe that Christ passionately desires to turn our day in history into a time of great revivals all around the world. If He does so desire it, what holds Him back? Only His people. Our wicked selfishness, coldness, and unbelief stays His hand. Christ has said He will build His Church! If you do not believe He will do it in our day, by great revivals, then what method do **you** think will work? The Church of our day has tried everything imaginable. Much of what is being done is good—even of God. But none of those things has produced the great advance necessary to save the masses of our day, or to save our society from total destruction.

Already Christ is stirring up His people to a new awareness of our desperate situation. May God open our understanding to see that the answer is a great revival of historic proportions. May the Holy Spirit melt our hearts to humble ourselves, pray, seek God's face, and turn from our wicked ways. Then our Christ will hear from heaven, forgive our sin, and heal our land.

While this is by no means a complete discussion of the major doctrines of the Christian faith, I trust it will suffice to show that seeking God for another great revival is doctrinally sound. The basic doctrines embraced by all evangelicals actually lay a sound foundation for expecting God to revive His work in our day.

CHAPTER FOUR

The Foundation of History

WHAT IS REVIVAL?

- When a wealthy businessman prays all night in intense agony, pleading with God to bless him—and confessing to God all the evil of his heart and life—and the rest of his life is dramatically changed—*that* is **personal** revival!

- When a top government official has a vision of the Lord that shows him the total spiritual bankruptcy of his own heart, and the people around him, and the result is a changed life and a divine commission to his nation—*that* is **personal** revival!

- When a family man in his thirties gives up the spiritual hypocrisy of six years, is saved, healed, and answers the call of God to the ministry—all in three weeks—*that* is **personal** revival!

- When professing Christians who would not speak to each other for years are totally reconciled, when dozens of sick marriages are healed, when self-righteous, carnal church members are transformed, when worldly Christians put God first, when God robbers began to give, when fearful Christians begin to witness—*that* is **church** revival!

• When a church seating 1,000 is packed every night for six weeks, and many of the services run all night—*that* is **church** revival!

• When an entire Sunday morning congregation sits quietly weeping and praying before God under deep conviction for sin—*that* is **church** revival!

• When the teenagers, in their own prayer meeting are on their knees for over an hour, weeping in agonizing prayer for the salvation of their friends—*that* is **church** revival!

• When there are so many people going to businesses to pay old bills, pay for things they have stolen, and pay for dishonest things they have done, that the newspapers run front-page stories about it—*that* is either **church** revival or the **revival of God's work** in the world!

• When 80 percent of the adults are converted in an industrial city—*that* is the **revival of God's work** in the world!

• When people are being converted in a large metropolitan city at the rate of 10,000 a week—*that* is the **revival of God's work** in the world!

• When the illegitimate birth rate drops 44 percent in one year, and judges are presented with white gloves in public ceremonies because there are no cases to try—*that* is the **revival of God's work in the world!**

Without a fairly good understanding of history, we cannot have a good understanding of our own day. All the narrative portions of our Bible are history. God could have given us a manual filled with rules and regulations which tell us how to live, without giving us any history, either past or future. That is not what He did. The very first book of the Bible gives us an historical account of creation in general and the creation of man in particular. It includes the fall of man into sin and the beginning of God's redemptive plan, with the call of Abraham and the establishing of the nation of Israel—through which would come the Scriptures and the Saviour of the world.

The rest of the Old Testament books until the Psalms are historical accounts. Once you are past the books of poetry and philosophy, you are back into history—even in the Prophets.

As you come to the New Testament, you find that the four Gospels are the history of the life of Jesus Christ, with the teachings of Jesus recounted in their settings. The Book of Acts is a brief history of the first days of the Church. The Epistles are letters written to real churches which existed in history—often these letters deal with situations in which those churches were involved. Finally, the Book of Revelation is a book of future history.

History, then, is essential in the mind of God! When it comes to revival, the same is true. We cannot rightly consider the truths of revival unless we see them in real life, in the settings when and where they were experienced. For this, we turn to history.

Even a quick survey makes it evident that history has been so filled with revivals that it would be impossible in a book of this scope to thoroughly cover them all. Nevertheless, we shall attempt to include enough to paint a strong picture of the historical reality of revival.

In his book, *We Can Have Revival Now,* Dr. John R. Rice, a powerful soul-winning evangelist of the past generation, wrote:

> Faint-hearted Christians, who watch the clouds so much they do not sow, and observe the wind so much they do not reap, are defeated by the manifest wickedness on every side, and do not believe that God can give revival now. Many people cite the coldness of the people of God, the modernism and infidelity in many of the pulpits and in many places of denominational leadership, the widespread appeal of pleasure, the outrageous wickedness on every hand, as evidence that God cannot now give great revivals as he once did. But such faint-hearted christians should make a study of the great revivals in Bible times, and they would find that these revivals came in most cases, in the midst of wickedness as great and apostasy and false religions as prevalent as those we face today. It is a most heartening study to observe some of

the great revivals in the Bible and see how, against amazing odds, God used one person or a few in each case, to turn a whole nation or a strategic city back to God.[1]

With that challenge, let us begin. The many revivals in both Bible and later history make it impossible to do more than briefly mention most of them, with some receiving a more intensive examination than others. For ease of handling, I will divide these revivals into two sections—*Biblical History* and *Church History*.

Revivals in Biblical History

These revivals generally encompass cities or nations. In every case, the leader or leaders of the revival were revived first. Then the larger revival followed. The revival of an individual seems to stand by itself in a few cases, without involving a city or nation. We will consider those examples first. Two of these, Jacob and Isaiah, have already been dealt with at some length in chapter 3 under the heading of Personal Revival. I will briefly consider a few others.

It is likely that the oldest book in the Bible is Job. The entire book is the account of Job's spiritual renewal. Since this is not a story of spiritual coldness, rebellion or backsliding, it does not seem to fit the classic pattern of declension and revival but is—on the contrary—the experience of a good man who is brought to a completely new relationship with the God he loved. Before his personal revival, God said of Job, "There is no one on earth like him; he is blameless and upright, a man who fears God and shuns evil" (Job 1:8). Nevertheless, Job had a problem with spiritual pride and self-righteousness. We read about it in Job 32:1,2; 34:5–9,12,36–37:

> So these three men stopped answering Job, because he was righteous in his own eyes. But Elihu son of Barakel the Buzite, of the family of Ram, became very angry with Job for justifying himself rather than God. "Job says, 'I am innocent, but God denies me justice. Although I am right, I am considered a liar; although I am guiltless, his arrow inflicts an incurable wound.' What man is like

Job, who drinks scorn like water? He keeps company with evildoers; he associates with wicked men. For he says, 'It profits a man nothing when he tries to please God.' ... It is unthinkable that God would do wrong, that the Almighty would pervert justice ... Oh, that Job might be tested to the utmost for answering like a wicked man! To his sin he adds rebellion; scornfully he claps his hands among us and multiplies his words against God."

In this case, Elihu is the man speaking, with prophetic authority, the truth of God to Job. He says that he is filled with the Spirit of God and cannot be silent. After Elihu's powerful sermon, God begins to reveal Himself to Job. Then we have the dramatic renewal that takes place in Job, spiritually, physically, and socially. We find Job's prayer of repentance in Job 42:2–6.

I know that you can do all things; no plan of yours can be thwarted. [You asked,] 'Who is this that obscures my counsel without knowledge?' Surely I spoke of things I did not understand, things too wonderful for me to know. [You said,] 'Listen now, and I will speak; I will question you, and you shall answer me.' My ears had heard of you but now my eyes have seen you. Therefore I despise myself and repent in dust and ashes.

This personal revival is very important, because we see that a child of God does not need to be backslidden in order to need revival. Indeed, Job was meticulous in all his religious observances, and was declared by God to be superior to all others in his fear of God and hatred of evil. Nevertheless, a new revelation of God to his heart showed Job himself in a new light which brought deep repentance and dramatic change to his life. The result was a new ministry of power to his friends and a new relationship to God that made it possible for God to bless Job in all other aspects of his life.

Some people in the Church today are similar to Job: they love God and hate evil. Outwardly, their lives are examples of Christian faithfulness and service to God. Neither these people nor their friends think they need revival. God may think differently. A new revelation of God

Himself to their hearts would, in many cases, give them a view of themselves. Like Job and Isaiah, they would cry out, "Woe to me! ... I am ruined! For I am a man of unclean lips, and I live among a people of unclean lips, and my eyes have seen the King, the LORD Almighty" (Is. 6:5). If we can get our eyes off of ourselves and other people, and fasten our attention upon the Lord, He will truly revive many of us who until now have not seen ourselves as being in need of revival.

The second individual revival I wish to consider is that of King David. David had been a great man of God, indeed, "a man after God's own heart." When he was anointed by the prophet Samuel, "the Spirit of the Lord came on David from that day forward." Even in those terrible days when he fled from King Saul, David stayed true to the Lord. He would not stretch forth his hand against the Lord's anointed when it appeared that God had placed Saul right in his hands. He would not take the kingdom by human means, but waited on God's timing and God's working. Finally, David was fully vindicated by God and established as the King of all Israel. God had taken him from the sheep-fold and given him the highest place.

But David became careless, in both his public and personal life. We find the terrible story in II Samuel 11. It was time for David to go to battle against his enemies. He stayed in Jerusalem and sent Joab to lead the armies of Israel. Then, in an hour of terrible temptation, he committed adultery. The woman, another man's wife, became pregnant! He tried to cover his sin but could not, since the woman's husband was more honourable than David. Now, completely trapped by his sin and unwilling to confess it, he ordered Uriah's execution to be carried out in such a way that it would look as though Bathsheba's husband had been a casualty of war. Then David took the "widowed" Bathsheba for his wife and she gave birth to the child that had been conceived in adultery. "But the thing that David had done displeased the LORD" (II Sam. 11:27).

David did these terrible things as a result of a slow progression into self-centredness and pride. He became spiritually lazy and full of self-importance. Satan set him up, and down he went! Fortunately, God loved David too much to let him go on in service to the Lord as if everything was all right. God sent Nathan, a prophet who dared to speak for God at the risk of his life! He trapped David with a made-up story about a rich man who stole his poor neighbor's little pet lamb. When David reacted with anger against the imaginary man, Nathan exposed his hypocrisy by saying, "You are the man!" Pierced to the heart with conviction, David collapsed before God in total brokenness and genuine repentance, crying out, "I have sinned!" A great revival followed in David's individual life. Though this revival appears to have been sudden, in reality it was the culmination of months of torment—David was pressed by his conscience and the Spirit of God. We see the agony of this struggle in Psalm 38:1–4,6,8–10,18:

> O Lord, do not rebuke me in your anger or discipline me in your wrath. For your arrows have pierced me, and your hand has come down upon me. Because of your wrath there is no health in my body; my bones have no soundness because of my sin. My guilt has overwhelmed me like a burden too heavy to bear. I am bowed down and brought very low; all day long I go about mourning. I am feeble and utterly crushed; I groan in anguish of heart. All my longings lie open before you, O Lord; my sighing is not hidden from you. My heart pounds, my strength fails me; even the light has gone from my eyes. I confess my iniquity; I am troubled by my sin.

Then in Psalm 51, we have David's great prayer of repentance. It goes right to the heart of what is essential for true revival.

> Have mercy on me, O God, according to your unfailing love; according to your great compassion blot out my transgressions. Wash away all my iniquity and cleanse me from my sin. For I know my transgressions, and my sin is always before me. Against you, you only, have I sinned and done what is evil in your sight, so that you are proved right when you speak and justified when you judge. Surely I was sinful at birth, sinful from the time my

mother conceived me. Surely you desire truth in the inner parts; you teach me wisdom in the inmost place. Cleanse me with hyssop, and I will be clean; wash me, and I will be whiter than snow. Let me hear joy and gladness; let the bones you have crushed rejoice. Hide your face from my sins and blot out all my iniquity. Create in me a pure heart, O God, and renew a steadfast spirit within me. Do not cast me from your presence or take your Holy Spirit from me. Restore to me the joy of your salvation and grant me a willing spirit, to sustain me. Then I will teach transgressors your ways, and sinners will turn back to you. Save me from bloodguilt, O God, the God who saves me, and my tongue will sing of your righteousness. O Lord, open my lips, and my mouth will declare your praise. You do not delight in sacrifice, or I would bring it; you do not take pleasure in burnt offerings. The sacrifices of God are a broken spirit; a broken and contrite heart, O God, you will not despise (Ps. 51:1–17).

Parts of this prayer establish a pattern for our own individual repentance and personal revival. David began by appealing to God's mercy and love—the only ground by which to approach God for forgiveness. In complete humility and honesty, he confessed his sin. He regarded his sin as principally against God, although he had sinned against Bathsheba, Uriah, Joab, all of Israel, and the enemies of God. He knew God would be justified in condemning him. He even understood the innate wickedness of his own being. Then he came to the main issue of his inner life, admitting that his outward deceit came from a deceitful heart—"You desire TRUTH in the inner parts." The hidden part, not seen by man, was where David needed deep change. He prayed to be cleansed by the blood (hyssop), so he would be made pure and all his sins would be blotted out. With the words, "Create in me a clean heart, O God, and renew a steadfast spirit within me," he prayed for inner change. Then he asked God to not remove the special anointing of the Holy Spirit from his life, but give him a willing spirit. Again he dealt with the primary path to a revived life, as he assured himself before God that the "sacrifices of God are a broken spirit; a broken and a contrite heart God will not despise." He reminded God that the result of a revived life is the conversion of sinners.

God's response was "I have put away your sin." However, some of the natural results of David's sin could not be changed! The child died. Immorality and violence repeated themselves in David's children. We must not think revival will bring in the Millennium. It will not. Nevertheless, David's individual revival was genuine and powerful, resulting in a changed life and renewed ministry.

The personal revival process follows this path: a genuine Christian becomes careless in his relationship to God and his daily life. Slowly, he is weakened until he falls into temptation and sin. He tries to hide his sin, but the resulting hypocrisy brings about a condition of increasing inner anguish in the presence of God's convicting Holy Spirit. The Word of God is eventually brought to the heart with convicting power. Sin is exposed! Deep repentance follows. The Christian in question sees in a new way that his problem has to do with the condition of his heart or spirit. At the center of his being, there is need for truth, wisdom, purity (singleness of heart), and brokenness. He appeals to the mercy and grace of God for cleansing from sin and a divine creative renewal in his innermost being. He pleads for the anointing of God's Holy Spirit to remain on him. He prays for emotional and possibly physical healing. Then, he reminds God that this personal revival will result in the conversion of sinners. These are two examples of individual revival! One of these two experiences is available now for every honest, hungry-hearted Christian. May God give us the courage to enter in!

As we turn our attention to the group revivals of the Old Testament, we find an interesting variety, but the same principles. We would not all necessarily agree as to which incidents are revivals—however, there should be enough agreement to lay aside our differences temporarily and look for some patterns that will provide principles upon which we can build for the revivals so desperately needed in our day. To do this, I am going to lay out a brief view of some of the major Old Testament revivals.

REVIVAL UNDER MOSES

The historical foundation for revival in the Old Testament reveals that most of these revivals follow similar patterns. Though some personal revivals do not seem to go beyond that, the majority of individual revivals result in some form of group revival—most of which are *national* revivals! A significant time lapse between the revival of the individual and his nation is notable in the following example. Nevertheless, the revival of the individual makes the revival of the nation possible! This is the great revival under Moses:

> *"I have seen these people," the* LORD *said to Moses, "and they are a stiff-necked people. Now leave me alone so that my anger may burn against them and that I may destroy them. Then I will make you into a great nation." But Moses sought the favor of the* LORD *his God. "O* LORD*," he said, "why should your anger burn against your people, whom you brought out of Egypt with great power and a mighty hand? Why should the Egyptians say, 'It was with evil intent that he brought them out, to kill them in the mountains and to wipe them off the face of the earth'? Turn from your fierce anger; relent and do not bring disaster on your people. Remember your servants Abraham, Isaac and Israel, to whom you swore by your own self: 'I will make your descendants as numerous as the stars in the sky and I will give your descendants all this land I promised them, and it will be their inheritance forever.'" Then the* LORD *relented and did not bring on his people the disaster he had threatened.... The next day Moses said to the people, "You have committed a great sin. But now I will go up to the* LORD*; perhaps I can make atonement for your sin." So Moses went back to the* LORD *and said, "Oh, what a great sin these people have committed! They have made themselves gods of gold. But now, please forgive their sin—but if not, then blot me out of the book you have written"* (Exodus 32:9–14, 30–32).

First—let us notice **three things**:

1. *The Need For Revival*;
2. *The Key To Revival*; and,
3. *The Process Of Revival.*

First then, *The Need For Revival.* An entire people had turned from the true and living God to idols! God's wrath was hanging over them. They had become lawless and were running wild. They were out of control. It was revival or ruin! The need for revival was imperative.

Next we come to *The Key To Revival*, which is always the same— an "Intercessor." Moses was that intercessor. God Himself has said this is the "key":

> *I looked for a man among them who would build up the wall and stand before me in the gap on behalf of the land so I would not have to destroy it, but I found none. So I will pour out my wrath on them and consume them with my fiery anger, bringing down on their own heads all they have done, declares the Sovereign* LORD (Ezek. 22:30,31).

The boldness of Moses' intercessory prayer is astounding! This is not to be confused with arrogance from "the most meek man on the face of the earth." It is a selfless prayer, devoid of pride, for God offered to make of Moses a great nation and he refused it. It is a prayer of identification with the people, for Moses said "save them or damn me with them"! It is a believing prayer, based on the Word of God, God's promises. It is a helpless prayer that seeks the presence of God, saying, "You go with us, or we are not going"! It is a focused prayer that seeks God's reputation and glory in the earth. Finally, it is a personal prayer that hungrily cries out for a new revelation of God to the heart and life of the intercessor.

Finally, we come to *The Process Of Revival.* Once the true inter-cessor knows he has the ear of God, he looks for others who will pay the price to stand with him. This Moses did, in his invitation to which the Levites responded. Next comes thorough dealing with sin. Then comes cleansing, forgiveness, and a renewed manifestation of the presence of God among His people. God's covenant is re-established, and a nation is revived and saved from destruction.

These are still the proper steps toward revival in our day.

REVIVAL UNDER SAMUEL

The next great national revival for Israel was the revival under Samuel. Judges 17:6 gives us the setting: "In those days there was no king in Israel; every man did what was right in his own eyes" (NASB).

Twice, the Book of Judges states this was a time in the history of Israel when everyone did what was right in his own eyes—a time of **fragmentation**, when society was falling apart. It was a day of personal independence and lawlessness—there was no **social glue**!

Israel had departed from God, and in so doing, they were no longer committed to any basic set of moral standards and values by which to live. The ensuing political and social chaos exposed them to oppression and destruction. In a battle with the Philistines, the Ark of God was captured. The two wicked sons of the priest Eli were killed. The wife of one of them, dying in childbirth,

> named the boy Ichabod, saying, "The glory has departed from Israel"—because of the capture of the ark of God and the deaths of her father-in-law and her husband. She said, "The glory has departed from Israel, for the ark of God has been captured" (I Samuel 4:21,22).

When Eli heard the news, he fell, broke his neck, and died. For twenty years, the Ark was gone—God's glory *had* departed from His people—and they languished in powerlessness and oppression.

Then they cried out to the LORD—and God raised up a Prophet and leader named Samuel, who called Israel back to God.

> And Samuel said to the whole house of Israel, "If you are returning to the Lord with all your hearts, then rid yourselves of the foreign gods and the Ashtoreths and commit yourselves to the Lord

and serve him only, and he will deliver you out of the hand of the Philistines." So the Israelites put away their Baals and Ashtoreths, and served the Lord only. Then Samuel said, "Assemble all Israel at Mizpah and I will intercede with the Lord for you." When they had assembled at Mizpah, they drew water and poured it out before the Lord. On that day they fasted and there they confessed, "We have sinned against the Lord." And Samuel was leader of Israel at Mizpah (I Samuel 7:3–6).

He said, "You must return to the Lord 'with all your heart.'" Half-hearted commitment produces a situation that requires revival, and God knows our hearts. His second requirement was for Israel to turn from every form of idolatry. His third requirement was an exclusive commitment to the Lord and His service. Next, Samuel called them to a solemn assembly in which they fasted, prayed, confessed their sins, and offered the required blood sacrifice to make atonement and reconciliation with God, whom they had so long offended. Finally, Samuel himself entered into a ministry of intercession on their behalf. The result was a great revival!

As they prayed and pled the Blood of the Lamb—God moved in supernatural power against the enemy. The Israelites left their place of comfort and safety and attacked! God gave them a great victory. They recovered lost territory. They set up a memorial to remind them of this great revival! Their memorial was named **Ebenezer**—"stone of help." Often we doubt God will work in our day, because we have not bothered to study the great revivals of the past. The hymn writer put it like this: "Here I raise my Ebenezer/ Hither by thy help I've come./ And I hope by thy good pleasure/ safely to arrive at home."

How does this apply to us today? The world as we know it is breaking up around us! Both government and business are fragmenting—downsizing and dividing into smaller units. Small business and job-changing will be the order of the day. Personal independence in belief and action is the direction of society. Loyalty and commitment to a larger entity have been discarded. "Multicultural" has been interpreted to mean "anti-moral and multi-value." **Lawlessness reigns—**

every person does what is right in his own eyes! Because the people of North America have turned away from God, they have **no social glue** to hold them together. Our whole society is falling apart. When this fragmentation reaches intolerable proportions, survival will force us to accept a **totalitarian form of government!** It will be **anti-Christian!** Then under oppression—like the Israelites—we will cry out to God. Will it then be too late? Wouldn't it be better to repent now? LET REVIVAL COME NOW!

WHAT SHALL WE DO? Let us follow the same steps laid out for the people of Israel. Today's Christians have put business, possessions, pleasure and self-fulfillment ahead of God. We must repent of our half-hearted Christianity. We need to get rid of our idols. God should be put first in our lives and have an exclusive place in our service. We need to come together in solemn assemblies, where we fast, pray, confess our sins and seek the cleansing of the blood of Christ. Rather than selecting our leaders from the ranks of business executives, we need men and women of prayer. Memorials of testimony that give glory to God, rather than man, should be set up. When we seriously do these things, revival will follow.

FOUR REVIVALS UNDER KINGS OF JUDAH

"Asa did what was good and right in the eyes of the LORD his God" (II Chron. 14:2). This statement about King Asa is a fitting introduction to four great national revivals in Judah, led by four great kings of Judah. They are Asa, Jehoshaphat, Joash, and Hezekiah. Any study of revival in Bible history makes it abundantly obvious that the leaders of God's people have a profound responsibility in the matter of revival. In these four revivals, certain procedures instituted by these four leaders become distinguishing marks. These four things may set precedent for steps toward revival in our time.

All of these revivals began with "Destroying Idols." The Scripture accounts are filled with statements like the following:

II **Chronicles 14:3**—"He removed the foreign altars and the high places, smashed the sacred stones and cut down the Asherah poles."

II Chronicles 14:5—"He removed the high places and incense altars in every town in Judah, and the kingdom was at peace under him."

II Chronicles 17:3–4—"The LORD was with Jehoshaphat because in his early years he walked in the ways his father David had followed. He did not consult the Baals but sought the God of his father and followed his commands rather than the practices of Israel."

II Chronicles 17:6—"His heart was devoted to the ways of the LORD... he removed the high places and the Asherah poles from Judah."

II Chronicles 23:17—"All the people went to the temple of Baal and tore it down. They smashed the altars and idols and killed Mattan the priest of Baal in front of the altars."

II Chronicles 31:1—"When all this had ended, the Israelites who were there went out to the towns of Judah, smashed the sacred stones and cut down the Asherah poles. They destroyed the high places and the altars throughout Judah and Benjamin and in Ephraim and Manasseh."

Are God's people guilty of idolatry today? I wonder what God thinks about all the things we put ahead of Him. God says greed is idolatry—Colossians 3:5. What about our inordinate preoccupation with pleasure, our obsession with sports, and a retired life of leisure? God says that in the last days, men will love pleasure more than they love God (II Tim. 3:1–5). Would God call our passion for personal fulfillment and success idolatry? Then there is the matter of man-worship. Many of God's people are devoted to religious leaders and systems, rather than to God. It is **all** idolatry! Which idol must I give up to experience revival?

On a hot September day in San Antonio, Texas, the temperature was 99 degrees. A woman accidentally locked her 10-month-old baby girl in her car. Frantically, the mother and aunt ran around, nearly hysterical, while a neighbor tried to unlock the door with a hanger wire, to no avail. The baby was turning blue and frothing at the mouth when a truck driver came along. Quickly, he solved the problem by smashing the window with a tire iron. He then delivered the baby into her mother's arms. Was the mother grateful? No! She was angry at him for smashing the window of her car. We say we want revival, but are we willing to give up our idols in order to have it?

The Old Testament accounts next describe the leaders "restoring public worship," which was not possible until the idols were destroyed. Please look at the exciting scriptural statements about what happened in II Chronicles 15:8–9.

> *When Asa heard these words and the prophecy of Azariah son of Oded the prophet, he took courage. He removed the detestable idols from the whole land of Judah and Benjamin and from the towns he had captured in the hills of Ephraim. He repaired the altar of the LORD that was in front of the portico of the LORD's temple. Then he assembled all Judah and Benjamin and the people from Ephraim, Manasseh and Simeon who had settled among them, for large numbers had come over to him from Israel when they saw that the LORD his God was with him.*

II Chronicles 24:4, 9–10 tells us that

> *Some time later Joash decided to restore the temple of the LORD.... A proclamation was then issued in Judah and Jerusalem that they should bring to the LORD the tax that Moses the servant of God had required of Israel in the desert. All the officials and all the people brought their contributions gladly, dropping them into the chest until it was full.*

II Chronicles 29:1–11 tells us how Hezekiah cleansed the temple of the Lord, and restored proper worship.

A scandalous neglect of commitment to the Church prevails in our day. Almost anything is a legitimate reason not to be involved— why is that? Why is it that half of most congregations never sing? Why do people scramble to sit in the back of the sanctuary? Why is there a problem getting proper board members? Why are church business meetings so poorly attended? Why must people be entertained in order to come to church services? Why is Sunday evening attendance a third or less than that of the morning? I thank God I was brought to Sunday evening services as a child. That is where I received Christ when I was seven. Why is it that the greater portion of Christians do not tithe into the church?

A number of years back, *The British Weekly* published the following letter:

> Dear Sir;
>
> It seems ministers feel their sermons are very important and spend a great deal of time preparing them. I have been attending church quite regularly for thirty years, and I have probably heard 3,000 of them. To my consternation I cannot remember a single sermon. I wonder if a minister's time might be more profitably spent on something else?

For a number of weeks, a storm of editorial response followed. Finally, it was all ended by the following letter:

> Dear Sir;
>
> I have been married for thirty years. During that time I have eaten 32,850 meals, mostly my wife's cooking. Suddenly I have discovered I cannot remember the menu of a single meal. And yet, I have the distinct impression that without them, I would have starved to death long ago![2]

The third mark of these revivals was "hearing and obeying God's Word." This is clear from the following Scripture passages:

> *The Spirit of God came upon Azariah son of Oded. He went out to meet Asa and said to him, "Listen to me, Asa and all Judah and Benjamin. The LORD is with you when you are with him. If you seek him, he will be found by you, but if you forsake him, he will forsake you. For a long time Israel was without the true God, without a priest to teach and without the law. But in their distress they turned to the LORD, the God of Israel, and sought him, and he was found by them* (II Chron. 15:1–4).

II Chronicles 18:13, "But Micaiah said, 'As surely as the LORD lives, I can tell him only what my God says.'"

King Jehoshaphat appointed Levites to go throughout the land and teach the people the Word of God. The result was astounding! We have the account in II Chronicles 17:9–10.

They taught throughout Judah, taking with them the Book of the Law of the LORD; they went around to all the towns of Judah and taught the people. The fear of the LORD fell on all the kingdoms of the lands surrounding Judah, so that they did not make war with Jehoshaphat.

Jesus said, "You have done away with the commands of God through the doctrines of men." Today, the commands of God are being mocked and ignored on every side. Even Christians often do what is right in their own eyes, rather than what God clearly says in His Word. The Kingdom of God is not a democracy—it is a Theocracy, and the authority of God's Word is final! George Will, in "Men At Work," writes the following:

Baseball umpires are made from granite and stuffed with microchips. They are professional dispensers of pure justice! Once when Babe Penelli called Babe Ruth out on strikes, Babe Ruth made a populist argument. He reasoned fallaciously from raw numbers to moral weight. He said, "There's forty thousand people here who know that last one was a ball, tomatoe head!" To which Penelli replied, with the measured stateliness of a judge, "Maybe so, but mine is the only opinion that counts!"[3]

Christians today are pressed by the weight of numbers to doubt God's moral standards. Remember—**only God's opinion counts!**

"Seeking God's Face" or "Prayer." is the fourth mark of these revivals. Among the overwhelming number of Scripture passages that indicate this are II Chronicles 14:11; 20:5–6; 20:12, and II Chronicles 32:20–22:

Then Asa called to the LORD his God and said, "LORD, there is no one like you to help the powerless against the mighty. Help us, O LORD our God, for we rely on you, and in your name we have come against this vast army. O LORD, you are our God; do not let man prevail against you."

Then Jehoshaphat stood up in the assembly of Judah and Jerusalem at the temple of the LORD in the front of the new courtyard and said: "O LORD, God of our fathers, are you not the God who is in heaven? You rule over all the kingdoms of the nations. Power and might are in your hand, and no one can withstand you.

"O our God, will you not judge them? For we have no power to face this vast army that is attacking us. We do not know what to do, but our eyes are upon you."

King Hezekiah and the prophet Isaiah son of Amoz cried out in prayer to heaven about this. And the LORD sent an angel, who annihilated all the fighting men and the leaders and officers in the camp of the Assyrian king. So he withdrew to his own land in disgrace. And when he went into the temple of his god, some of his sons cut him down with the sword. So the LORD saved Hezekiah and the people of Jerusalem from the hand of Sennacherib king of Assyria and from the hand of all others. He took care of them on every side.

There has never been a revival that did not come in answer to prayer! Oh, how desperately the Church of Jesus Christ needs to pray today—there is too much talk, and not enough prayer. We need to talk less and pray more.

Years ago, a church in Hartford, Connecticut had a very brilliant pastor, but he was not sound in doctrine. Three godly men in that church realized that their pastor was not speaking the truth. They did not go about talking and stirring up trouble. Instead, they covenanted together to meet every Saturday night to pray for him. They did this many nights, sometimes long into the night. Then, Sunday morning they would go to church and listen, to see if God had answered their prayers. One Sunday morning, all was changed. The sermon was filled with truth. The pastor was obviously changed in person and convictions. Through that pastor and that church followed the greatest revival the city of Hartford had ever seen!

What shall we say to these things? Nations have not changed! People have not changed! **God has not changed!** Let us search our hearts before God. Are we guilty of idolatry? Do we neglect the Church of the living God? Are we striving to live according to the Word of God? Are we a people of prayer who seek God's face? I believe when we can answer these questions properly, the revival will come!

THE REVIVALS UNDER ELIJAH AND JONAH

No study of revivals in the Old Testament would be complete without including the revivals under the leadership of the prophets Elijah and Jonah. These revivals increase in importance when we realize that one was a revival involving the people of God, and the other was a revival involving the salvation of a pagan nation and city.

Before the revival led by Elijah, Ahab ruled Israel. "There was never a man like Ahab, who sold himself to do evil in the eyes of the LORD, urged on by Jezebel his wife" (I Kings 21:25). Because these two had led Israel into a totally backslidden and idolatrous state, God had brought the judgement of a drought lasting over three years on all the land, through the prophetic word of Elijah. Ahab sought to kill Elijah, who had hidden during this time. When the time was ripe for the revival, God sent Elijah to Ahab for a spiritual confrontation. I Kings 18:16–39 tells the story.

From this account, we learn seven things about revival:

1. Revival demands decisions. "How long will you waver?" It means serious change of commitment.

2. Revival is a time of conflict, between God and Satan, the Church and the world, the Spirit and the flesh.

3. Revival is a time of repairing broken altars, the altars of the Lord that have been broken down. Altars of personal and family devotions, church attendance, tithing, and witnessing to the lost.

4. Revival is a time when we set things in order. The stones and the sacrifice were to be arranged in a particular order as com-

manded by God. There are things that need to be straightened out in our lives. Some of those things involve human relationships and some involve restitution. Revival is God's finger pointing at me! In a real revival, God will find me!

5. Revival is precipitated by earnest, believing prayer. Elijah prayed desperate prayers that had to get answers. "Answer me O Lord, answer me!"

6. Revival will always include miracles. Then the fire of the Lord fell! This revival included both physical and spiritual miracles.

7. Finally, revival will mean the restoration of God's people, the conversion of sinners, and a definite impact on society. May God see fit to give us such a revival in our day among the people of God!

Humbly now O Lord I pray, send revival here today.
All my coldness, all my sin, all my doubting deep within,
Forgive them Lord, cleanse them away.
O send revival here today!
Humbly Lord I ask of thee, send revival now through me.
Emptied out of self and pride, no longer do I wish to hide.
O dear Lord use me I pray, to bring revival here today!

Let us consider the revival led by the prophet Jonah. This story is found in the Book of Jonah—a book of only four chapters. I will quote here only small portions which apply directly to my subject matter. The setting for this revival is unique in the Old Testament. Assyria, the great world power of that day, was a totally pagan nation immersed in idolatry. Its seemingly invincible army had a reputation for cruelty beyond imagination.

Nineveh was Assyria's capital, a very large city for that day, and considered impregnable. A constant source of fear and dread was Assyria's armies, even the thought of which raised disgust and hatred in the hearts of God's people! The prayer of most Israelites was that God would destroy Nineveh. Jonah was commanded by God to go and preach to them, that they might repent and avoid His just judgement. It was the last thing on earth that any patriotic Jew wanted to do. Jonah argued with God, and when that didn't work, he flatly refused to go. Indeed, he set off in the opposite direction. God sent a great storm and a great fish to stop him. Down in the bottom of the sea, in the fish's stomach, Jonah repented. The fish vomited Jonah up on the land, and God renewed His call to bring revival to the pagan city of Nineveh. Jonah went.

He preached what God told him to preach: "Forty days, and Nineveh will be destroyed!" A great revival followed—even the King believed and led the nation in genuine repentance. So, God did not destroy Nineveh as He had said. Jonah became so angry over this that he wanted to die! But God rebuked Jonah for his carnality and lack of love. This revival confronts us with a painful and demanding question: "Can our world be changed?" Is it too far gone? Can God change my life, my family, my church, my city, my nation? Do I really want that kind of change enough to obey God and pay the price needed to bring it about? Please look with me at these questions as they are answered in the Book of Jonah. The answer divides itself into three issues about God Himself:

> *God's Nature,*
> *God's Priorities,* and
> *God's Signs.*

1. God's Nature

God cannot and does not change! People can and do change. In this account the sailors change, Jonah changes, and Nineveh changes. It may appear that God changes, but He does not. God changed His actions, but not His purpose. The Nineveh that God said He would destroy in forty days no longer existed. In this entire revival, God was always the same, always acting like Himself in each situation. It was like God to send Jonah to Nineveh. It was like God to stop Jonah when he disobeyed. It was like God to save the sailors and rescue Jonah when he repented. It was like God to give Jonah a second chance. It was like God to spare Nineveh when they repented. And it was even like God to deal gently with his pouting prophet.

2. God's Priorities

God's priorities are eternal rather than temporal. Man's priorities are often "creatures of a night." God is concerned about eternal souls. God said about the gourd, "You did not tend it or make it grow." Men are God's creation. God loves people we Christians do not think deserve His love or salvation. Somehow we have forgotten our own sin and need of God's grace. The poet has put it this way: "For the love of God is broader than the measure of man's mind; And the heart of the Eternal is most wonderfully kind!"

3. God's Signs

The Ninevites were no doubt deeply impressed by the miraculous experience of Jonah, who had in a way experienced death and resurrection. This experience of Jonah was so great a sign of God, that Jesus spoke of it in Matthew 12:39–41:

> He answered, "A wicked and adulterous generation asks for a miraculous sign! But none will be given it except the sign of the prophet Jonah. For as Jonah was three days and three nights in the belly of a huge fish, so the Son of Man will be three days and three nights in the heart of the earth. The men of Nineveh will stand up at the judgment with this generation and condemn it; for they repented at the preaching of Jonah, and now one greater than Jonah is here.

This of course is the "sign of the cross." Christ crucified is the message at the heart of every revival—His death for us, and our death with Him. God's sign, the cross, has never changed. Do we Christians really want a revival, or do we just want to make our lives easier? Do we want the pagan world around us to change because we are afraid of what is going to happen to us if it doesn't, or do we want revival because men are lost, under God's judgment, and on their way to an eternal hell?

THE POST-EXILE REVIVAL

Can a city be revived?
In Rome, New York, where my parents were married, 80% of the adults were converted in a revival!

In the Great Revival of 1905, the pastors of Atlantic City, New Jersey reported that of a population of 50,000, only 50 adults remained unconverted!

Can a city be revived?
Let us consider the city of Jerusalem, about 538 years before the birth of Jesus Christ. Jerusalem had been conquered by Nebuchadnezzar of Babylon in 609 B.C. The puppet kings he put in place rebelled against him, so in 587 B.C., he destroyed Jerusalem—breaking down the walls, burning the Temple, and destroying all the leading homes of the city. He deported all the leaders of the country, along with the craftsmen and soldiers that were left. The land and the city were stripped.

In 538 B.C., King Cyrus of Persia sent Zerubbabel and a large group of Jews back to Jerusalem to rebuild the Temple. They began with enthusiasm, but opposition from their enemies, personal selfishness, and indifference on the part of God's people brought the work to a halt.

In their first excitement, the Jews who returned also started to repair the walls and gates of the city. The Jews' enemies put a stop to that, and broke down their repairs and burned their repaired gates.

Sixteen years passed, during which no proper worship could be carried on. The people were totally exposed to their enemies and roving bands of robbers. Into this desperate scene came the prophets Haggai and Zechariah, under whose preaching the people were revived. Quickly, the rebuilding of the Temple was finished and the worship of God was restored, but the city still lay wasted and exposed. The Jews in the land were living sinful lives, filled with selfishness and compromise.

Eighty more years went by. Then, in 458 B.C., Ezra came from exile, leading a large group of Jews and bringing money and help of all kinds. A great spiritual revival followed! Ezra was a great preacher and teacher of the Word of God! As the people got right with God, God prepared for their restoration. Now that the spiritual walls were restored, it was time to restore the physical walls of the city.

Twelve more years went by. God then laid His hand on a man high up in the government of the Persian Emperor, and Nehemiah was sent to Jerusalem to rebuild the walls and totally REVIVE the city! The year was 446 B.C.

The REVIVAL that followed speaks directly to you and me! Nehemiah was faced with 42,000 people paralyzed by past failure and defeat. Even the thought that they could save their city brought scorn and mockery from the world around them. Their enemy, Sanballat, asked:

What are these feeble Jews doing? Will they restore their wall? Will they offer sacrifices? Will they finish in a day? Can they bring the stones back to life from those heaps of rubble—burned as they are? (Neh. 4:2).

Yes Sanballat, that was exactly what they would do, by the power of Almighty God! **How did they do it? What were the key issues in that great revival? I see eight issues:**

First—Nehemiah did a thorough and honest evaluation of the situation. Things were indeed desperate (Nehemiah 1:3, Nehemiah 2:13–17).

Second—Nehemiah organized the people to clear away the rubbish (Neh. 4:10).

Third—They began to build with the stones that were fallen down (Neh. 4:3).

Fourth—They separated themselves from the world in doing God's work (Neh. 2:20).

Fifth—They worked separately where they lived, but came together as a congregation for worship, encouragement and instruction (Neh. 3:23, 8:1,3,6).

Sixth—They learned how to work and war at the same time. (Neh. 4:16–20).

Seventh—Nehemiah insisted that God's people be right with one another (Neh. 5:1–7).

Eighth—Nehemiah bathed the entire movement in earnest prayer (Neh. 1:4; 4:9). There are thirteen references in this book to the prayer life of Nehemiah.

These same issues are absolutely key to revival in our day. Any honest evaluation of our situation makes it clear that only God can save us! God's people must be convinced to pay the necessary price for revival. Then we need to humble ourselves for the dirty work and clear all the rubbish from our lives and our churches. Raising up people and godly practices which have been broken down, we then must separate ourselves from the world. After that, we will be ready to go to work for God right where God has placed us. At the same time, we will restore public worship and honour the preaching of the Word of God. Also, our people must be taught how to carry on spiritual warfare. We must insist that God's people get right with each other, and we must bathe everything we do with earnest prayer and even fasting until the revival comes!

NEW TESTAMENT REVIVALS

Malachi is the last call to revival in the Old Testament. God's people were living once more in Jerusalem following their return from exile. Under the leadership of men like Zerubbabel, Joshua the High Priest, Ezra, Nehemiah, Haggai, and Zechariah, the city of Jerusalem had been physically and spiritually revived.

Nevertheless, with their comfort and safety restored, the people tended to drift into coldness and a spirit of materialism and religious boredom. Malachi's message was a sharp call to return to their first love for God and give the Lord absolute priority in their lives. Along with all other Jews, the hope of these people was the long-awaited coming of the Messiah—the Christ. **Malachi warned them that the coming of Christ would be a time of refining.** His words are in Malachi 3 and 4.

Those words about the Lord's coming were God's last words of divine revelation to His people for 400 years! The next true Prophet of God was John the Baptist.

That brings us to the **New Testament revivals.**

Israel was now an occupied country, controlled by the Roman Empire, with a puppet king totally subject to Rome. Their Temple and Jewish religion, full of corruption, was a tool of the ruling politicians. **Into this scene came John, and a great revival followed!** After John's execution, the revival continued through the ministry of Jesus and His disciples. This movement became so widespread that there was talk of taking Jesus and making Him King of Israel by force! The account of this revival has been considered at some length in chapter 2 of this book. **John was beheaded, Jesus was crucified, and this great revival movement came to a crashing halt.**

Then came the Resurrection and PENTECOST! From that great outpouring of the Holy Spirit came a revival that lasted 300 years, survived nine major persecutions by Rome, and preached the gospel to basically the entire civilized world of that day!

The first wave of that revival, described in the Book of Acts, deals with **six major Spiritual awakenings:**

1. A Jewish Awakening

The movement of God's Spirit recounted in Acts 1 and 2 launched all the others. It involved **only Jews.** Please notice the distinguishing marks of this awakening, which was preceded by a period of intense prayer (Acts 1:13–14; 2:1–47). Those praying were together both in heart and location. A powerful visitation of the Holy Spirit occurred and thousands of conversions and baptisms took place.

These new Christians devoted themselves to assembling together for the teaching of God's Word, fellowship, the Lord's Supper, prayer, miracles, giving, hospitality, and constant Church growth. They had a powerful impact on the pagan world around them, that produced admiration in some and persecution from others. What happened there is an ideal picture of true revival!

2. A Christian Awakening

The second spiritual awakening in this great revival came soon after the first one—preceded by similar activities and with similar results. This was **a Christian awakening** due to the fact that those directly involved in its precipitation were those who had experienced, or were the fruit of, the first awakening after Pentecost.

Acts 4 describes how an outburst of persecution resulted in the arrest of the Apostles Peter and John. Upon their release, a second filling—a fresh outpouring of the Holy Spirit—took place. This was to be expected, since God had already said, through Peter in Acts 3:19–21, that refreshing would come from the Holy Spirit, time after time, until Jesus' return.

3. A Samaritan Awakening

The next spiritual awakening in this spreading revival was a **Samaritan awakening**. That seems logical, since the Samaritans were a mixture of Jews and Gentiles, and God intended this revival to reach the Gentile world. We have the account in Acts 8:5–17.

These Samaritans were people of whom it was said "They feared the Lord and served other gods." Jesus said of them, "You do not know what you worship." Nevertheless, they were a people open to God and ready to respond to the truth. It was a Samaritan woman whom Jesus reached at the well. A Samaritan leper, healed by Christ, returned to give thanks when the others did not. It was a Samaritan who came to the rescue of the man who fell among thieves in Jesus' parable, leading to our contemporary phrase "being a good Samaritan."

Somewhat different than the others, this awakening indicates a progression we should note for our own encouragement. First, no apostles were involved in this moving of God until after the fact. Second, the man God used was not a pastor, but a deacon in the Church. Third, the miracles were **among** precipitating factors, rather than **a result**, as was the case in the first two awakenings. They were coupled with the powerful preaching of Christ and resulted in thousands of conversions, baptisms, and a powerful impact on the society in which this awakening occurred. The Church thought it important that these new believers should be immediately led into the Spirit-filled life. Surely this is an example for us to note today!

4. A Gentile Awakening

This brings us to the fourth awakening of this revival, and the opening of the Gentile world to the gospel and all the blessings of being part of the Kingdom of God. The account is found in Acts 10.

Cornelius, an officer in the wicked military machine of Rome, refused to be swallowed up by the evil in which he lived and moved. He sought God to the best of his knowledge, leading to **a family awakening**. This revival became cross-cultural, and opened the door to world-wide missions.

All great missionary movements have been precipitated by revival! This spiritual awakening was marked like all the rest by a powerful outpouring of the Holy Spirit, the conversion of a number of people, water baptism for the new converts, and the filling of the Holy Spirit—this time immediately concurrent with their conversion.

5. A Congregational Awakening

The fifth awakening in this revival movement is one that should encourage all of our churches today, since it is **a congregational awakening**. We find the particulars in Acts 19:1–10. A congregation of believers, converted through the message of John the Baptist, believed in Christ, though imperfectly—they knew nothing about the powerful work of the Holy Spirit available to them. Paul instructed them more completely in the truth of the gospel and they believed, were baptized, and filled with the Holy Spirit.

Some opposition followed from the obstinate Jews in that city, so Paul left the Jewish synagogue and rented a neutral hall in which to preach. This action laid the foundation for other places to be used for worship, fellowship, prayer, teaching and the assembly of Christians. So powerful was this spiritual awakening that in two years' time, all the people in Asia had heard the Word of God—they had been evangelized!

6. A Personal Awakening

These five spiritual awakenings precipitated a revival that lasted for 300 years. One of the most significant among many **personal spiritual awakenings** was that of Saul of Tarsus. His full story is contained in most of the Book of Acts, and most of the epistles of the New Testament. I will list two passages for you to read: Acts 8:1–3, and Acts 9:1–22.

Saul was proud, stubborn, cruel, self-righteous, educated, wealthy, powerful, and extremely religious. A brilliant theologian, a graduate of the best schools, and a zealous defender of the Jewish religion of his day, Saul was a representative of the Jewish religious hierarchy, and a vicious persecutor of the Church. He would easily have been voted as the most unlikely man on earth to become a Christian! Not one man for whom I am praying was as impossible as Saul—nevertheless, God saved him, healed him, filled him with the Holy Spirit, and called him into the ministry. Saul is a dramatic picture of what God can do in the midst of revival! How many Sauls are among us, waiting for us to pay the price for revival, so that their hard hearts will be broken and they will become giants of spiritual power for God? Everywhere this man went, there was either a riot, a revival, or **both!** That is the kind of commitment and anointing our world and our times desperately need.

CHAPTER FIVE

The Foundation
of Church History

W hen we turn from the history of revival in the Bible to the history of revival in Church history, we run into some difficulty, because the history of revival *is* the history of the Church—and the history of the Church is the history of revival. Every major advance in Church history was precipitated by revival. Church historians have, for the most part, made no distinction in these matters. Those powerful advances in the Kingdom of God that were the result of unusual movings of the Holy Spirit have not been given the special treatment they deserve. Nevertheless, revivals have occurred throughout the entire history of the Church.

The revival that began with John the Baptist, continued with Jesus, and exploded at Pentecost continued until A.D. 300, when Constantine made Christianity the state religion. That began the decline of the spiritual life of the Church in general, and brought that revival to an end. From there, the Church moved into what has been called "the dark ages." The Roman and later, the Orthodox Church became enmeshed in politics, ensnared by wealth, and smothered by ritualism and formalism. This condition prevailed almost universally until the Reformation. However, in spite of this widespread declension, there were some bursts of light in the darkness. Some of these were revivals. We will touch on a few briefly.

Within sixty years following the deaths of the apostles, a powerful revival was led by Justin Martyr (103–165 A.D), who founded a disciple training school in Rome and documented many miracles in the Church, such as healings, exorcisms and prophesyings. He stated that, "There is no people, Greek or Barbarian, or any other race, by whatsoever appellation or manner they may be distinguished, however ignorant of art and agriculture, whether they dwell in tents or wander about in covered wagons, among whom prayers and giving of thanks are not offered through the name of the crucified Jesus, to the Father and creator of all things."[1]

Surely, such a revival matches that of Paul in Asia, where every person had heard the Word of God! Between A.D. 185 and 254, there was such a powerful revival that Origen states,

> In all Greece and in all barbarous races within our world, there are tens of thousands who have left their national laws and customary gods for the Law of Moses and the Word of Jesus Christ; though to adhere to that Law is to incur the hatred of idolaters and to have embraced that Word is to incur the risk of death as well. And considering how, in a few years with no great store of teachers, in spite of the attacks which have cost us life and property, the preaching of that Word has found its way into every part of the world, so that Greeks and Barbarians, wise and unwise, adhere to the religion of Jesus—doubtless it is a work greater than any work of man.[2]

Eusebius, who lived from A.D. 266 to 340, describes another great advance of the Kingdom of God in these words: "There flourished at that time many successors of the apostles, who reared the edifice on the foundation which they laid, continuing the work of preaching the gospel, and scattering abundantly over the whole earth the wholesome seed of the heavenly kingdom. For a very large number of disciples, carried away by fervent love of the truth, which the divine Word had revealed to them, fulfilled the command of the Saviour to divide their goods among the poor. Then taking leave of their country, they filled the office of evangelists, coveting eagerly to preach Christ and to carry the glad tidings of God to those who had not heard the Word of faith. And after laying the foundations of faith in some remote and barbarous countries, establishing pastors among them and confiding to them the care of those young settlements, without stopping longer they hastened on to other nations, attended by the grace and virtue of God."[3]

This is in spite of the fact that about 1.9 million Christians, out of a possible 120 million believers, had been martyred for Christ since A.D. 33. He also documented numerous miracles, such as healings and exorcisms. This revival was in progress 300 years after the death of the last of the apostles.

From around A.D. 510 to 900, wandering Irish evangelists and preachers spread across Europe. Many were converted in one of the greatest Christian movements of all time as the revival proceeded to the Alps, Germany, Danube, Italy, Orkneys, Faeroes, and Iceland!

A detailed study of the first thousand years after the apostles will show many powerful revival movements fired the Church of that day and advanced the Kingdom of God on earth.

FRANCISCAN REVIVAL—A RETURN TO SIMPLICITY

Ecclesiastes 7:29 is translated in the Living Bible with these words: "God made us plain and simple, but we have made ourselves very complicated." It seems to me then, that a return to God should include a "Return To Simplicity."

God's call to "revival" is constantly a call to "RETURN":

*Let the wicked forsake his way And the unrighteous man his thoughts; And let him **return** to the LORD, And He will have compassion on him, And to our God, For He will abundantly pardon* (Is. 55:7, NASB; emphasis by the author).

Then again, in Jeremiah 3:22, "**Return,** faithless people; I will cure you of backsliding." "Yes, we will come to you, for you are the LORD our God," and Jeremiah 24:7,

I will give them a heart to know me, that I am the LORD. They will be my people, and I will be their God, for they will return to me with all their heart.

Hosea repeats the theme in 14:1–2:

RETURN, O Israel, to the LORD your God. Your sins have been your downfall! Take words with you and return to the LORD. Say to him: "Forgive all our sins and receive us graciously, that we may offer the fruit of our lips."

The complication of our lives is often caused by a sinful preoccupation with the things of this world. Fleshly desires, materialism, pride of human accomplishment, or obsession with self-fulfillment is all part of "the world" referred to in I John 2:15–17: "Do not love the world or anything in the world." Every true call to **revival** has been a call to turn away from the complication of living like the world around us, and to come back to the **simplicity** of following Jesus Christ! **One of the greatest examples of this kind of revival occurred in the twelfth century:**

It was 1182 and all of Europe was filled with unrest and insecurity, with war as the only serious occupation. Russia was in a struggle with the Mongols. The Roman Empire was staggering under attacks from the Turks, Arabs, and the Bulgarians. The Moors had swept over the sunny plains of Spain, and continued to hold sway. The Germanic Tribes were ruled by the Warrior, Frederick Barbarossa. England too was torn by unrest and civil war.[4]

With the fall of the Empire, the Normans, the Huns, the Wends, and the Czechs rushed forth over the plains of Europe, pillaged its cities and devastated its civilization. In these misfortunes, Italy was the greatest sufferer. The fruitfulness of her soil and the age and wealth of her cities made her an object of envy and betrayal. So appalling was the ruin that the population began to decline, fear took possession of the hearts of the people, and the whole population was gripped by gloom and apathy. During this time, the feudal system came into being as people gathered into cities for protection. One of these cities was **Assisi**.

But what of the Church? As bad as other things were, the Church was even worse! These were the Middle Ages, when the Pope of Rome held absolute sway over the nations and rulers of Western Europe. To say the Roman Church was corrupt is a gross understatement. Living in kingly luxury and immorality, the princes of the Roman Church were totally given to intrigue and violence. The priesthood, for the most part, was ignorant and lived in open vice of every kind. Naturally, the common people had no instruction, and lived in sin and superstition. To them, Christ was a dim and distant figure on a cross who could not be reached except through priests who were often more debased than those who came to them. In these conditions, the general population lived captive to sensuality, materialism, and violence.

Into this situation came a young man named Francis Bernardone. His father, a wealthy merchant, traveled constantly and gave no guidance to his son. Francis found himself totally free to run his own life, and available to him all the money he wanted. He dressed and acted like a prince, and lived in constant gaiety and sinful indulgence. Eventually, a war arose between Assisi and the city of Perugia. Francis, now 20 years old, eagerly joined the forces, and marched out of Assisi like a young knight, only to be captured and imprisoned for a year. Even then, his spirits never failed him—he remained cheerful throughout. When released, Francis returned to Assisi, and plunged back into revelry and dissipation with such zeal that he became ill and for weeks at a time hovered between life and death.

During his recovery, Francis began for the first time to think seriously about life. He went to a hill where he could see the beauty that used to thrill him, but the thrill was gone—replaced by a great darkness which rose up within him. It seemed to him that life was wretchedly empty. His heart was sick within him.

A deep self-disdain, restlessness, and great unhappiness of mind filled Francis, who at 25 still had no thought of God. When he was well again, his friends enticed him back to his old ways. Once more, he plunged into a life of sensuality and pleasure. Francis heard of a war being fought in south Italy and made great preparations, boasting that he would return as a great prince. He was gone for only one night before returning without his armour and sword. Sickness again descended upon him, and this time his old friends could no longer entice him back into the ways of dissipation and sin! For some time longer, Francis remained in darkness and anguish of soul. He wandered over the fields, praying at shrines, seeking peace.

One day, as Francis knelt in prayer in a wayside chapel, his heart full of agony, he cried out—"Great and glorious God, and thou Lord Jesus, I pray ye, shed abroad your light in the darkness of my mind!"[5] As he looked up, he seemed to see the eyes of Christ fixed upon him in tender love. Immediately, his spirit leaped to embrace the Saviour! From that hour, his heart was transfixed by the love of Christ. His friends denounced him and fled from him. Then his own father, who did not mind him ruining his life in sin, was filled with wrath! His father now entreated him, threatened him, and flogged him. Finally, he disinherited him. Francis renounced all his possessions, and laying them in a large pile in the public square, he made this confession:

> Listen, all of you, and understand it well; until this time I have called Peter Bernardone my father; but now I wish to obey God. I return him the money about which he is so anxious, and all my garments, and all he has ever given me. From this moment I will say nothing but 'Our Father in heaven'![6]

Francis then left his home, never to return.

On February 24, 1209, Francis knelt in prayer at the altar of a church, listening to words of Scripture as they were read. The Gospel for the day was the tenth chapter of Matthew. He heard the words of Jesus—

> *As you go, preach this message: 'The kingdom of heaven is near.'*
> *Heal the sick, raise the dead, cleanse those who have leprosy,*

drive out demons. Freely you have received, freely give. Do not take along any gold or silver or copper in your belts; take no bag for the journey, or extra tunic, or sandals or a staff; for the worker is worth his keep (Matt. 10:7–10).

These words burst upon Francis as if spoken to him by God Himself—to Francis, this was his calling! As he went, preaching the simple gospel, others began to follow. His disciples grew in number and enthusiasm, and he eventually founded the Franciscan Order. The sermons which Francis preached were simple and direct. He proclaimed the need for repentance, the joy of obedience to the will of God, the shortness of human life, and the certainty of judgement to come. Behind the sermons was a heart flaming with ardent love for God—a man who had relinquished every earthly ambition, and whose consuming passion was to awake in men's hearts the joy and rapture that burned in his own. His words were like fire, piercing the heart!

Francis sent his disciples out two by two, as done by Jesus. And so they traveled over Europe—preaching, serving, living by faith. Thousands of the common people along with many of the rich and powerful came to Christ through this preaching and example of faith and love and total commitment to Jesus Christ! So widespread and profound was this movement that it brought about a deep spiritual change in the very fibre of society.

The end of the tenth through the first half of the eleventh centuries may justly be regarded as the darkest period in the whole history of the Christian Church! When Francis and his followers appeared before men in the garment of poverty, when they preached repentance and the love of God, when outside the church they proclaimed the willingness of God to forgive, independent of all forms and ceremonies, they announced **good news** which the world had waited for long years to hear. Their voices fell on eager ears.

Over the face of the earth, the Spirit of God had been hovering, a new Pentecost was being prepared, and when, at length, the fire descended, it passed from city to province with a joyous leap and rush. A new joy dawned in the world, and men were brought back to simplicity. It not only broke the fetters on the human spirit, but also the mind. This revival was the **real** precursor of the Renaissance! This grassroots revival literally changed the world of that day!

As usual, there were reports of widespread healings, signs, and miracles. By A.D. 1270, there were Franciscan missionaries in almost every part of the known world. By A.D. 1400, this movement had spread from Lapland to Congo, from the Azores to China, boasting 60,000 Franciscan preachers! In spite of the fact that the Roman Church was still corrupt, the world of that day had been touched and changed by revival.

THE REFORMATION REVIVAL—A Return to Scripture

It is likely that what Church historians call "The Reformation" was **the** greatest revival of the work of God in human history, since that greatest of all revivals at Pentecost. It was so far-reaching that it literally changed the social order and governments of most of Europe. A number of smaller revival movements led up to, and indeed, contributed significantly to it. In each case, these movements were influenced by the ministries of godly leaders.

One such man was John Wycliffe—a philosopher, theologian, and reformer. He lived from 1330 to 1384 A.D., and helped to set the direction of the entire Reformation. John Wycliffe has often been called the "Morning Star" of the Reformation. If the Franciscan revival could be called "A Return To Simplicity," the Reformation revival could be called "A Return To Scripture." This was the key to Wycliffe's ministry, and was the centrepiece of the entire Reformation revival. The cry of these men became "Scripture only!" They truly believed such Scripture statements as those penned by the Apostles Paul and Peter: II Timothy 3:16–17 and II Peter 1:20–21:

All Scripture is God-breathed and is useful for teaching, rebuking, correcting and training in righteousness, so that the man of God may be thoroughly equipped for every good work.

Above all, you must understand that no prophecy of Scripture came about by the prophet's own interpretation. For prophecy never had its origin in the will of man, but men spoke from God as they were carried along by the Holy Spirit.

Because the Roman Church was the official state religion in most of Europe, it had great political power. Any Christian movement with which that Church did not agree was an object of persecution by both Church and state. When a disagreement arose between the Roman Church and the English Parliament, Wycliffe defended the right of Parliament, and thereby made friends in government and enemies in the Roman Church.

Wycliffe taught in Oxford for most of his career, and also served as priest for a number of churches. He sent out disciples called "Poor Preachers." As they traveled across England, people responded to their simple gospel in large numbers and the revival was on! In 1378, Wycliffe and some of his friends had begun a translation of the Bible into English, so the Scriptures could be read by the common man. It was published in 1388, along with many other of his writings, four years after his death.

Both John Huss and Martin Luther were strongly influenced by Wycliffe's teachings. Lollards, as Wycliffe's followers called themselves, believed that the Bible was the only rule of faith and practice. The revival of true Christianity, through the ministry of Wycliffe and the Lollards, spread across England with such power that it became a political force the government of that day could not ignore.

By 1408 another reformer, John Huss, was furthering the cause of revival in Europe. He was a lecturer in theology at the University of Prague, a priest, and the preacher at Bethlehem Chapel where he preached in the Czech language rather than Latin. Though not as radical as Wycliffe, Huss nevertheless agreed with him concerning the authority of Scripture and the corruption of the Roman Church. Eventually Huss was excommunicated, and the city of Prague was placed under interdict. So great was his support among the people that riots broke out in the streets in defense of his cause. Eventually,

Huss was summoned to the Council of Constance for trial, with the promise of safe conduct by the Roman Emperor. It meant nothing. He was charged with heresy and burned at the stake. His execution resulted in the Hussite Wars in Bohemia. This man's preaching, writing, and martyrdom helped to fan the flames of revival and reformation in Europe.

Now God called another man to further the cause of revival in Europe, this time in Italy. He was a monk by the name of Girolamo Savonarola. In 1482, he began his ministry as a preacher in the Priory of San Marco in Florence. He brought reform to the Dominican Order in Tuscany, and was appointed its first vicar-general. Savonarola had spent a great deal of time studying the Scriptures and in prayer. Becoming greatly stirred by the sin of the populace and the corruption of the Roman Church, he began to preach fiery sermons in which he warned the people of Florence and Italy that the judgment of God would fall upon them unless they repented. So powerful were his sermons that people were terrified, wept in his presence, and repented by the thousands. Savonarola's denunciation of sin made no exception for the Medici family, which controlled Florence, or the Pope himself.

When the French king, Charles VIII, marched on the city, it was Savonarola who mediated a treaty with him, so that Florence was allowed to form a republic. Although Savonarola had no political position, he was for a time the actual leader of the city. Under his leadership, Florence became an example of righteousness. He organized the children of the city and preached to them, rescuing street boys by the thousands. Powerful families in Florence, however, who loved their sin and hated Savonarola, waited for an opportunity to rebel against him and his reforms. His attacks on the Roman Church and the Pope led to Savonarola's eventual excommunication.

Finally, in 1498, Savonarola was declared guilty of heresy and sedition and was sentenced to death. He and two of his closest associates were hanged, and their bodies burned. Another martyr was added to the glorious list. The heat of revival was now greatly increased. Shortly, that fire of God would burst forth in a spiritual conflagration that would change not only Europe, but the whole civilized world!

Many things besides strictly Christian issues contributed to the vast upheaval of the Reformation. The entire medieval and feudal system—political, cultural and economic—was ripe for destruction. God raised up men who dared to challenge the false beliefs which held the minds of men subject to the system. When the Scriptures were re-established as the standard of belief and practice, the truth of God brought new freedom to the minds of those in bondage to both Church and state, so that they could shake off their shackles and create a new world in which to live.

Thousands who were not Christians were involved in this explosion. The wars and bloodshed that took place were not strictly Christian. They were the natural results of a population who, sitting in darkness, was suddenly given a glimpse of light. That light came from the truth of God, as the reformers called the Church back to the Scriptures, and thousands upon thousands of people, from the nobility to the peasants, were truly converted.

On this point, James Burns, in his book, *Revivals, Their Laws and Their Leaders*, makes this comment:

> The Reformation may be regarded from two aspects. First it may be viewed from its intellectual side, as the dawn of a new period in history, marking the emancipation of the human mind, and the first great step in the march of freedom. On the other hand it may be regarded from the religious side, as a revival of spiritual life after a long period of darkness; as a return to Biblical Christianity in opposition to the sacerdotal system which had grown around it. It is with the latter—the Reformation as a revival of spiritual religion—that we have to do; and whatever further steps the movement once initiated was forced to take, it is well to remember that the reformers had this at first solely in view... The supreme fact with which we are concerned is that the Reformation was supremely a revival; that it marked for a vast multitude, the recovery of

faith; that it was a rebirth in the world of primitive and evangelic Christianity, and lighted myriads of human hearts with the flame of spiritual joy.[7]

In such a movement many remarkable men were involved, but some stand out as definite leaders in different countries of Europe. We will briefly consider only a few.

Our thoughts go first to Martin Luther, who came from peasant stock and a home filled with hardship and stern discipline. He graduated from one of the best universities in Germany in 1502, and in 1505, entered the Augustinian Convent in Erfurt to become a monk. While most monasteries of the time were centers of the most shocking sin of every kind, the one Luther entered was a model of piety in that day, headed by John Von Staupitz—a mystic, a writer, and a good man.

Luther wanted above all things to be at peace with God, and fasted, prayed, wept, agonized, and practiced the greatest austerities to try to make himself acceptable to Him. Staupitz advised him to study the Scriptures, giving special attention to the Epistles of Paul. Slowly, Luther began to understand the truth of justification by faith. Suddenly he realized that he was forgiven and accepted by God through the work of Christ. Faith became real. He was born of God. Joy flooded his heart!

At first, Luther had no idea of where this new relationship with God would take him. He continued in his old practices without seeing any contradiction. In the fall of 1510, Luther was sent by his convent on a matter of business to Rome. He undertook that journey with the greatest joy, fully expecting to see Christianity at its highest and holiest. He saw the very opposite. Rome and the Pope himself were given over to every kind of corruption and evil!

As he crawled up the steps of Scala Santa in order to obtain the indulgence given to the faithful, Luther heard within his heart the words of Scripture—"the just shall live by faith" (Heb. 10:38). Filled with horror, Luther fled from Rome. He returned to Wittenberg to study and lecture. After earning his doctorate in 1512, Luther began to deliver lectures on the psalms and the Pauline epistles. It was in this process that the theological foundation for the coming revival was laid. Those who listened to these lectures were strongly aware that they were being exposed to something new in both philosophy and power. As he listened, Dr. Pollich said, "This monk will revolutionize the whole scholastic teaching!" Another professor said, "There is here a divine, who explains the epistles of the man of Tarsus with wonderful genius." And still another, "This monk is a marvelous fellow. He has strange eyes, and will give the doctors trouble by and by."[8] That turned out to be an understatement. Luther's convictions solidified, his gifts developed, and his ministry and reputation grew. Then came the event which changed Luther's life dramatically and precipitated the revival that would follow.

The Pope needed large sums of money to build a great cathedral he was designing in Rome. He decided to raise this money by selling indulgences on a massive scale. One of the Pope's most successful salesmen was a man named John Tetzel, whose brazen manner of making fantastic promises to those who bought the indulgences brought in great sums of money.

When Luther heard that this con artist was coming to the area where he lived, he attacked his methods directly. First, he appealed to the Archbishop of Mayence to do something to stop this monster. He received no reply. Next, he went directly to the people by publishing a thesis with 95 propositions, and nailing it to the church door in Wittenberg. Now the die was cast! News of this publication went throughout Germany in a matter of fourteen days and raised the most extraordinary excitement, along with throwing Luther into the leadership of a vast movement of which he had never dreamed.

Nor did the Pope have any idea of what lay ahead. When Luther's thesis was brought to him, he smiled and said, "A drunken German wrote them. When he has slept off his wine, he will be of another mind."[9] The purpose of this book does not include repeating subsequent events, which have been recounted in large volumes many times. Let it be sufficient to say that both princes and common people gathered to Luther's banner. A great conflict arose between Luther and his followers, and the Church of Rome. Many powerful men supported Luther, and sought to protect him from those who would have gladly put him to death. Prince Frederick of Saxony was one of these.

Luther preached and wrote continually on the subjects of dispute between him and Rome. Many received his words gladly. The gospel of Jesus Christ and His saving grace was proclaimed widely. Thousands left the darkness of Roman bondage to enter the Kingdom of God by faith. Luther was finally brought to trial at Augsburg, but easily won the day. Then he was summoned to the Diet, at Worms, to face the Pope's representatives and the Emperor of the Roman Empire. Here, he was ordered to recant. He replied, "Unless convinced by Holy Scripture, or by clear reasons from other sources, I cannot retract. To Councils or to Pope I cannot defer, for they have often erred. My conscience is a prisoner to God's Word. Here I stand. I cannot do otherwise. God help me."[10]

The Council broke up. Luther headed back to Wittenberg. His friends discovered a plot to assassinate him on the way home, so they themselves captured him in the woods, and carried him away to the castle of Wartburg in the forest, where he was kept hidden until the immediate danger was past. While in the castle, Luther translated the Scriptures into the German language, so many of his people could read the Word of God for themselves. The invention of the printing press also helped to spread both the Scriptures and other Christian literature. The speed with which this revival spread can only be described as explosive. Burns put it well when he said,

> Only three years and a half have now elapsed since Luther nailed his thesis to the door of the church at Wittenberg. The extraordinary commotion which that act created is an illustration of the state of public feeling. The minds of men were like fuel only waiting for a spark to set it ablaze. When Luther supplied the spark the conflagration was immediate, and it swept with incredible swiftness over Europe. Although the result differed in different countries, being stamped by

national characteristics, yet over the whole it made for a reformation in morals, for a cleansed church, and for a purified spiritual vision. Even within the Catholic church itself the result was to regenerate and to revive....

So great, however, was the upheaval when it did come, so many-sided was it, so full of fury were its political, intellectual, and theological conflicts, that the reader is in constant danger of having obscured for him the real spiritual awakening which took place, and which lifted the whole church of Christ into higher spiritual levels. So vast was the upheaval caused by Luther and his supporters that it was impossible to confine it to the vicinity in which it took place. A wave of spiritual awakening swept across Europe, agitating nations, threatening dynasties, arousing joyful acceptance or implacable opposition wherever it went.[11]

The final result in Germany was a complete break with the Roman Church, the establishment of the Lutheran Church, and a broad Protestant movement across Europe. Christians had a new and open Bible, a new hymnody, and a new form of worship. The pure gospel was preached widely, and hundreds of thousands were converted through simple faith in Christ.

In other countries of Europe, the masses were ready also for truth and freedom. Other gifted men of God were encouraged and inspired by Luther's example and teaching. These rose up by God's power and became the spark to ignite similar revivals in their own countries. As Lutheranism moved northward, the Reformation took place in Scandinavian countries peacefully, since the governments of those countries, led by monarchs, responded to the spreading revival gladly. Sweden, Denmark and Norway broke with the authority of the Roman Church and established Protestantism by government decree.

As early as 1518, Switzerland was introduced to the revival through the preaching and discussions of a Swiss pastor by the name of Huldreich Zwingli. His break with Rome was even more severe than that of Luther. In a war that grew out of the Reformation, Zwingli was killed. Another man, whose influence would reach throughout Europe and extend to this very day, soon took his place. Born in France in 1509, John Calvin received his beginning education in what was one of the best universities of the day—the University of Paris, called the "Sorbonne." He excelled in his studies, and from there, his father sent him to Orleans to study law. Again he attracted attention by his diligence and keen intellect. Calvin, like Luther, had discovered that the rituals, ordinances, and disciplines of the Roman Church could not bring him peace with God.

About this time, Calvin came in contact with the teachings of the Reformation revival. As he read and studied the Epistles of Paul, he became convinced of the truth. A great struggle followed, culminating in the surrender of his heart and a genuine conversion experience which he saw as the direct work of the Holy Spirit through the truth of the living Word of God. The Scriptures became for Calvin—as was true with other reformers—the only rule of faith and practice. To know the Word of God and to make it known became, to him, a worthy object for his life.

At this time France was already in turmoil over the teachings of the reformers. Luther's writings were being read, accepted by many, and were causing much conflict. The truth had found acceptance in high places, even winning the Queen Mother and the Chancellor, Duprat. Upon his conversion, Calvin stepped into this arena as a champion of the Protestant cause. He was immediately accepted as a leader, and found others gathering around him to learn, though he himself was only a beginner. This is often the case in revival.

Soon, Calvin found it necessary to flee from Paris and wander about in hiding. Many were hungry for the truth, he found, but had nothing or no one to teach them. His response to this was the writing and publication of his famous "Institutes." Calvin was now 27 years old. It seemed to him that what was needed in this great revival was a careful setting forth of intellectual truth concerning the Scriptures and the Protestant cause. He wanted peace and quiet to study and write.

He again wandered about Europe. In his travels he visited Geneva. Here, through the ministry of William Farrel, a reformer, the city had adopted Protestantism by public vote. Much dissension had followed. Now through the persuasion of Farrel, Calvin sensed the call of God to remain there and give the city the godly leadership it needed. So began an association that would only be broken by Calvin's death. The revival that followed here was a revival of the Word of God in practice. Geneva became a sort of model of what was possible if the Scriptures were taken seriously. It is true that there were mistakes and extremes. Nevertheless, what was done and taught here profoundly influenced the entire revival movement all across Europe. The study and teaching of theology based entirely on the Bible helped to bring down the entire structure of Roman scholasticism, with its false emphasis on the authority of the Church, and to exalt the Word of God to the supreme place, as the only rule of faith and practice in the Church of Jesus Christ. This was, indeed, truly revival.

At that time, Scotland was one of the darkest countries in Europe. There were three basic classes of people: the feudal lords, the clergy of the Roman Church, and the peasant class who were serfs held in bondage and ignorance by the two other classes. The majority of the population was enslaved in spirit, mind, and body. Into this universal darkness, some rays of light were slowly penetrating from the Reformation in other countries of Europe. Because this light was the light of the gospel, it had divine power to touch the hearts and minds of the Scottish people.

Long-standing conflicts between the kings and the nobility also made the Lairds of Scotland open to new ideas. The Church of Rome in Scotland was grossly corrupt and debased and the common people were ripe for the Word of God. All that was needed was a leader who could ignite the fire of God among them. As always, God had his man. His name was John Knox. Born in 1505, Knox began his education at one of the few decent village schools in his homeland. He entered the University of Glasgow at the age of seventeen. Around 1530, he was ordained to the Catholic priesthood and was a tutor rather than a pastor. Knox was strongly influenced toward the truth of the Word of God by his friend, George Wishart, who was one of the early reformers in Scotland, later martyred for his faith. After being converted, Knox followed Wishart everywhere, and after Wishart's death was forced to flee for his life. At length he reached St. Andrew's Castle, where other reformers were gathered. With one voice, they called on him to be their minister. Knox was astounded, but became convinced that it was the call of God, and finally accepted. From the very first, Knox's sermons were powerful and direct, sparing nothing and no one! Because of the strong connections between the royal families of Scotland and France, the French sent a fleet to attack the Castle of St. Andrew. The garrison was quickly overcome, and all reformers were imprisoned. Many, Knox among them, were sent to the galleys. Knox remained there for 19 months suffering so severely during that time that his health was permanently damaged.

In 1549, he was released, but forced into exile. Some of those years he spent as a minister in the English Church. In 1552, he was summoned to London as King's Chaplain, where he participated in helping to formulate what became the "Thirty-Nine Articles" of the Church of England. When Edward VI died, Mary ascended to the throne and began to persecute the reformers in England. Knox, with others, was forced to flee the country. His wanderings finally brought him to Geneva, where he met John Calvin for the first time. Calvin had a powerful effect on Knox. Eventually Knox returned to Geneva, where he pastored an English congregation for three years.

All this time, the revival was spreading in Scotland. In 1559, the call came from the reformers in Scotland for Knox to return. From the time of his return, Knox became the undisputed leader of the Reformation in Scotland. His passionate preaching and undaunted courage carried all before him. Serious men and patriots gathered to him. So strong was the spiritual revival that followed that by the next year Parliament met in Edinburgh, voted for the Protestant faith, and abolished Roman Catholicism. In the same year, the first General Assembly of the Church of Scotland was held. In 1561, the beautiful and proud Mary, Queen of Scots, became the ruler of Scotland. She had been brought up in Paris among Catholics, and was determined to crush Protestantism in Scotland. She tried every way possible to entrap John Knox, but utterly failed. During these years, John Knox was the real leader of the country. If not a historical fact, it would be hard to believe an entire nation could change so completely in a few short years! No purely political or philosophical movement could ever produce what happened there. This was a spiritual revival which affected the entire population—from the grassroots peasant to the highest nobility of the land. Scotland became a Christian nation! The people of Scotland became a people of a book, and that book was the Bible. Their values, morals and lifestyle were all shaped by the Word of God.

One more area must be mentioned in dealing with the Reformation revival. That is one of the places where it first began—England itself, from whence had come John Wycliffe, called "The Morning Star" of the Reformation. Those seeds of the Reformation were sown as early as the 1300s, but never produced the total change in the 1500s that took place in most of the rest of Europe. In 1534, Parliament passed an act making the King and his successors the supreme head of the Church of England. This broke the power of the Roman Church in England, but was not accompanied by a deep and universal spiritual change. In 1547, Martin Bucer and other reformers were invited to England to preach, and in 1549, a Book Of Common Prayer was issued. Queen Mary I persecuted the reformers for a short time, but in 1563, under Queen Elizabeth I, Protestantism was restored. Nevertheless, real revival was not to come to England until the Evangelical Revival in the 1700s.

Thorough assessment of the Great Reformation has already been tried by many. I am not about to attempt it except to say this—no explanation on a purely human level will suffice. The changes wrought in Europe—at all levels of society, and in the political, intellectual, and moral realms—could not have been possible without a deep basic change in the people themselves. So profound was this change that nothing but Christian conversion can begin to explain it. In other words, this was above all else, a true Christian revival, and all the rest either was made possible by, or flowed from, this revival!

THE EVANGELICAL REVIVAL—
A Return to Individual Conversion and Holiness

Because the Reformation in England was not based on a broad spiritual renewal, it did little to change the moral character of the people or the nation. Outwardly there was a new freedom in both the political and religious aspects of society. This freedom did not elevate that society, but only opened the door to every kind of evil. This is a classic example of the fact that freedom cannot be maintained without God! As the conflict continued between Catholicism and the Church of England, neither one had any true biblical Christianity to offer. The Church became a laughing stock to all. The advance of Deism degenerated from liberty to license. Clergymen, for the most part, were ignorant, immoral, and totally unconcerned about the spiritual lives of their people. Their sermons were weak and empty. Bishop Butler, who lived at that time wrote,

> Christianity is not so much a subject for inquiry, but that it
> is now at length discovered to be fictitious.... Men treat it as
> if in the present age this were an agreed point amongst all
> people of discernment, and nothing remained but to set it up
> as a principle subject of mirth and ridicule.[12]

Scientific skepticism was the order of the day among intellectuals. Green says, "At the other end of the social scale lay the masses of the poor. They were ignorant and brutal to a degree which it is hard to conceive."[13]

Into this desperate situation came three young men, whom God used to precipitate one of the greatest revivals of modern history. They were George Whitfield, and John and Charles Wesley. These three young men met at Oxford, and began a search for God that resulted in a spiritual cataclysm. All were trained for the ministry and were high churchmen. None of them knew God personally. Each one was trying, by spiritual disciplines, to gain peace with God. They formed a society which others jokingly called "The Holy Club." Eventually, all were ordained to the ministry without being truly converted. Each one, in his own way, laboured for God—and tried, by strict austerities, to make himself acceptable to God. George Whitfield pursued such a course of self-denial that he became ill and almost died. In this process, he read a book by Henry Scougal, a young Scotsman of the previous century, entitled *The Life of God in the Soul of Man*. This book was such a contradiction to all that he believed that he wrote,

> God showed me that I must be born again or be damned! I learned that a man may go to church, say his prayers, receive the sacrament, and yet not be a Christian.[14]

Finally he came to the place where he understood, and was born of God. This is his testimony:

> God was pleased to remove the heavy load, to enable me to lay hold of his dear Son by a living faith, and by giving me the spirit of adoption, to seal me even to the day of everlasting redemption. O! with what joy—joy unspeakable—even joy that was full of and big with glory, was my soul filled, when the weight of sin went off, and an abiding sense of the pardoning love of God, and a full assurance of faith, broke in upon my disconsolate soul! Surely it was the day of mine espousals—a day to be had in everlasting remembrance![15]

And so, one of the greatest preachers the world has ever seen was born into the family of God, and thereby began that life of God which was to be shared with thousands.

John and Charles Wesley went through a similar struggle. Charles was to find deliverance before John. As Charles lay in bed, seriously ill, he was attended by a deeply spiritual Christian woman. Though poor and ignorant in many ways, she knew Christ. She became strongly convinced that God wanted her to speak to this sick man. She struggled against the conviction for a while, but finally overcome by the pressure of the Holy Spirit, she entered his room and said with an intense voice, "In the name of Jesus of Nazareth, arise! Thou shalt be healed of all thy infirmities!" These words struck Charles with startling effect. He said, "They struck me to the heart. I never heard words uttered with like solemnity. I sighed within myself and said, 'O, that Christ would thus speak to me!'" Suddenly the light pierced his heart. He seemed to be caught up in God's power. At that moment he was born again.[16]

John and Charles Wesley had previously gone to Georgia as missionaries. At that time, neither was a true child of God. On their return trip, a small group of Moravian missionaries was also on the ship. Their simple faith aroused John's curiosity and admiration. When back in London, John sought out the Moravian settlement, and there he met Peter Bohler, a friend and follower of Count Zinzendorf. Bohler had an immediate and profound influence on John Wesley. As John listened to Bohler preach, he was deeply shaken at the doctrine of the grace of God. John said, "Bohler amazed me more and more in the account he gave of fruits of faith, the love, holiness, and happiness that he affirmed to attend it."[17] Wesley said that on March 4, he spent a day with Bohler, "by whom, in the hands of the great God, I was clearly convinced of unbelief; of the want of that faith whereby alone we are saved." On the 24th of May, 1788, John spent the evening with the Society in Aldersgate street. Someone was reading Luther's preface to the Epistle to the Romans. Here is his own testimony;

> About a quarter before nine, while he was describing the change wrought by God in the heart through faith in Christ, I felt my heart strangely warmed. I felt I did trust Christ, Christ alone, for salvation; and an assurance was given me that he had taken away my sins, even mine, and saved me from the law of sin and death. I began to pray with all my might for those who had in a more especial manner despitefully used me and persecuted me. I then testified openly to all there what I now first felt in my heart.[18]

Many spiritual struggles were to follow for all three men, but one thing was certain—they now knew Christ in reality, were truly born of God, and could in sincerity preach the unsearchable riches of Christ. This they immediately began to do with astounding results. London was filled with large church buildings. Everywhere these men preached, the churches quickly became packed to suffocation. Their passionate and thorough preaching of the true gospel was so completely different that their audiences sat stunned. Very soon the devil raised his head and the Church of England clergy began to oppose these upstarts, partly through guilt and partly through jealousy. When they were cast out of the churches, Whitfield decided to do what for a high churchman was unthinkable. He decided to preach in the open air. Soon, between 5,000 and 10,000 people were listening to him in the fields. John Wesley was shocked and would have none of it at first. One day however, Whitfield managed to drag John out to the field where he was preaching. As John stood by his side, he was overcome with what he saw happening. He went back to his room and wrote in his diary, "Tomorrow I will be more vile than Whitfield!" And so, he and Charles began the same kind of ministry. All three preached to great crowds in city squares and the open fields, the numbers sometimes reaching 20,000 and 30,000 people. Whitfield was a colorful and passionate preacher who could move whole crowds to tears. One day as Whitfield was preaching, Lord Chesterfield was in the audience. Whitfield was illustrating the terrible, lost condition of a sinner by describing a blind beggar led by a dog. The dog left him, and he was forced to grope his way along with only the help of his blind man's cane.

> "Unconsciously he wanders to the edge of a precipice; his staff drops from his hand down the abyss, too far to send back an echo; he reaches forward cautiously to recover it; for a moment he poises on vacancy, and—"

"Good God!" shouted Chesterfield, as he sprang from his seat to avert the catastrophe, "he is gone!" [19]

John Wesley, on the other hand, was a careful theological preacher whose logical presentation of the truth of God brought deep conviction for sin and broken-hearted surrender to Christ. John was also an administrator who was able to organize the work of God among the masses for long-lasting effect. Charles, while also a warm-hearted preacher, was best known for his ability to put the truth of God to music so that the thousands of new Christians could express their love and praise to God in joyful song.

As this revival gained momentum, multiplied thousands came to Christ and were soundly converted. Under the leadership of John Wesley, the great Methodist movement came into existence. Both Whitfield and Wesley preached also in the Colonies, where thousands responded to the gospel of Christ. So widespread and profound was this revival that it literally transformed England at every level of society.

During the Reformation, France was another European country which did not experience a deep spiritual revival. The result was the horrible bloodbath of the French Revolution. England was, without a doubt, headed in the same direction. The Evangelical revival, under the leadership of Whitfield and the Wesleys, wrought such a change in the character of the people from the grassroots up that the whole nation was changed—thereby avoiding France's experience.

In many national crises, there are only two choices—revival or revolution. May God help His people to be willing to pay the necessary price in our day that we may experience revival instead of revolution. Another consideration is this: even after the Reformation had brought such change, individual salvation did not have the emphasis it needed. The Church still held too much power over the individual Christian. The Evangelical revival addressed this imbalance by its great stress on an individual relationship with Christ through personal conversion and spiritual birth.

Though Wesley preached this message, it was Whitfield who sounded the gospel note with the greatest power and effect. John Wesley added to that a fresh emphasis on holiness of life for the Christian. He not only preached and wrote about this, but established class meetings wherever the Methodist Church spread, in order that Christians might be accountable to one another, and encourage one another in living a holy, Christian life. Thus, this great revival was a "return" to individual conversion and holiness.

The Great Protestant Reformation, which began in approximately 1517, launched a constantly-progressing series of revivals that have continued to multiply until today. These revivals are so many, and so widespread, that it would not be possible in a volume such as this to deal with all of them in detail. Richard Owen Roberts has made an excellent list of most of these, published by Tyndale House in their *Almanac Of The Christian World*, 1993–1994 edition.

THE GREAT AWAKENING

Jonathan Edwards was the main instrument used of God in this revival. Though his preaching produced the dramatic effects, it is also true that those sermons were powered by a life of intense and persistent prayer. He spent the whole night before he preached his now-famous sermon, "Sinners In The Hands Of An Angry God," in prayer. As people listened to him preach, they were filled with the fear of God, some gripping the pew for fear that they were about to fall into hell. There was in some of his meetings such a moaning and weeping that he had to ask the people to be quiet so others could hear the sermon. George Whitfield visited Edwards in 1740. Together, they were used of God to start a revival movement known as the "Great Awakening." This revival penetrated all of the New England states, and its effect was felt in the United States for the next sixty or seventy years. Jonathan Edwards wrote a number of theological works that are still widely read today.

Among those used of God in this revival, Charles Finney is one of the best known. At the time he became a Christian, Mr. Finney was a practicing attorney, his education having been entirely in law. He experienced a remarkable conversion of which the following is his own testimony:

I was powerfully converted on the morning of the 10th of October, 1821. In the evening of the same day I received overwhelming baptisms of the Holy Ghost, that went through me, as it seemed to me, body and soul. I immediately found myself endued with such power from on high that a few words dropped here and there to individuals were the means of their immediate conversion. My words seemed to fasten like barbed arrows in the souls of men. They cut like a sword. They broke the heart like a hammer. Multitudes can attest to this.[20]

So great was the conviction of sin and the fear of God in some of Mr. Finney's meetings, that some people could not sit up, and so fell on the floor from weakness. Multiplied thousands were converted, and whole cities were affected. In the city of Rome, New York, where my parents began their married life, 80 percent of the adults became Christians! Charles Finney established a college for the training of ministers, and authored a number of books. His best-known books are *An Autobiography* and *Lectures On Revival*, both of which are still widely read and studied today. A lesser-known book by him is *Systematic Theology*, which deserves to be more widely studied by those who want a balanced view of biblical doctrine.

THE PRAYER MEETING REVIVAL

The "Prayer Meeting Revival," as it is called, is described by Dr. J. Edwin Orr in these words:

In September 1857, a man of prayer, Jeremiah Lamphier, started a prayer meeting in the upper room of the Dutch Reformed Consistory Building, in Manhattan. In response to his advertisement, only six people out of a population of a million showed up. But, the following week there were fourteen, and then twenty three, when it was decided to meet every day for prayer. By late winter they were filling the Dutch Reformed Church, then the Methodist Church on John street, then Trinity Episcopal Church on Broadway at Wall street. In February and March of 1858, every church and public hall in downtown New York was filled. Horace Greeley, the famous editor, sent a reporter with horse and buggy racing around the prayer meetings to see how many men were praying. In one hour he could get to only twelve meetings, but he counted 6100 men attending. Then a landslide of prayer began, which overflowed to the churches in the evenings. People began to be converted, 10,000 a week in New York city alone. The movement spread throughout New England, the church bells bringing people to prayer at eight in the morning, twelve noon, and six in the evening. The revival raced up the Hudson and down the Mohawk, where the Baptist, for example, had so many people to baptize that they went down to the river, cut a big hole in the ice, and baptized them in the cold water; when Baptists do that they are really on fire.... Trinity Episcopal Church in Chicago had 121 members in 1857; in 1860, 1400.[21]

More than a million people were converted in one year. That revival was so unusual that even the areas where it was taking place seemed to be filled with the Spirit of God. On one occasion, a ship sailed into an American harbor and seemed to cross an invisible line inside of which the power of God was at work. Conviction for sin fell on the officers and crew, and by the time they disembarked, every one of them were converted. Says J. Edwin Orr,

> That same revival jumped the Atlantic, appeared in Ulster, Scotland and Wales, then England, parts of Europe, South Africa and South India.... Effects were felt for 40 years; it was sustained by a movement of prayer.[22]

THE WELSH REVIVAL

The Welsh revival took place less than a hundred years ago, and deserves careful study by all those longing to see it happen in our day. I will include here only a skeleton of what happened, again from Dr. J. Edwin Orr:

> Most people have heard of the Welsh Revival which started in 1904 ... Seth Joshua, the Presbyterian evangelist, had come to the New Castle Emlyn College where Evan Roberts was studying for the ministry. Evan Roberts, then 26, had been a coal

miner. The students were so moved that they asked if they could attend his next campaign nearby, so they cancelled classes to go to Blaenanerch, where Seth Joshua prayed publically, "O God, bend us." Evan Roberts went forward, where he prayed with great agony, "O God, bend me." Upon his return he could not concentrate on his studies. He went to the principal of his college, and explained: "I keep hearing a voice that tells me I must go home to speak to our young people in my home church. Principal Phillips, is that the voice of the devil or the voice of the Spirit?" Principal Phillips answered very wisely, "The devil never gives orders like that. You can have a week off." So he went back home to Loughor and announced to the pastor, "I've come to preach." The pastor was not at all convinced, but asked: "How about speaking at the prayer meeting on Monday?" He did not even let him speak to the prayer meeting, but told the praying people, "Our young brother Evan Roberts, feels he has a message for you, if you care to wait." Seventeen people waited behind, to be impressed with the directness of the young man's words. Evan Roberts told his fellow members: "I have a message for you from God. You must confess any known sin to God, and put any wrong done to man right. Second, you must put away any doubtful habit. Third, you must obey the Spirit promptly. Finally, you must confess your faith in Christ publically." By ten o'clock, all seventeen had responded. The pastor was so pleased that he asked, "How about your speaking at the mission service tomorrow night? Midweek service Wednesday night?" He preached all week, and was asked to stay another week; and then "the break" came. I have read the Welsh newspapers of the period.... Suddenly there was a headline, "Great Crowds Of People Drawn To Loughor." For some days a young man named Evan Roberts was causing great surprise. The main road between Llanelly and Swansea on which the church was situated was packed, wall to wall, people trying to get into the church.... Every grocery shop in that industrial valley was emptied of groceries by people attending the meetings, and on Sunday, every church was filled. The movement went like a tidal wave over Wales, in five months there being a hundred thousand people converted through the country.... It was the social impact that was astounding. For example, judges were presented with white gloves, not a case to try; no robberies, no burglaries, no rapes, no murders, and no embezzlements, nothing. District councils held emergency meetings to discuss what to do with the police now that they were unemployed.... As the revival swept Wales, drunkenness was cut in half. There was a wave of bankruptcies, but nearly all taverns.... That revival also affected sexual moral standards. I had discovered through figures given by British government experts that, in Radnorshire and Merionethshire, the actual illegitimate birth rate had dropped 44% within a year of the beginning of the revival. That revival swept Britain. It so moved all of Norway that the Norwegian Parliament passed special legislation to permit laymen to conduct Communion because the clergy could not keep up with the number of converts desiring to partake. It swept Sweden, Finland and Denmark, Germany, Canada from coast to coast, all of the United States, Australia, New Zealand, South Africa, East Africa, Central Africa, West Africa, touching also Brazil, Mexico and Chile.[23]

CONCLUSIONS TO THE HISTORY OF REVIVAL

As we look at the history of revival, whether in the Bible or Church history, there should be some very important lessons for us to learn. What kind of lessons? What are the questions we should ask of revival history? Let me suggest the following:

- *Were these revivals the work of God, or man, or both?*
- *In what kinds of situations did these revivals occur?*
- *Are there any reasons to believe similar revivals might occur again in our time and place?*

What should we do about these answers? Please consider with me the answers to these questions in the order they are stated above.

1. Were these revivals the work of God, or man, or both?

The revivals recounted in both biblical and Church history were pre-eminently the work of God. The unusual visitation of the Holy Spirit in power, and the miraculous changes which followed establish these revivals as instances of God bringing new manifestations of His life to individuals, groups and nations. These revivals could not be produced by any work of man. The deep and dramatic changes in the lives of sinful, weak human beings, often by the thousands—such as at Pentecost, or the Evangelical revival under Whitfield and the Wesleys, or the Great Awakening in the United States, or the Welsh revival of 1904–1905—have no other realistic explanations. Those involved in these revivals constantly speak of the awareness of the presence of God.

David Brainerd recounts the revival among the American Indians in 1745 this way: "The power of God seemed to descend upon the assembly like a mighty rushing wind, and with astonishing energy bore down all before it. I stood amazed at the influence that seized the audience almost universally, and could compare it to nothing more aptly than the irresistible force of a mighty torrent."

Describing the revival in Northampton, Mass. in 1735, Jonathan Edwards wrote, "The town seemed to be full of the presence of God. It never was so full of love, nor so full of joy, and yet so full of distress as it was then. To cleansed hearts it is heaven, to convicted hearts hell, when God is in the midst."

Charles Finney describes the scene in the village schoolhouse near Antwerp, N.Y.:

> An awful solemnity seemed to settle upon the people; the congregation began to fall from their seats in every direction, and cry for mercy. If I had had a sword in each hand, I could not have cut them down as fast as they fell.[24]

In the Welsh Revival of 1904–1905, a meeting continued through the night near the town of Gorseinon. At about four in the morning, a godless miner, hardened in his sin, was going home from his night shift in the mines. He saw the light in the chapel and turned aside to see what was happening at so strange an hour. The moment he opened the door, he was overwhelmed with a sense of the presence of God. He was heard to exclaim, "Oh! God is here!" He was so full of fear that he did not dare to enter or leave, and so he fell down in the doorway and was converted on the spot.

I do not see how anyone could study the history of revivals and come to any other conclusion but that revival is a work of God. Does this mean then, that man has no responsibility in the matter? Does the sovereign work of God's grace exclude man's direct involvement? Certainly not.

Revivalist Charles Finney describes it this way.[25] A man is walking toward a 1,000-foot cliff in the dark. It is so dark he cannot see the abyss before him. Another man, familiar with the area sees him headed for destruction, and cries out, "**Stop!**" The man stops just in time. He looks down and sees that he is standing on the edge of a precipice. He sits down, trembling. A small crowd gathers around him. The man gives his testimony. He says, "Thank God, I'm saved!" He is saying God saved him. Then he turns to the man who shouted to him to stop, and says, "You are the one who saved me. I will ever be grateful to you for what you have done. If it hadn't been for you I would be lost!" He is saying the other man saved him. Then he says, "If I hadn't stopped when you shouted, I would have been lost!" He is saying he saved himself. Finally he says, "It was that word which saved me. That word 'stop' was my salvation." Now, he is saying the word saved him. Which is true? Of course, all are true! That is the experience of most who are saved. That is the way of revival!

In all the history of revival, whether biblical or Church history, man's believing, obedient action is obviously present. The revivals in Old Testament history were precipitated by earnest prayer, confession of sin—both personal and national—destruction of idols, and a return to the true worship of Jehovah. All appear to be part of the cause of revival rather than its results. Pentecost itself was preceded by ten days of obedient, believing prayer. The second outpouring of the Holy Spirit in Acts 4 seems to have been precipitated by another period of earnest, united prayer.

The great revivals of Church history are all preceded by one person, or a group of persons, getting right with God and seeking His face in prayer. The Welsh revival is a good example, as we find Evan Roberts praying in great agony, "O, God, bend me!" Then as he spoke to the small group in Loughor, he gave careful instruction to them for their action. He said,

> "You must confess any known sin to God and put any wrong done to man right. Second, you must put away any doubtful habit. Third you must obey the Spirit promptly. Finally, you must confess your faith in Christ publically."[26]

As these Christians believed and obeyed, the Holy Spirit came upon them in great power, and the revival was in progress.

The Canadian Revival of 1971–1972 was the result of repentance and protracted prayer. The mighty moving of the Spirit of God in Saskatoon followed two years of intense prayer by a congregation, led by their pastor, Bill McLeod, who had himself met God at the cross and had his life transformed. The history of revival makes it clear that revival, though a work of God, usually tarries until God's people are willing to pay the price to be ready to receive what only God can give! My second question is:

2. In what kinds of situations did these revivals occur?

The simple answer is that, for the most part, these revivals occurred in the worst possible circumstances. This is obvious on the face of the subject—generally speaking, the very reason for a revival is that there is a desperate need for one! In Old Testament history, most revivals came at a time when God's people were in dire straits, either spiritually or politically, and often it was both. The reason for this was that when they turned away from God, they got into trouble socially, economically, and politically.

When revival came in New Testament times, through John the Baptist, Jesus Christ, and the apostles, Israel was living in political bondage to Rome and struggling with a religious leadership filled with corruption and hypocrisy. The Franciscan revival came at one of the darkest periods of Europe's entire history. The Reformation revival faced a Church that was so evil that it was doing more harm than good. Again, the Evangelical revival took place in circumstances that were desperate and hopeless, with sin and unbelief rampant both in the Church and in the population generally. All of history proclaims with one voice that revival can be expected in the worst possible situations. The question that naturally arises from this conclusion is:

3. Are there any reasons to believe that similar revivals might occur again in our time and place?

I believe there are. We are living in days of almost universal wickedness. In the public sphere, almost every semblance of moral standards and decent values have been discarded. Much of the evangelical church is worldly, entertainment-focused, self-satisfied, prayerless, and unconcerned about the lost in its midst. Individual Christians are often totally self-centered and pleasure-driven. In spite of all this, or maybe because of it, there is a stirring among God's people.

I have been involved in the revival movement since 1972. Ten years ago, most evangelical denominations were not interested in revival. Some leaders even opposed it. The church was preoccupied with church growth, seminars, and religious personality cults. That is now changing. On every side in the evangelical church, there is an interest in revival. Denominational leaders are speaking out as to the need. Christians are coming together to pray and seek God's face. Church leaders are calling in revivalists to speak at church conferences. Nothing we face today is as bad as what prevailed at most times in history when revival came. The interest in and call for revival is much broader than was the case in most of those situations in the past. There is *every* reason to believe that we can and will experience a great revival in our day!

Finally, we come to the last question:

4. What should we do about these answers?

We should do exactly what the people of God did in those times past, that seemed to precipitate those great revivals. What were the steps they took in believing obedience to God? That is the subject matter of the second division of this book: "**Experiencing Revival.**"

EXPERIENCING
REVIVAL

STEPS TOWARD EXPERIENCING REVIVAL

The second half of this book focuses on practical application of what we have learned in the first half. Therefore, it is **absolutely essential that you are familiar with the material in the first half**, in order to be able to understand and put into practice that with which you will now be confronted.

Early in this book, I explained that what is set forth here is not intended to absolutely bring revival, but rather to move you in that direction. I want to add that the following steps toward revival are not necessarily to be taken in the order they are given. Indeed, some of them you will want to take concurrently.

Before we proceed, I believe it is time to revisit our definition of revival.

A REVIVAL DEFINITION

- In the biblical sense, a revival is a new or fuller manifestation of the presence of God Himself in an individual, a church, a city, or a nation.

But how shall we know in practical terms if such a revival has taken place?

- When the manifestation of the life of God is adequately expressed in the renewal of a person or a group, God will be glorified, and God's people will be restored to biblical standards of experience and practice. If the restoration is thorough and permanent, this will result in the conversion of the ungodly around them. If this process affects large numbers of people of both classes, the society of which both are a part will, to some degree, be reformed.

Such have been those great works of God among men in the past, that have been known as the "Great Revivals." Just such a great revival is needed in North America today!

With this in mind, we will now consider some of the steps that will move us in the direction of this kind of revival.

CHAPTER SIX

The Step of Humbling Ourselves

*If my people, who are called by my name, **will humble themselves**, and pray and seek my face and turn from their wicked ways, then will I hear from heaven and will forgive their sin and will heal their land.*

~ II Chronicles 7:14

More than 2,500 years ago a great empire was ruled by a very unusual king. His capital city, sixty miles in circumference, was enclosed by a wall that was 300 feet high, eighty feet thick, and which extended thirty-five feet below the surface of the ground. This wall was studded with 250 towers and 100 gates of brass. A half-mile long bridge, thirty feet wide, on stone piers spanned the great river Euphrates which bisected the city. Under the river was a tunnel, fifteen feet wide and twelve feet high.

In this city was the Temple of Murdock, where a golden image of the god Bel and a golden table that together weighed twenty-five tons were housed. There were also two golden lions, a golden table forty feet long and fifteen feet wide, and a human figure of solid gold, eighteen feet high. This city had 53 temples and 180 altars. The Hanging Gardens, made of several tiers of arches, supported solid platforms 400 feet square. They were filled with beautiful gardens of trees, shrubs, and flowers. Beneath the arches were luxurious apartments. A reservoir at the top was filled from the river below by hydraulic pumps.

Designed and built by the genius of one man, that city was Babylon, and the man of which we speak was the great Nebuchadnezzar.

It is not surprising that this man was filled with pride over his many accomplishments. He did not understand that God had given him every ability—even the empire itself. Angered by his pride, God called upon Nebuchadnezzar to repent and humble himself. God spoke to him through a dream and a prophet, but he would not listen. Nebuchadnezzar was judged by God with the outcome that he lost his mind and his kingdom. He was driven out into the fields, where he became like an animal for seven years before he finally repented thoroughly. God restored his mind, health and kingdom. When Nebuchadnezzar repented, this is what he said:

> At the end of that time, I, Nebuchadnezzar, raised my eyes toward heaven, and my sanity was restored. Then I praised the Most High; I honored and glorified him who lives forever. His dominion is an eternal dominion; his kingdom endures from generation to generation. All the peoples of the earth are regarded as nothing. He does as he pleases with the powers of heaven and the peoples of the earth. No one can hold back his hand or say to him: "What have you done?" At the same time that my sanity was restored, my honor and splendor were returned to me for the glory of my kingdom. My advisers and nobles sought me out, and I was restored to my throne and became even greater than before. Now I, Nebuchadnezzar, praise and exalt and glorify the King of heaven, because everything he does is right and all his ways are just. And those who walk in pride he is able to humble (Dan. 4:34–37).

Jesus tells us that pride comes from the heart, and makes a man unclean (Mark 7:21–23). God also says that "A high look and a proud heart is sin" (Prov. 21:4). We want to call it dignity, or culture, but God calls it sin. The Apostle James reminds us that "God resists the proud, but gives grace to the humble" (Jas. 4:6, Prov. 3:34, NKJV). God holds the proud at arm's length, but dwells with the humble:

For thus says the High and Lofty One who inhabits eternity, whose name is Holy: "I dwell in the high and holy place, with him who has a contrite and humble spirit, to revive the spirit of the humble, and to revive the heart of the contrite ones (Is. 57:15, NKJV).

God's refusal to accept our pride is dramatically stated in these words:

"For behold, the day is coming, burning like an oven, and all the proud, yes, all who do wickedly will be stubble. And the day which is coming shall burn them up," says the LORD *of hosts, "That will leave them neither root nor branch"* (Mal. 4:1, NKJV).

What is pride? Pride is misdirected love. It is love that belongs to God only, turned in upon one's self. This pride is described in II Timothy 3:1–5. Please notice that those who are lovers of themselves are also proud, and involved in many other terrible sins that go along with self-love. This was the sin of Nebuchadnezzar. It was also the sin of Satan! This is seen in the words from Isaiah 14:12–15, which describe Satan's fall. Pride is self-exaltation. Jesus asked the question, "How can you believe, when you receive glory from one another and you do not seek the glory that is from the *one and* only God?" (John 5:44, NASB).

The Pharisees did everything to be seen of men. They made long prayers on the street corners. They wore long robes to accent their holiness. They made public their gifts to gain attention. They loved recognition in public, and sought the most honoured seats at religious gatherings. This pride that was so manifest among the religious leaders of Jesus' day is just as evident today in the Church and is a major hindrance to revival! Christian "celebrities" among us, whether preachers or musicians, are an abomination to God! God will not give His glory to another even if we will. God is not morally free to bless our exaltation of man. The Apostle Paul put it this way:

I say to every one of you: Do not think of yourself more highly than you ought, but rather think of yourself with sober judgment, in accordance with the measure of faith God has given you (Rom. 12:4).

Pride is caused by an inaccurate estimate of one's self. When Job saw himself in comparison with God, he said, "My ears had heard of you but now my eyes have seen you. Therefore I despise myself and repent in dust and ashes" (Job 42:5,6).

Egotism and timidity are two sides of the coin of pride. They are both a preoccupation with what others think about us, a focus on self rather than God. One of the marks of revival is people being liberated from egotism and timidity. In the Canadian Revival of the early 1970s, we saw this happen constantly. It was almost a trademark of that revival.

Pride goes before a fall, and that was surely true of Peter. He proclaimed loudly, "I will die for you!" But in a few hours, he had denied his Lord three times. Jesus' disciples were quarreling among themselves as to who would be the greatest. This culminated in James and John actually asking Jesus for the highest places in His coming Kingdom. They glibly said they could drink of Jesus' cup, but had no idea that He was referring to the cross.

How does pride manifest itself in our daily lives? Since pride is loving self rather than God, it tends to make self a god by taking to itself many of the attributes of God. Here are a few: **Infallibility:** "I am always right." **Omniscience:** A know-it-all attitude. **Omnipotence:** Finding it necessary to talk about my accomplishments in order to be glorified among men. **Superiority:** I am more important than that other person. God asks the question,

For who regards you as superior? And what do you have that you did not receive? But if you did receive it, why do you boast as if you had not received it? (I Cor. 4:7, NASB).

Of being critical about other Christians, God says,

Brethren, even if a man is caught in any trespass, you who are spiritual, restore such a one in a spirit of gentleness; {each one} looking to yourself, lest you too be tempted. Bear one another's burdens, and thus fulfill the law of Christ. For if anyone thinks he is something when he is nothing, he deceives himself (Gal. 6:1–3, NASB).

Moral Perfection: Self-righteousness or self-justification. Not calling sin—*sin!* Wrong concepts about sanctification. If I claim to have a spiritual experience that does not allow me to fail, I will be locked into a position where I cannot admit that I have sinned. I may call sin "mistakes," or "my temperament," or "human weakness," or "my personality." "If we say that we have no sin, we deceive ourselves, and the truth is not in us" (I John 1:8, KJV).

HOW DO MEN FALL INTO THE SIN OF PRIDE?

1. Prosperity can contribute to it

God gave his people a solemn warning about this possibility in Deuteronomy 8:11–14,17,18:

Be careful that you do not forget the LORD your God, failing to observe his commands, his laws and his decrees that I am giving you this day. Otherwise, when you eat and are satisfied, when you build fine houses and settle down, and when your herds and flocks grow large and your silver and gold increase and all you have is multiplied, then your heart will become proud and you will forget the LORD your God, who brought you out of Egypt, out of the land of slavery. You may say to yourself, "My power and the strength of my hands have produced this wealth for me." But remember the LORD your God, for it is he who gives you the ability to produce wealth, and so confirms his covenant, which he swore to your forefathers, as it is today.

2. Comparisons Between People

God warns us of this danger in II Corinthians 10:12.

"For we dare not class ourselves or compare ourselves with those who commend themselves. But they, measuring themselves by themselves, and comparing themselves among themselves, are not wise (NKJV).

3. Imbibing the Spirit of the World

God has commanded, "Do not love the world or anything in the world" (I John 2:15–17). One of the "wicked ways" I will deal with later in this book is worldliness, which is a major hindrance to revival today!

WHAT IS THE CURE FOR PRIDE?

A clear answer is found in the attitude of Christ, as set forth in Philippians 2:5–8.

Have this attitude in yourselves which was also in Christ Jesus, who, although He existed in the form of God, did not regard equality with God a thing to be grasped, but emptied Himself, taking the form of a bond-servant, {and} being made in the likeness of men. Being found in appearance as a man, He humbled Himself by becoming obedient to the point of death, even death on a cross (NASB).

Here are five aspects of the attitude of Christ:

1. A sober self-estimate

Christ knew exactly who He was, and why He came into the world. He did not promote His position with God.

2. He did not seek a reputation

Dr. F.B. Meyer, in writing to a friend, said that he had heard that he (Dr. Meyer) had of late developed a reputation as a teacher of the "deeper Christian life." He said it made one want to crawl into heaven through the back door.[1] Amen!

3. He made Himself a servant

Christ said He came not to be ministered unto, but to minister, and to give His life!

4. Christ humbled Himself

It was not necessary for God to humble Him. We must humble ourselves. If God has to humble us, we will be sorry. Nebuchadnezzar would not humble himself, so God humbled him. And what a humbling it was! He lost his mind and his kingdom for seven long years.

What a terrible lesson to learn. Finally, we find that,

5. Christ was obedient unto death—the death of the cross!

So it is with us—SELF MUST DIE! The doctrine and experience of the cross is essential to adequate preparation for revival! Those who experienced the Canadian Revival of 1971–1972 saw clearly that their main problem was the self-life. They humbled themselves at the feet of Christ, and agreed with God about their own death with Christ. It was not just a mental ascent, but a real dying. Self had to get off the throne, and Christ was made Lord in the fullest sense of the word. Lives, marriages, families, and churches were transformed by this approach to the Christian life. This has been true in every revival of history and must become true in God's people today if we are to see the great revival we so desperately need.

We are willing to sing about the cross, preach about the cross, and even wear gold crosses around our necks, but many who are praying for revival would stop immediately if they realized the answer to their prayers meant dying upon that instrument of torture and death. That is exactly what it will mean! God has said that if His people will "humble themselves," He will heal their land. When we discover humbling ourselves to the point of death on the cross is required, will we be willing to do it? I pray we will! Now, let us ask ourselves a further question about humbling ourselves:

IN WHAT AREAS DO WE, AS CHRISTIANS, NEED TO HUMBLE OURSELVES?

I want to deal with three such areas.

1. Transparency, or Honesty

Christians must become honest and open, walking in the light of God with nothing to hide, as God says in I John 1:5–9.

And this is the message we have heard from Him and announce to you, that God is light, and in Him there is no darkness at all. If we say that we have fellowship with Him and {yet} walk in the darkness, we lie and do not practice the truth; but if we walk in the light as He Himself is in the light, we have fellowship with one another, and the blood of Jesus His Son cleanses us from all sin. If we say that we have no sin, we are deceiving ourselves, and the truth is not in us. If we confess our sins, He is faithful and righteous to forgive us our sins and to cleanse us from all unrighteousness (NASB).

For many years I heard this Scripture used to support the idea that sin breaks our fellowship with God. That is not what it says. It says that **hiding** our sin is what breaks our fellowship with God. Making it our regular practice to live a life in the dark keeps us from having fellowship with God as well as with men. Confessing our sin to God, and where indicated to man also, brings cleansing and restoration of fellowship with God and man.

The blood of Jesus Christ is adequate for all our sin. Praise God! Many, many Christians are walking in darkness—they are not living transparent lives. Pride often keeps them from coming into the light. We must humble ourselves, come into the light, confess our sins, and start living in fellowship with God and man if we are to see true revival.

If you are serious about revival, I challenge you right now to put down this book and get a pencil and paper. Ask God to show you everything you are hiding, and every area of your life where you are walking in darkness. Make a list. Humble yourself before God, and where necessary before man—confess each hidden thing and accept the cleansing of the blood of Christ. If you do this, I promise you that revival will begin in your heart and you will experience a fullness of joy that you may have never known. God's Word states: "He who conceals his sins does not prosper, but whoever confesses and renounces them finds mercy" (Prov. 28:13). King David found this to be true. Some of his confessions of sin, especially Psalms 38 and 51, are striking examples of this truth.

A story is told about a woman who acquired wealth and decided to have a book written about her genealogy. The well-known author she engaged for the assignment discovered that one of her grandfathers had been electrocuted for murder in Sing Sing Prison. When he said that it would have to be included in the book, she pleaded for a way of saying it that would hide the truth. When the book appeared, that section read as follows: "One of her grandfathers occupied the 'Chair Of Applied Electricity' in one of America's best known institutions. He was very much attached to his position, and literally died in the harness." That is what pride will try to do with the truth!

When I was a young pastor, I thought that unless I appeared to be nearly perfect before my people, they would neither trust me nor follow me. The very opposite, I soon discovered, was true. If they believed my facade of perfection, they threw up their hands in despair, saying they could never be like that! If they did not believe in my false facade, they considered me a hypocrite—which was even worse. When I finally decided to walk in the light, I and my people began to have fellowship with one another as well as with God. They were willing to follow an honest man even though he was imperfect. Fifty years of experience with pastors leads me to believe very few of them are walking in the light. As to the man in the pew, his record is probably worse than his pastor.

The danger of this situation was brought home to me quite forcefully through an experience with a member of the church of which I was, at that time, the pastor. This man gave approximately $30,000 a year to God's work. In his giving to certain people, he wanted a tax credit that was not allowed by the Revenue Service. He had done this for a number of years before I came along, and was quite angry when I put a stop to it. Then another matter arose in which he wanted to follow a procedure definitely contrary to our church bylaws. Again, I said he could not do what he wanted to do. So he went around the church talking, blaming me for his frustration. I thought, *I will fix his wagon!* So I printed in the bulletin a copy of the bylaw in question. Everyone read it and it made him look like a fool. I say, to my sorrow, that was exactly what I wanted. I enjoyed my revenge for about two days before the Holy Spirit convicted me of my bad motives, showing me that I had not handled this man with the love of God. So I went to his house to confess my sin and ask his forgiveness. What a disappointment! He would not hear what I had to say, for he said, "My pastor can do no wrong. Whatever you did must be right, since you are a man of God." It was very frustrating. I wondered why he took this position when I had humbled myself before him. Then I realized that if he admitted I had done wrong, he would need to admit that he had done wrong. His distorted idea of what a pastor should be was helping to keep him from what he should be.

Walking in the light often includes making restitution. All revivals are filled with instances of people going back to make things right. Proprietors of businesses are amazed as people come streaming in to pay for things stolen, or pay old debts, or even to correct a dishonest business deal. Some Christians find themselves talking to the tax man as they pay up that which they dishonestly avoided. All this makes it necessary to humble ourselves.

As we move deeper into the areas that underlie dishonesty, cover up, or hiding, we encounter the problem of **fear**. Much of the dishonesty in our lives arises from our perception that we will in some way be harmed if the truth is known. What we fear may be physical harm, or the fear of rejection, which brings emotional harm. This kind of fear is as old as the first sin of man. Adam and Eve had a completely open and transparent relationship with God. They knew God face-to-face. Then they sinned against God. What happened? We find the answer in Genesis 3:8–12. Immediately, Adam and Eve hid from God, and each other. They felt naked, and wanted to hide from each other. They were afraid, and hid from God. Why? They were afraid of rejection and harm, and with good cause. This kind of fear has its roots in doubting God's love (unbelief), breaking God's laws (guilt), and trying to avoid God's judgement (self preservation). Sinful human beings try to protect themselves by building a house to hide in, a house called "FEAR." The materials out of which it is built are deceit, lies, hypocrisy, self-righteousness, and suspicion. The roof shuts out God and the walls shut out other people. To experience true revival, the roof must come off and the walls must come down! We must humble ourselves and come out into the open. This will mean honest confession to God and man. I John 1 tells us that we will then not only have true fellowship with God, but also with one another.

I am not talking about "washing our dirty linen in public" and exposing all the sinful secrets of our lives, as is being done on television talk shows. I am talking about becoming honest men and women before God and man. I am talking about humbling ourselves. In the biographies of the Bible, there is no attempt to paint unreal pictures of plaster saints. The truth is told. And so we know about Abraham's lies about his wife Sarah, and his false step with Hagar. We know about Jacob's deceitful treatment of others, Elijah's prayer to die, David's adultery and murder, and Peter's fearful behaviour with the legalistic Christians of his day, even after Pentecost! These are all people whom God blessed, when they walked in the light.

One of the strongest illustrations of this truth is found in Jacob's personal revival. All the deceit of his life finally culminated in the coming confrontation with his brother, Esau. Esau had threatened to kill Jacob, and now was coming to meet him with an army of 400 men. That night, Jacob met with God in prayer. He wrestled with God, saying, "I will not let you go until you bless me!" Then God said, "What is your name?" The name Jacob means "trickster, or heel grabber." It was time for total honesty. When Jacob finally admitted what he really was, God blessed him. So it is with us; when we come to the end of our self-effort, and are willing to be totally honest with God about ourselves, God will bless us!

We do not need more knowledge, or better methods, or greater opportunities, or finer skills. **We need God!** After this experience, Jacob was given a new name. He was now a prince with God and men. Through all Jacob's failure, God loved him, and longed to revive him and bless him.

O, my brother, sister, God loves us still. It is true we have failed Him. It is true that pride, dishonesty, and fear have kept us back from God's full blessing. Nevertheless, God loves us still. Let us lay hold of God, let us confess our true nature, let us refuse to let go of God until He gives us a new name of blessing and power!

Too many of God's people live their lives in compartments: one life is lived at church, another is lived at work, and still another at home. Then there is a totally private life lived only in their thoughts, or possibly in their actual experiences, but unknown to the other compartments of their lives. The Word of God states that a double minded man is unstable in all he does (James 1). This kind of life is fragmented. This Christian is walking in darkness and must come into the light and begin to live an honest transparent life by God's grace in order to be made whole. This will be a humbling experience, but is absolutely essential to experiencing God's full blessing. This is what happens in every true revival. In the process of coming into the light, it may be necessary to go to someone other than God to make something right as far as possible. This brings us to the second area in humbling ourselves.

2. Restitution

When human beings commit sins, they create situations which are impossible for them to ever make perfectly right again. If it were possible, we would not need the forgiveness of God through substitutionary atonement. Only the blood of Christ can take away sin!

God's Word tells us, "But if we walk in the light, as he is in the light, we have fellowship with one another, and the blood of Jesus, his Son, purifies us from all sin" (I John 1:7). Nevertheless, in some situations, there are other people who have in some way been hurt by our sins. There is also the question of being truly repentant. Some of these situations require effort to make restoration, which may be a costly process involving sums of money, or a confession that may lead to criminal charges. I have seen a number of such situations. Let me share one with you.

In one of the churches I pastored there was a man who sincerely wanted the blessing of God on his life. God dealt with him in a number of different instances where he needed to make restitution. One day he came to me to discuss one of these situations. He said that before he became a Christian, he and another man had gone to another city, broken into a house, and stolen many items. This had happened ten years before. Now he believed God was leading him to go back there, find the house, and try to make restitution as far as possible.

The other man who had helped in the robbery was not a Christian, and would not want to be involved in the restitution in any way. What should he do? We prayed together. I advised him to prayerfully make a list of all he could remember of what they had taken, try to set an honest price on it and write it down. Then I suggested he go to that city, try to find the house, see if the same people lived there, confess his crime to them, and offer to pay for all the items listed. If those people could think of other items taken, add those to the list. He agreed, and away he went. He found the house and rang the doorbell.

A woman came to the door. He introduced himself, and asked if she had lived there ten years before. She said yes. He asked if she remembered when her house was broken into. Again she said yes. He told her that he was one of the thieves, that he had become a Christian, and that he had come to make restitution. She invited him in and called her husband. They sat in the living room while he told the story of his changed life. He gave them his list. He offered the cheque, but they did not want it, saying the insurance had paid them long ago. It was with some difficulty he persuaded them to take it. The lady served him cake and coffee, and it was a wonderful evening as he shared the grace of God in his life.

In a similar incident, a young man came to me for advice about a crime he had committed that not only tormented his conscience but filled him with fear of arrest. He had purchased some items of equipment for his business while in the United States. When he came back to Canada, he had his wife and mother-in-law carry these items, which were small but expensive, in their purses. They all stated they had nothing to declare, and so avoided paying the duty. What should he do?

We prayed together, then I made a call to the customs office, explaining the situation but not giving his name. They said if he would come in and bring his receipts, they would figure the duty he owed, he could pay the bill, and that would be the end of it. They told me that if they caught him, he would face a fine and/or imprisonment. If he confessed and paid what he owed, there would be no punishment.

This kind of humble action on our part is often a powerful testimony not only to other Christians, but to people of the world. Evan Roberts was the instrument God used to launch the great revival in Wales that went around the world. The night it began, he was speaking to seventeen people in the church in Loughor. He challenged them with four steps to take. The first one stated, "You must confess any known sin to God, and put any wrong done to man right." That still stands as an absolute requisite for revival, whether personal or corporate!

Sometimes public confession will be indicated, though as a general rule the confession of sin needs only to be made to God, and possibly the person or persons against whom we have sinned. Revivalist Ralph Sutera has put together some excellent guidelines for restitution and public sharing. With his permission, I am including them at the end of this book as Appendix B, under the heading, **"Forgiveness, Confession And Restitution."**

The whole question of restitution leads us very naturally to another area.

3. Forgiveness and Reconciliation

In order to humble ourselves and begin to walk in the light, the walls between us and other people must come down. This is only possible through forgiveness and reconciliation. This process strikes a major blow at pride and fear.

When the Canadian Revival was at its height, a large revival meeting was in progress in Winnipeg, Manitoba, Canada. Night by night the prayer rooms were filled with people seeking God. Harry and Evelyn Thiessen are a married couple who had met God and had their lives and marriage transformed through the revival. One night a woman in a very sad condition entered a prayer room where Evelyn was working. Afflicted with a stomach problem for twenty years, at this point the woman could not keep a normal meal down, and had wasted away to skin and bones. She could not do her housework, take care of her family, or be a wife to her husband.

Numerous doctors could not find anything wrong with her. Her condition, meanwhile, gradually worsened. Evelyn was asked to counsel with her, but at first could not discover her problem. The woman was in a terrible state of mind. As Evelyn prayed, asking God for guidance, she was led to ask the woman if there was anyone in her life with whom she had a bad relationship.

Finally, the woman admitted to Evelyn something she had never told anyone else: she was filled with bitterness toward her mother and sister. She related how they had both dominated her life, telling her how to treat her husband, how to bring up her children, how to keep her house, and even how to dress.

Evelyn said she would have to forgive them in order to find peace and healing. At first the woman didn't see how she could, but eventually with many tears, confessed her sin to God, and made the decision to forgive her mother and sister. Evelyn asked if either of them could be reached by phone. Yes, one could be reached. They went to a phone and called that person. On the spot, that woman confessed her bitterness and forgave her family member. What rejoicing! She went home that night, ate a normal meal, and soon returned to normal health. That is a splendid illustration of what forgiveness can do!

When we were just into the revival we experienced in Brown Street Church in Akron, Ohio, where I was pastor, I saw another example of the same thing. The visitation of God in revival power had begun on Sunday morning. Monday morning, I was in my office and received a phone call from the wife of a young man in the church who had been a Christian only a short while. She wanted to know if she could bring her husband over to see me. I asked her why she needed to bring him. She said he was bent over with stomach pains and could not straighten up.

It sounded like he had a physical problem, so I suggested she take him to Emergency. She said that he didn't think it was physical and neither did she. I said they could come over. He came in bent over, holding his stomach, and sat in a chair. I asked a number of questions trying to discover the problem, but was not making any progress. I stopped and prayed, asking God to show me the problem. It seemed to me that the Holy Spirit told me to ask him about his relationship with his father, whom I did not know. He flared at me, saying with great intensity, "I hate him!" I questioned him about that, and found out that his father had raised him with great sternness and no love. I said, "You will have to forgive him." He said, "Never!"

I shared with him what God has to say about Christians forgiving those who have wronged us. After a while, he agreed to forgive his father. I asked where his father lived. I discovered he lived about ten miles from town on a farm. I then told this young man that I thought he should go out there immediately and be reconciled with his father. He agreed. His wife drove the car and they went to the farm. As soon as he saw his father, his heart broke, and with tears he rushed into his father's arms. At once, he could straighten up. They wept on each other's shoulders. My friend confessed his bitterness, asked his father to forgive him, and declared his forgiveness for his father. All his pain was gone, and he was reconciled with his father. That incident illustrates the terrible power of bitterness, and the wonderful, healing power of forgiveness. Three of the most striking passages in Scripture about forgiving others who have wronged us are found in the Gospel of Matthew and Paul's epistle to the Ephesians:

"If your brother sins against you, go and show him his fault, just between the two of you. If he listens to you, you have won your brother over. But if he will not listen, take one or two others along, so that 'every matter may be established by the testimony of two or three witnesses.' If he refuses to listen to them, tell it to the church; and if he refuses to listen even to the church, treat him as you would a pagan or a tax collector" (Matt. 18:15–17).

Then Peter came to Jesus and asked, "Lord, how many times shall I forgive my brother when he sins against me? Up to seven times?" Jesus answered, "I tell you, not seven times, but seventy-seven times.
"Therefore, the kingdom of heaven is like a king who wanted to settle accounts with his servants. As he began the settlement, a man who owed him ten thousand talents was brought to him. Since he was not able to pay, the master ordered that he and his wife and his children and all that he had be sold to repay the debt.
"The servant fell on his knees before him. 'Be patient with me,' he begged, 'and I will pay back everything.' The servant's master took pity on him, canceled the debt and let him go.
"But when that servant went out, he found one of his fellow servants who owed him a hundred denarii. He grabbed him and began to choke him. 'Pay back what you owe me!' he demanded.
"His fellow servant fell to his knees and begged him, 'Be patient with me, and I will pay you back.'
"But he refused. Instead, he went off and had the man thrown

into prison until he could pay the debt. When the other servants saw what had happened, they were greatly distressed and went and told their master everything that had happened.

"Then the master called the servant in. 'You wicked servant,' he said, 'I canceled all that debt of yours because you begged me to. Shouldn't you have had mercy on your fellow servant just as I had on you?' In anger his master turned him over to the jailers to be tortured, until he should pay back all he owed.

"This is how my heavenly Father will treat each of you unless you forgive your brother from your heart" (Matt. 18:21–35).

Let all bitterness and wrath and anger and clamor and slander be put away from you, along with all malice. And be kind to one another, tender-hearted, forgiving each other, just as God in Christ also has forgiven you (Eph. 4:31,32, NASB).

From these Scriptures, please consider carefully with me:

THREE ISSUES IN FORGIVING OTHERS

1. The Goal of Forgiveness

The goal of forgiveness is **reconciliation**. Jesus said, "Go and confront your brother." If he will hear you, you have won your brother. You are reconciled. That is God's goal in forgiving you and me. We are ambassadors for Christ, as though God were pleading through us, "Be reconciled to God!" (Rom. 5:9–11). God loves us and wants to remove the enmity between us. That is our goal in forgiving others. Sometimes the other person may refuse to be reconciled, even as many refuse to be reconciled to God. Nevertheless, our responsibility to forgive is unchanged.

Seeking to be reconciled, when it involves a Christian brother, may necessitate the involvement of church leaders and church discipline as Jesus stated. When church leaders do not have the courage to deal with Christians at odds with one another, revival tarries in many churches. Jesus said that a person who refuses to forgive and be reconciled should be treated as an unbeliever. If he is an unbeliever, he should have his membership removed. If this procedure were followed with carefulness, wisdom, and love, a different atmosphere would prevail in many of our churches. The way would be open for God to move in revival power!

How does this work? First, the person who has been wronged should go to his brother, confront him in a loving manner, showing him exactly what he has done, declare his full forgiveness for the wrongdoer, and seek reconciliation with his brother. If that fails, he should now go to the church leaders, such as Deacons or Elders, and explain his problem. Those church leaders should then send two of their number with him to help solve the problem. If the other person still refuses to be reconciled, he should be brought before the entire governing body of the church (church board or board of Elders). If he still refuses to be reconciled, he should be warned by the church leaders, and if still obstinate, should be treated as an unbeliever and have his membership removed. Through all this, we must act with the greatest gentleness and love, and keep in mind that the goal of this procedure is forgiveness or reconciliation.

During the Korean war, a South Korean Christian, a civilian, was arrested by the communists and orders were given to shoot him. However, when the young communist officer discovered that the prisoner was in charge of an orphanage full of small children, he decided to spare the man and kill his son instead. So the nineteen-year-old son was apprehended and shot in the presence of his father. Later, the fortunes of war changed, and the young communist officer was captured by the United Nations Forces. He was tried and condemned to death. Before the sentence could be carried out, the Christian whose boy had been killed pleaded for the life of the killer. He declared that the officer was too young, and did not really know what he was doing. "Give him to me," said the Christian, "and I'll train him." His request was granted. That Christian man took his son's killer into his home, and made him his son. There he cared for him, loved him, and led him to Christ. Today that young former communist is a Christian pastor in South Korea. That is true biblical forgiveness! The second issue in forgiving others is:

2. The Method of Forgiveness

The biblical method of forgiveness is through vicarious suffering. In the parable given by Jesus, the one who was wronged paid the debt to set the sinner free. When the master fully forgave the servant, the great debt that he could never pay, it was the master who suffered the loss. Ephesians 4:32 states that we are to forgive just as God forgives through Jesus Christ. And how is that? We are all sinners against God. We have wronged Him beyond our ability to ever pay the debt. God, in Christ, accepted the wrong we did to Him, and bore it for us on the cross, fully paying the debt, so we might be free and be reconciled to God. Justice must be done! The law must be fully satisfied! Someone must pay the debt! But who? We cannot pay it. God in love for us fully paid the debt Himself.

When Alexander was Tzar of Russia, he often camped with his army in the battle zone. In his army was a young officer whose parents were friends of the Tzar. This young man had entangled himself in serious debt through gambling. The debt was so great there was no way he could pay it. He could not stand to think of the disgrace he was about to bring upon his family and himself, so he decided to take his life. Late one night, when all others within the encampment were asleep, he sat in his tent, a candle burning, and the list of debts on a small table before him. He had added up the debts, placed the total sum at the bottom, and then beside this wrote, "Who can pay so much?" He loaded his service revolver and placed the end of the barrel against his temple. Then suddenly he thought of his sister, who loved him dearly. He put his head down on his arms and wept. He fell asleep. Alexander was out walking through the encampment, and seeing a light burning in an officer's tent, went to investigate. He entered the young man's tent quietly and approached the table. He saw the young man asleep, saw the revolver in his hand, read the list of debts, and immediately understood the situation. He stayed a few moments more, and then left the tent. Soon the young man awakened. He picked up the revolver. He decided to read the list once more. He came to the bottom where he had written, "Who can pay so much?" Then he saw one word had been added. In a different handwriting, the word read "Alexander." He recognized that signature and leaped to his feet, shouting, "I'm saved, I'm saved!" The next morning, a messenger came from Alexander with a bag of gold to pay his debts.

When I look at the list of my sins, I know it is hopeless. I ask, "Who can pay so much?" Then I look again, and I see a signature, signed in blood: "Jesus Christ." And I, too, shout, "I'm saved, I'm saved!" Even so, on our behalf, Christ was willing to bear the offense that was against Him, pay the debt, and set us free. So I, too, must be willing to accept the hurt done to me, bear the offense, and set my fellow servant free. It will cost me something. I, too, must take up the cross! I must follow my Lord. I must forgive all who have wronged me. This is a very, very important step toward experiencing revival!

During the Revolutionary war, there lived in Pennsylvania a pastor by the name of Peter Miller. Although Miller was greatly loved by everyone in the community, there was one man who lived near the church who hated him, and had earned a bad reputation for his abuse of the minister. This man was not only a hater of the church, but it also turned out that he was a traitor to his country. He was convicted of treason, and sentenced to death by hanging. The trial was conducted in Philadelphia. No sooner did Miller hear of it, than he set out on foot to visit General Washington, and interceded for the man's life. But Washington told him, "I'm sorry that I cannot grant your request for your friend."

"Friend?" Miller cried, "Why that man is the worst enemy I have in the world!"

"What?" the general exclaimed in surprise, "Have you walked sixty miles to save the life of an enemy? That, in my judgement, puts the matter in a different light. I will grant him a pardon for your sake." The pardon was prepared, and Miller set out at once on foot to a place fifteen miles away, where the execution was to take place that afternoon. He arrived just as the man was being carried to the scaffold. When the man saw Miller hurrying toward the place, he remarked, "There is old Peter Miller. He has walked all the way from Ephrata to have his revenge gratified today by seeing me hanged." But scarcely had he spoken the words, when Miller pushed his way through to the condemned man, and handed him the pardon that saved his life.[2] That is biblical forgiveness! That brings us to the final issue in forgiving others:

3. The Result of Forgiveness

The result of forgiving is inner peace. This is true even though forgiving another is not based on feelings, but on a careful biblical decision. That decision is followed by a process which eventually brings inner peace.

As a young Christian, I heard many times that God forgets our sins—a belief which seemed to be backed up by Scripture. However, there was a problem with that concept. I heard many Christians saying, "I try to forgive, but I can't forget. I have asked God to take it out of my mind, but He hasn't." It seemed unfair for God to expect me to forgive without forgetting, when *He* was able to forget.

Then I discovered that God's Word did not teach that concept at all, but something quite different, something possible to achieve. A Scripture often used to support the "God forgets our sins" concept turned out to teach something much better, upon careful consideration. It is Isaiah 43:25. God says: "I, even I, am the one who wipes out your transgressions for My own sake; and I will not remember your sins" (NASB). God does not say He forgets our sins, but rather that He **chooses not to remember** them. God does not forget anything! God knows the end from the beginning, and died for our whole lifetime of sin before we were even born.

What God does is something we also can do. To take the wrongs done to us out of our memory would necessitate Him to damage our brains—something He is unlikely to do. I **cannot immediately forget**, but I **can choose not to remember**. When I choose to forgive someone, I make the choice not to think or talk about it anymore. When some situation jogs my memory and all the old thoughts and feelings come rushing in, I can say, *no, I have forgiven that person and I refuse to think or talk about it anymore*. Sometimes other people who mean well will bring up the subject, trying to sympathize with you for the hurt you have suffered. You must not allow it! Say kindly but firmly, "Please stop. I have forgiven that person and do not wish to talk about it anymore." All the poison and pain will eventually drain away, and though you will not totally forget the wrong, you will almost never think about it, and will be effectually healed from the hurt.

When the Moravian missionaries first went to the Eskimos, they could not find a word in their language for forgiveness, so they had to compound one. This turned out to be: "Issumagijoujungnainermik." It is a formidable-looking assembly of letters, but an expression that has a beautiful connotation for those who understand it. It means, "Not-being-able-to-think-about-it-anymore."

Another wonderful truth about forgiveness exists in this verse. God says "I will wipe out your transgressions **for My own sake**." Forgiveness is something good I do for myself! In Jesus' parable, He states that the servant who would not forgive would be tormented until he did. Refusing to forgive someone hurts me more than the other person. Indeed, he may not be hurt in the least by my unforgiving spirit. Because my bitterness hurts me and robs me of inner peace, the one who wronged me continues hurting me over and over. I can only get free by forgiving him. In Hebrews 12:14,15, God says,

Pursue peace with all men, and the sanctification without which no one will see the Lord. See to it that no one comes short of the grace of God; that no root of bitterness springing up causes trouble, and by it many be defiled (NASB).

It is true that the root bears fruit—our bitterness defiles us and other people around us. This problem in Christian families and churches is one of the greatest hindrances to revival today!

Leonardo da Vinci, one of the outstanding intellects of all history, excelled as a draftsman, engineer, inventor and artist. William Edward Biederwolf recounts, in "The Man Who Said He Would"[3] how just before da Vinci commenced work on the "Last Supper," he had a violent quarrel with a fellow artist. So enraged and bitter was Leonardo that he decided to paint the face of his enemy into the face of Judas. In that way, he would vent his spleen and get revenge, by handing the man down in infamy and scorn to succeeding generations. The face of Judas was, therefore, one of the first that he finished. Everyone who saw it could easily recognize it as the face of the man with whom Leonardo had quarreled.

Finally, he began to paint the face of Christ, but could make no progress. Something seemed to be baffling him, holding him back, frustrating his best efforts. At length, he came to the conclusion that the thing which was checking and frustrating him was the fact that he had painted his enemy into the face of Judas. He therefore painted out the face of Judas, and commenced anew on the face of Jesus. This time he had the success which the ages have acclaimed. You cannot at the same time be painting the features of Christ into your own life, and painting another face with the colors of enmity and hatred!

A little boy was asked, "What is forgiveness?" He replied, "It is the odour that flowers breathe when they are trampled upon." So it will be with us. Revival is costly! Will we who name the name of Christ be willing to pay that price?

Forgiveness is a big but essential step toward revival. We must humble ourselves and become totally honest with ourselves, with God, and with others. Where it is indicated, we must be willing to make restitution, and even share publically what God is doing in our lives. Finally, we must forgive others and seek to be reconciled with those who have wronged us. All of this will bring revival into our lives and the lives of others.

The Word of God gives us numerous accounts of those who humbled themselves. One that speaks directly to our hearts is II Kings 5:1–15.

Now Naaman was commander of the army of the king of Aram. He was a great man in the sight of his master and highly regarded, because through him the LORD had given victory to Aram. He was a valiant soldier, but he had leprosy.

Now bands from Aram had gone out and had taken captive a young girl from Israel, and she served Naaman's wife. She said to her mistress, "If only my master would see the prophet who is in Samaria! He would cure him of his leprosy."

Naaman went to his master and told him what the girl from Israel had said. "By all means, go," the king of Aram replied. "I will send a letter to the king of Israel." So Naaman left, taking with him ten talents of silver, six thousand shekels of gold and ten sets of clothing. The letter that he took to the king of Israel read: "With this letter I am sending my servant Naaman to you so that you may cure him of his leprosy."

As soon as the king of Israel read the letter, he tore his robes and said, "Am I God? Can I kill and bring back to life? Why does this fellow send someone to me to be cured of his leprosy? See how he is trying to pick a quarrel with me!"

When Elisha the man of God heard that the king of Israel had torn his robes, he sent him this message: "Why have you torn your robes? Have the man come to me and he will know that there is a prophet in Israel." So Naaman went with his horses and chariots and stopped at the door of Elisha's house. Elisha sent a messenger to say to him, "Go, wash yourself seven times in the Jordan, and your flesh will be restored and you will be cleansed."

But Naaman went away angry and said, "I thought that he would surely come out to me and stand and call on the name of the LORD his God, wave his hand over the spot and cure me of my leprosy. Are not Abana and Pharpar, the rivers of Damascus, better than any of the waters of Israel? Couldn't I wash in them and be cleansed?" So he turned and went off in a rage. Naaman's servants went to him and said, "My father, if the prophet had told you to do some great thing, would you not have done it? How much more, then, when he tells you, 'Wash and be cleansed'!" So he went down and dipped himself in the Jordan seven times, as the man of God had told him, and his flesh was restored and became clean like that of a young boy. Then Naaman and all his attendants went back to the man of God. He stood before him and said, "Now I know that there is no God in all the world except in Israel."

This great man found that he had to go down seven times in order to be cleansed. Some of us may find it necessary to do the same. Maybe it will be seventeen times! Whatever is required for our cleansing, may God help us to be willing to do it so the revival may come!

CHAPTER SEVEN

The Step of Prayer

If my people, who are called by my name,
*will humble themselves **and pray and seek my face***
and turn from their wicked ways, then will I hear
from heaven and will forgive their sin
and will heal their land.

~ *II Chronicles 7:14*

Revivalist Armin Gesswein has said, "Prayer is not everything, but everything is by prayer!" In the Christian life that is true. Is that stated in Scripture? It most certainly is. We read in Philippians 4:6,7:

Do not be anxious about anything, but in everything, by prayer
and petition, with thanksgiving, present your requests to God.
And the peace of God, which transcends all understanding, will
guard your hearts and your minds in Christ Jesus.

So let me say it again, "In the Christian life, prayer is not everything, but everything is by prayer." Does that describe my Christian life? Do I really want revival? If I secretly hope for God to bring about great revival without great praying, it will not happen! Wait a minute! Why all these extravagant statements? What is so important about prayer? **Why should I pray?** I want to give you three biblical answers to that question.

1. I Should Pray Because God Commands It

In fact, the Word of God commands me to pray first, last and always. Paul said to Timothy,

> *I urge, then, first of all, that requests, prayers, intercession and thanksgiving be made for everyone. I want men everywhere to lift up holy hands in prayer, without anger or disputing* (I Tim. 2:1,8).

For many of us, prayer is the method of last resort, when nothing else has worked and we are desperate. Writing to the Thessalonians, Paul said, *"**Finally**, brothers, pray for us that the message of the Lord may spread rapidly and be honored, just as it was with you"* (II Thess. 3:1, author's emphasis). All things in the Christian life should be concluded with prayer. First and last, we should pray. Then again, Paul writes, *"And pray in the Spirit **on all occasions** with all kinds of prayers and requests. With this in mind, be alert and **always keep on praying** for all the saints"* (Eph. 6:18); *"**pray continually**"* (I Thess. 5:17, author's emphasis).

Jesus Himself had something to say on this matter as we see in Luke 18:1: *"Then Jesus told his disciples a parable to show them that they should always pray and not give up."* God's command to us is that we are to pray first, last, always, everywhere, for all people in our lives, and in every circumstance. There is a motto which reads, **"You can do more than pray after you have prayed, but you cannot do more than pray until you have prayed."** Not to live a life of prayer is to live a life of disobedience! I should pray because God commands it. If I am a serious Christian, that should be enough.

2. I Should Pray Because Jesus Set the Example

That Jesus was a man of prayer, I am sure will not be disputed. In order to fasten this fact securely upon our minds, however, I will include a number of Scripture passages that clearly state it:

> *After he had dismissed them, he went up on a mountainside by himself to pray. When evening came, he was there alone* (Matt. 14:23).

Very early in the morning, while it was still dark, Jesus got up, left the house and went off to a solitary place, where he prayed (Mark 1:35).

After leaving them, he went up on a mountainside to pray (Mark 6:46).

When all the people were being baptized, Jesus was baptized too. And as he was praying, heaven was opened and the Holy Spirit descended on him in bodily form like a dove. And a voice came from heaven: "You are my Son, whom I love; with you I am well pleased (Luke 3:21–22).

But Jesus often withdrew to lonely places and prayed (Luke 5:16).

One of those days Jesus went out to a mountainside to pray, and spent the night praying to God (Luke 6:12).

About eight days after Jesus said this, he took Peter, John and James with him and went up onto a mountain to pray (Luke 9:28–29).

One day Jesus was praying in a certain place. When he finished, one of his disciples said to him, "Lord, teach us to pray, just as John taught his disciples" (Luke 11:1).

After Jesus said this, he looked toward heaven and prayed (John 17:1).

I Pray for them. I am not praying for the world, but for those you have given me, for they are yours (John 17:9).

My prayer is not that you take them out of the world but that you protect them from the evil one (John 17:15).

My prayer is not for them alone. I pray also for those who will believe in me through their message (John 17:20).

Then Jesus went with his disciples to a place called Gethsemane, and he said to them, "Sit here while I go over there and pray (Matt 26:36).

Going a little farther, he fell with his face to the ground and prayed (Matt 26:39).

He went away a second time and prayed (Matt 26:42).

Think what these statements about Jesus really mean! He went off into the mountains so He could be alone to pray. He arose early in the morning to be alone to pray. Jesus sometimes spent all night in prayer! It was after one of these nights in prayer that Jesus chose His disciples. When He withdrew with the disciples, He spent significant time in prayer in their presence. At His water baptism, He was praying when the Holy Spirit came upon Him. It was while He was praying with three of His inner circle that He was transfigured before them. In the evening of the last supper with His disciples, He prayed for them and for us. In the garden shortly before His crucifixion, He prayed in such agony that He sweat blood! Even on the cross Jesus prayed for the forgiveness of His murderers, and that God the Father would receive His spirit as He died.

Stop! Think! What does this all mean? Here is the Creator, Sustainer and Ruler of the universe, on earth in human form. He has all power, knowledge, and wisdom. He is very God of very God. In Him dwells all the fullness of the Godhead in bodily form. But—He needed to live a life of constant prayer. To Jesus, prayer had priority.

What about you and me? If Jesus could not get along without this life of prayer, how do we poor sinful, weak, ignorant mortals think we can live and serve without it? How can we be so deceived? We say we are too busy. Not one of us has ever been as busy as Jesus! He was thronged by thousands of people, so constantly that the Scriptures say the disciples did not have time to eat.

Why should I pray? Why should I pray? WHY SHOULD I PRAY? One serious look at the prayer life of Jesus tells me that prayer must become a number-one priority! Jesus said, "Without me you can do nothing!" The Psalmist said, "Power belongs to God!" The greatest revival the world has yet seen took place under the leadership of John the Baptist, Jesus Christ, and the apostles—all of whose lives were saturated with constant, passionate, believing prayer.

Revival will come in our day when God's people stop playing and start praying! God says, "when my people ... pray and seek my face ... then will I hear from heaven, and will heal their land." This brings me to my third reason for prayer:

3. I Should Pray Because Prayer Changes Things

Someone says, "Well, prayer doesn't really change anything but the person who prays. After all, God is sovereign and knows all things and determines all things. Nothing I can do will change one iota of what God will do. He has predestined all things in such a fashion that man's actions have no part in it." In Africa, Muslims who believe that allow flies to eat the eyeballs of their babies, which causes blindness. They shrug and say, "It is the will of God."

No Christian I have ever met has claimed to believe in that kind of sovereignty *and* supported it with daily practice. Christian parents wouldn't allow a baby to play on the freeway, drink poison, or reach for fire—they know better than to apply this faulty theology to such situations. But because it is costly to pray, they hide behind that doctrine, refuse to pray, and let lost sinners around them go to hell! My dear brother and sister, there are spiritual laws, instituted by a righteous and sovereign God, that bind Christians to unbelievers in such a way that God is not morally free to bring revival without our prayers. Does the Bible teach that? Yes it does! Let us examine a few examples from Scripture.

The Prayer of Moses in Exodus 32:9–14 states clearly that "the LORD relented and did not bring on his people the disaster he had threatened." Did God know of the actions Israel would take and what Moses would do in response? Of course He did! Notice, however, that God knew about Moses' prayer, which saved an entire nation from destruction! Who will do that today for *this* nation?

In Ezekiel 22:30–31, we hear God say,

I looked for a man among them who would build up the wall and stand before me in the gap on behalf of the land so I would not have to destroy it, but I found none. So I will pour out my wrath on them and consume them with my fiery anger, bringing down on their own heads all they have done.

Notice, please, that this is the sovereign LORD speaking. Consider another example:

The Prayers of the Ninevites: Jonah 3:4–4:1. Jonah was angry because the salvation of the Ninevites contradicted his theology and hurt his reputation. Nevertheless, that city would have been destroyed as God said if they had not fasted and prayed and repented of their sins. Prayer made the difference!

Please look with me at two examples from the life of King Hezekiah. The first one is in II Kings 19. Sennacherib of Assyria had invaded Judah, and had Jerusalem under siege. He sent King Hezekiah a letter in which he mocked God and called upon Hezekiah to surrender. We read what happened in II Kings 19:14–19,35–37. Does prayer change things? Ask Sennacherib! The poet tells this story in striking language:

Assyria came down like the wolf on the fold,
His cohorts were gleaming in purple and gold;
The sheen of their spears was like stars on the sea,
When blue waves roll nightly on deep Galilee.
Like the leaves of the forest when summer is green,
That host with their banners at sunset were seen;
Like the leaves of the forest when autumn has blown,
That host on the morrow lay withered and strown.
For the angel of death spread his wings on the blast,
And breathed in the face of the foe as he passed;
The eyes of the sleepers waxed deadly and chill,
Their hearts but once heaved and forever are still.
There lay the steed with his nostrils all wide,

But through it there rolled not a breath of his pride;
The foam of his gasping lay white on the turf,
And cold as the spray of the rock beating surf.
There lay the rider distorted and pale,
With dew on his brow and rust on his mail;
The tents were all silent—the banners alone—
The lances unlifted—the trumpet unblown.
The widows of Ashur are loud in their wail,
The idols are broke in the temple of Baal;
The might of the gentile, unsmote by the sword,
Has melted like snow in the glance of the Lord![1]

We hear God saying through Isaiah, in the striking account of Hezekiah's healing, that Hezekiah was to die of that particular illness (Is. 38:1–6). In this case, when Hezekiah prayed, God used the same Prophet to say that he would not die, but live fifteen more years! Does prayer change things? Yes it does!

There is a place where you can touch
the eyes of blinded men to instant perfect sight;
There is a place where you can say "Arise,"
to dying captives bound in chains of night;
There is a place where you can touch the store
of hoarded gold and free it for the Lord;
There is a place upon some distant shore
where you can send the worker and the Word;
There is a place where heaven's resistless power
responsive moves to faith that's true;
There is a place—a silent, trusting hour
when God Himself descends and fights for you;
Where is this blessed place? Do you ask where?

It is the place of true, believing prayer!

O, my brother and sister, this is one of the main answers to our desperate need for revival. We must pray for revival because prayer changes things! Alfred Lord Tennyson put it this way:

Pray for my soul!
More things are wrought by prayer than this world dreams of.
Wherefore, let thy voice rise like a fountain night and day.
For what are men better than sheep or goats
that nourish a blind life within the brain,
If knowing God, They lift not hands in prayer,
Both for themselves and those who call them friends?
For so the whole wide world with golden chains is bound
about the feet of God!

Now all this raises the question, "What can I do to develop a personal prayer life?" The truth of the matter is, that we shall never experience adequate group prayer unless those who come together to pray, already have learned to pray in private. I am convinced that this is the reason church prayer meetings and concerts of prayer have largely failed in our day. To explore this question, we will turn to Luke 11:1–14.

One day Jesus was praying in a certain place. When he finished, one of his disciples said to him, "Lord, teach us to pray, just as John taught his disciples."

He said to them, "When you pray, say: 'Father, hallowed be your name, your kingdom come. Give us each day our daily bread. Forgive us our sins, for we also forgive everyone who sins against us. And lead us not into temptation.'"

Then he said to them, "Suppose one of you has a friend, and he goes to him at midnight and says, 'Friend, lend me three loaves of bread, because a friend of mine on a journey has come to me, and I have nothing to set before him.'

"Then the one inside answers, 'Don't bother me. The door is already locked, and my children are with me in bed. I can't get up and give you anything.' I tell you, though he will not get up and give him the bread because he is his friend, yet because of the man's boldness he will get up and give him as much as he needs.

"So I say to you: Ask and it will be given to you; seek and you will find; knock and the door will be opened to you. For every-

one who asks receives; he who seeks finds; and to him who knocks, the door will be opened.

"Which of you fathers, if your son asks for a fish, will give him a snake instead? Or if he asks for an egg, will give him a scorpion? If you then, though you are evil, know how to give good gifts to your children, how much more will your Father in heaven give the Holy Spirit to those who ask him!"

Jesus was driving out a demon that was mute. When the demon left, the man who had been mute spoke, and the crowd was amazed.

The disciples had asked Jesus to teach them to pray. What follows is the teaching of the Son of God on this subject! This is, in my estimation, the most important teaching in the Bible on how to develop a personal prayer life. Jesus answers the question with five guidelines.

1. LEARN TO PRAY ROUTINELY (VERSES 2–4)

In the very first answer to the disciples' question, Jesus gave a simple outline of subject matter that one might follow in regular daily prayer. It is a perfect outline, but I don't believe Jesus was trying to get them to practice a memorized prayer. I believe He was saying that there are some things we should pray about on a regular basis. This is what I call "routine praying."

Many Christians who try to develop a regular prayer life run out of things to say after ten minutes. This is because they have not learned routine praying. If they had learned this they would have found that the real problem is finding time to pray about **all** they want to include in their prayers. I have never listened in on some other person's private prayers, so I cannot give you an illustration from someone else. All I know about is my own practice, so I will share that with you, to help you understand what I am talking about.

I begin my regular prayer times with worship of God, telling Him how much I love Him, and giving Him thanks and praise in detail. Next I pray for myself and my wife, regarding our spiritual and physical needs. I follow that with prayers for my children and their families, dealing in detail with their needs as I see them. Then I branch out to pray for myself and my wife's brothers and sisters and their families. I have now been praying for at least thirty minutes.

My next expansion will have to do with my work. Since I am in the Christian ministry, that will include the church I serve in, and other speaking and business engagements. I pray for my staff and their families, and various aspects of the church, including church finances, and our present building program. I now pray for our Bible College and Seminary, and the Canadian Revival Fellowship in which I serve as an associate evangelist. After that, I pray about our house and personal finances, and various projects in which my wife and I may be engaged. Next, I include my writing ministry, and my art hobby.

Now I am ready to pray for individuals with special problems and needs, such as missionaries or other servants of God. Here I include prayer for certain people I want to see come to Christ as Saviour, or surrender their lives completely to God. At the present time, I have fifteen people for whom I pray routinely in this category. At some point, I will attempt to minister to these fifteen face-to-face, and expect to see some of them yield to the Lord

That is a basic outline of my routine praying. When I am finished with that, I am ready to expand my praying in all kinds of directions for issues not a part of my regular prayer time.

Someone may ask if that kind of praying ever becomes boring? The answer is yes. Do I get tired of doing it? Yes. Isn't this kind of praying difficult and exhausting? Yes! Then why do I do it? Because Jesus taught it, and it works! As far as I am concerned, this is the most difficult, exhausting aspect of a personal prayer life. If you win this battle, you will win the war. If you do not, you will never develop an effective prayer life! Next Jesus taught that we should:

2. LEARN TO PRAY PERSISTENTLY (VERSES 5–8)

The old saints used to talk about "praying through." What did they mean? They meant that God wants us to pray until we get an answer. Most of us give up too easily. The answer may be "no," or "wait," or "not that way, but this way," or "yes." Whatever the answer, we ought to pray until we know we have reached God, and we also know what the answer is. This not "vain repetition." Vain repetition is repeating words endlessly and without thought. When someone prays, "Jesus, Jesus, Jesus, Jesus, Jesus," that is vain repetition like the heathen do. Persistence in prayer is an altogether different thing. The Apostle Paul understood this, and practiced it when praying about his thorn in II Corinthians 12:7–9. In the illustration Jesus gave, the man in need of bread thought friendship would be adequate for his need to be met.

Is God my friend? Most certainly He is! But Jesus taught that is sometimes not enough. This man did not get the bread because of their friendship, but because of his persistence! Why would that be? Because there are many things involved in getting prayers answered that are more complicated than simple friendship. The great Prophet Daniel discovered this. We find this excellent illustration in Daniel 10:1–14. Was God Daniel's friend? Yes. The angel said Daniel was greatly loved by God. Did God hear Daniel the first day he prayed? Yes. Was it important for Daniel to persist? Yes. Did Daniel get an answer to his prayer? Yes!

George Mueller was a great man of prayer. He supported two thousand orphans by praying in all their needs. A businessman in London, who gave to Mueller's work on a regular basis, had a son who was in the business with him, but was not a Christian. Mr. Mueller and his associates prayed regularly for the younger man's salvation. Nothing happened. The father died, and the son was still an unbeliever. At this point, Mr. Mueller had prayed for this man thirty-two years.

After the death of his father, the son was going over his father's business affairs and noticed that his father had given regularly to the Mueller orphanage. He decided that he should continue something so important to his father. He made out a check for the regular amount and went to the orphanage early in the morning to see how the money was being used. He asked to see Mr. Mueller, but was told that Mr. Mueller was busy at the moment, and was asked to wait in a small parlour. In the next room, Mr. Mueller was having morning devotions with his staff. He did not know of the young man's presence. The young man could hear every word in the next room. As he sat, stunned, he heard them praying for his salvation. By the time Mr. Mueller came into the room, the young man was broken and ready to receive Christ. So a persistent prayer was answered.[2]

The third thing Jesus taught was that we should:

3. LEARN TO PRAY SPECIFICALLY (VERSES 9–13)

"Ask, seek, knock" are very specific words. They indicate the importance of praying carefully and thoughtfully. When we ask, we put our petition into definite words. When we seek, we are looking for something. This involves vision, or seeing in our minds exactly what we want from God. The Word of God tells us that "Moses endured as seeing him who is invisible." When we knock, we have positioned ourselves so as to be ready when the door opens.

If God answered some of our prayers, we would not be ready to receive the answer. Some of us would be so surprised we would fall on our faces. All of this means very specific prayer. When Jesus asked the blind man, "What do you want me to do for you?" the blind man did not say, "Lord please bless me." He said, "Lord, that I might receive my sight."

As we pray for revival, we need to stop being general and get specific. What do we really want God to do? We need to think through what we are going to pray about. Then we need to take careful words and go to God in prayer. Those who pray casually for revival would find the real thing to be an unpleasant shock. If the specifics of what revival would mean to them were actually laid before them and they were asked to pray regularly and earnestly for those specifics, they would flatly refuse.

I am challenging every person who reads these words to take seriously the steps set forth here, and to begin to pray daily that these specific steps might be fulfilled in their own life, and in the lives of those around them.

The fourth thing Jesus taught His disciples about prayer was to:

4. LEARN TO PRAY AUTHORITATIVELY (VERSES 14–26)

Even though the incident recorded in verse 14 was an action of Jesus not directly connected with this teaching passage, the Holy Spirit saw

176

fit to include it here, and to follow it with some further teaching of Jesus that relates directly to praying with authority. This opens up the entire matter of "spiritual warfare." That is a large subject that needs special attention, so I will deal with it only briefly here. The Scripture passage that I included above, from the Book of Daniel, makes it clear that spiritual warfare is one aspect of a ministry of personal prayer.

We Christians are both physical and spiritual beings who actually operate in both the physical and the spiritual world at the same time. A vast kingdom of spiritual beings, with Satan as their head, directly opposes the Kingdom of God and all that it stands for. When Jesus walked in Galilee, He was constantly in conflict with them. When He died and rose again, He permanently defeated them. They hold their power among us only by deception. Through the power of the shed blood of Christ and in Jesus' name, we Christians have complete authority over them.

As we enter into the arena of prayer we must be willing, where necessary, to engage the powers of darkness in direct confrontation, and defeat them through the authority given us in Christ. In his little book *Quiet Talks On Prayer*, Dr. S.D. Gordon gives a classic description of this conflict. Here is one paragraph: "Now prayer is this; A man, one of the original trustee class, who received the earth in trust from God, and who gave its control over to Satan; a man, on the earth, the poor old Satan-stolen, sin-slimed, sin-cursed, contested earth, with his life in full touch with the Victor (Christ), and sheer out of touch with the pretender-prince (Satan), insistently claiming that Satan shall yield before Jesus' victory, step by step, life after life."[3] That is revival praying!

Finally, Jesus taught that we must:

5. LEARN TO PRAY REGULARLY (VERSE 1)

In the first part of this chapter, I made the point that Jesus set a strong example by praying regularly. Our present passage merely mentions as an introduction that Jesus was praying one day in a certain place. His disciples were there listening. Because they saw this as a regular practice they were moved to want to do the same thing. Regular praying is implied in the routine praying that Jesus taught. Also we find the practice of praying regularly in the lives of other great men and women of God in Scripture as well as more recent history. Psalm 5:2–3:

> *Listen to my cry for help, my King and my God, for to you I pray. In the morning, O LORD, you hear my voice; in the morning I lay my requests before you and wait in expectation.*

"Evening, morning and noon I cry out in distress, and he hears my voice" (Ps. 55:17). Early in his life he prayed every morning. Later on we find him praying regularly three times a day. Daniel 6:10,

> *Now when Daniel learned that the decree had been published, he went home to his upstairs room where the windows opened toward Jerusalem. Three times a day he got down on his knees and prayed, giving thanks to his God, just as he had done before.*

This was the regular practice of this great man of God. Another example, given in Luke 2:36–38, is the Prophetess Anna's recognition of the baby Jesus, because of her regular habits of prayer. A more recent example is that of Dr. J. Sidlow Baxter.[4] Let me give his story in his own words:

> Most of us need to lift our prayer life from the tyranny of our moods. Let me give one illustration, a leaf out of my own diary.
>
> When I entered the ministry in 1928 I determined to be the most "Methodist" Baptist in the history of the world. Talk about perfectionism! Talk about making plans for the day! They must have been a marvel to both angels and demons.
>
> But, just as the stars in their courses fought against Sisera long ago, so the stars in their courses seemed set on smashing my well made plans to smithereens. Oh, I would start you know. I'd rise at 5:30; fifteen minutes to wash and dress; then an hour and a half for prayer and Bible reading; half an hour

for breakfast; thirty minutes for a constitutional (that means to walk in the woods, breathe deep, and when no one was looking to run now and again), that's a constitutional.

I had everything all planned out; it was wonderful. Now I won't take time telling you all the subtle subterfuges which Satan used to trip me up and trick me out of keeping my plans. But I found that with increasing administrative duties and responsibilities in the pastorate my plans were going haywire. My time for prayer was getting crowded out and my periods of study with the Bible were getting scarcer.

That was bad enough, but it was worse when I began to get used to it. And then I began excusing myself. My prayer life became a case of sinning and repenting. Every time I got down to pray I had to start weeping and asking the Lord's forgiveness. I had to repent that I hadn't prayed more and ask him to help me to do better in the future. All such things really take the pleasure out of praying.

Then it all came to a crisis. At a certain time one morning I looked at my watch. According to my plan, for I was still bravely persevering, I was to withdraw for an hour of prayer.

I looked at my watch and it said, "Time for prayer Sid." But I looked at my desk, and there was a miniature mountain of correspondence. And conscience said, "You ought to answer those letters." So as we say in Scotland, I swithered. I vacillated. Shall it be prayer? Shall it be letters? Prayer? Letters? Yes, no, yes, no. And while I was swithering a velvety little voice began to speak in my inner consciousness; "Look here Sid. what's all this bother? You know very well what you should do. The practical thing is to get those letters answered. You can't afford the time for prayer this morning. Get those letters answered."

But I still swithered, and the voice began to reinforce what it had said. It said, "Look here Sid, don't you think the Lord knows all the busy occupations which are taking your time? You're converted. You're born again, and you're in the ministry. People are crowding in; you're having conversions. Doesn't that show that God is pleased with you? And even if you can't pray, don't worry too much about it. Look Sid, you'd better face up to it. You're not one of the spiritual ones." I don't want to use extravagant phrases, but if you had plunged a dagger into my bosom it couldn't have hurt me more! "Sid, you're not one of the spiritual ones."

I'm not the introspective type, but that morning I took a good look into Sidlow Baxter. And I found that there was an area of me that did not want to pray. I had to admit it, I didn't want to pray! But I looked more closely, and I found that there was an area of me that did. The part that didn't was the emotions, and the part that did was the intellect and the will. Suddenly I found myself asking Sidlow Baxter, "Are you going to let your will be dragged about by your changeful emotions?" And I said to my will, "Will are you ready for prayer?" And Will said, "Here I am, I'm ready." So I said, "Come on Will, we will go." So Will and I set off to pray. But the minute we turned our footsteps to go and pray, all my emotions began to talk; "We're not coming, we're not coming, we're not coming." And I said to Will, "Will, can you stick it?" And Will said, "Yes, if you can." So Will and I, we dragged off those wretched emotions and we went to pray, and stayed an hour in prayer. If you had asked me afterwards, "Did you have a good time?" do you think I could have said yes? A good time? No, it was a fight all the way!

What I would have done without the companionship of Will, I don't know. In the middle of the most earnest intercession I suddenly found one of the principle emotions, way out on the golf course playing golf. And I had to run to the golf course and say, "Come back!" And a few minutes later I found another of the emotions; it had traveled one and a half days in advance, and it was in the pulpit preaching a sermon

I had not even yet prepared. And I had to say, "Come back!" I certainly couldn't have said we had a good time. It was exhausting, but we did it.

The next morning came. I looked at my watch and it was time. I said to Will, "Come on Will, its time for prayer." And all the emotions began to pull the other way, and I said, "Will, can you stick it?" And Will said, "Yes, in fact I think I'm stronger after the struggle yesterday morning." So Will and I went in again. The same thing happened. Rebellious, tumultuous, uncooperative emotions. If you had asked me, "Have you had a good time?" I would have had to tell you with tears, "No, the heavens were like brass. It was a job to concentrate. I had an awful time with the emotions."

This went on for about two and a half weeks. But Will and I stuck it out. Then one morning during that third week I looked at my watch and said, "Will, its time for prayer, are you ready?" And Will said, "Yes, I'm ready." And just as we were going in, I heard one of my chief emotions say to the others, "Come on fellows, there's no use wearing ourselves out; they'll go on whatever we do." That morning we didn't have any hilarious experience, or wonderful visions with heavenly voices and raptures, but Will and I were able with less distraction to get on with praying. And that went on for another two or three weeks. In fact, Will and I had begun to forget the emotions. I would say, "Will, are you ready for prayer?" And Will replied, "Yes, I'm always ready."

Suddenly one day while Will and I were pressing our case at the throne of the heavenly glory, one of the chief emotions shouted, "Hallelujah!" And all the other emotions suddenly shouted, "Amen!" For the first time the whole territory of James Sidlow Baxter was happily coordinated in the exercises of prayer, and God suddenly became real, and heaven was wide open, and Christ was there, and the Holy Spirit was moving, and I knew that all the time God had been listening.

The point is this; the validity and the effectuality of prayer are not determined, or even affected by the subjective psychological condition of the one who prays. The thing that makes prayer valid and vital and moving and operative is, "My faith takes hold of God's truth." Brothers and sisters, soon now, we shall be meeting him. When you meet him, and I speak reverently, when you feel his arms around you, and when you embrace as well as adore him, don't you want to be able to look into that wonderful face and say, "Lord, at last I'm seeing face to face the one I have for years known heart to heart?" Why don't you resolve that from this time on you will be a praying Christian? You will never, never, never regret it! Never!"

I repeat my earlier statement: group prayer fails because individual Christians have not developed a personal prayer life. I believe that. If people who have learned how to pray come together, they have no problem praying collectively, or as a group. Nevertheless, I believe it will be helpful to establish the validity and effectuality of group prayer. Many of the most powerful revivals of history have come as a direct result of group prayer. Quite often I meet people who have been Christians for many years, but have never prayed aloud with any other person, sometimes not even with their husband or wife. This is a great tragedy for a number of reasons.

The most important reason is that the Bible has many examples of this kind of prayer, and it is obvious that those who do not practice it are definitely failing God. Sometimes the excuse given is that Jesus condemned the public prayers of the Pharisees, and said to go into a private place and pray in secret. That is true, but it does not teach that group prayer is wrong.

The Pharisees were not involved in group prayer. They stood in public places and made loud, long prayers to be seen of men, and to be thought spiritual. The fact is that some of those same men were devouring widow's houses. Jesus rightly condemned such practices.

His admonition to pray in secret still stands as of primary importance. But, it must be said that Jesus Himself prayed aloud in the presence of His disciples, so much so that they begged Him to teach them to do the same. On one occasion, as Jesus stood at the tomb of Lazarus, He prayed aloud before that group, and said in His prayer that He was praying thus so that those who were listening to Him pray might believe! When Jesus went up on the mountain where He was transfigured, He took three disciples with Him and prayed in their presence. When He prayed in the garden of Gethsemane, He took the same three disciples to pray with Him, and rebuked them because they fell asleep instead of helping Him in prayer. His long prayer, recorded in John 17, was prayed in the presence and hearing of His disciples at the Passover supper.

So, what was the practice of those same disciples and their followers? They spent long periods of time in private prayer like their Master, but also met together for group prayer. The Book of Acts records those first activities of the disciples and their converts after Pentecost.

This brief history will help you to discover the constant practice and power of group prayer. In order to make it easy to follow, I will state a proposition about group prayer, and then follow it with the incident from Scripture which I believe illustrates that proposition.

1. Through group prayer, believers were Spirit-filled and empowered for ministry, and unbelievers were converted (Acts 1:13–14, Acts 2:1–4, Acts 2:41–42).

After Jesus ascended to heaven, the disciples and other believers spent the next ten days in constant group prayer. The result was that those who had quarreled before were now of one accord. The result of that ten-day group prayer meeting was a mighty outpouring of God's Holy Spirit on them and the unbelievers around them. Three thousand were converted the first day, and in the next few weeks, thousands more. Is that what we want to see? At what price? I can hear someone say, "but you must understand that what happened at Pentecost was a special work of God and is not to be repeated." Then explain to me, please, why it was repeated in the "Prayer Revival" of 1857, when it reached such proportions that people were being converted in New York City at the rate of ten thousand a week! That revival touched all of North America. That revival began with six people who met to pray together for revival. That revival was a group prayer movement. The work of God going on in South Korea today is primarily a group prayer movement.

2. Through group prayer, bodies were healed, miracles were performed and finances were provided for God's work (Acts 4:23–24, Acts 4:31–34, Acts 5:12–14).

Here is another dramatic example of the power of group prayer. This is after Pentecost, but has many of the same marks. Some of the disciples had been arrested and threatened for preaching the Gospel. When released they went back to the assembly of Christians and had another group prayer meeting, with powerful results. There was another outpouring of God's Holy Spirit upon them, followed by new boldness, power, miracles, and many conversions. The people of the world around them were filled with awe at the reality of the power of God in their midst. Many of the great revivals of history have been marked by all the same things. In the Canadian Revival of the early 1970s, there was no preaching about healing or miracles, but they occurred. This has been true of every great moving of God in the history of the Church. It is not my intention in this book to promote or support any theological position on the subject of healing or miracles. I simply want to point out that when God is moving by His Holy Spirit in revival power, miracles seem to take place easily. Do you need a miracle? Does your church need some miracles? I believe that group prayer for revival is one of the primary answers. As we move on through this revival recorded in the Book of Acts, we see further proof of the validity of group prayer.

3. Through group prayer, God's people were delivered and their enemies in the world were confounded.

This is illustrated in Acts 12:1–12, in the imprisonment and miraculous deliverance of the Apostle Peter. Here again we see the great power in group praying. The situation looked hopeless. One church leader had already been executed, and it seemed inevitable that the next would be Peter. From the incidents recorded, it seems clear that the church not only prayed very earnestly, but they prayed all night, and a large number of them were still engaged in group prayer when Peter was delivered. As great as this deliverance was, it is not the end of the story. God's response went far beyond their prayers, and God struck down the perpetrator of these crimes, as we read in Acts 12:20–24. As the Word of God increased and spread in this great revival, it was time to launch the first missionary movement. So we see that:

4. Through group prayer, a great missionary project was launched.

This account is in Acts 13:1–4. Here are five men, leaders in the church at Antioch, something like a board of Elders. They are gathered together for prayer and fasting. This is not a public gathering. This group of godly men have come together to spend some serious time in the presence of God. Not only are they speaking to God, but they are waiting on God while He speaks to them. Out of this group prayer meeting came the great missionary journeys of Paul and his companions. In fact, this was the springboard from which that great revival was spread abroad, until the Scriptures say that everyone in Asia heard the Word of God! This is the power of group prayer! This great missionary thrust was sure to plant new churches wherever it went. One such account is given in Acts 16.

5. Through group prayer, a new church was born.

We find this in Acts 16:12–15. As Paul began his ministry of evangelism in this place, he did not go to the synagogue or a temple, but to a place down by the river where some women made a habit of gathering together for group prayer. In that setting, he shared the good news. It was in that setting that God opened the heart of Lydia, a businesswoman, whose home became the center of an expanding work of God, that culminated in the planting of a new church in that part of the world. That church was born in the warmth of group prayer.

As that church grew, that group prayer meeting still was the source of power to which the missionaries regularly returned, as we see in Acts 16:16–18. These men were on their way to the place of prayer when confronted by an evil spirit. Going to this group prayer meeting was a daily practice, which is made clear by the statement that this confrontation took place for many days. After this girl was delivered from this spirit, Paul and Silas were thrown in prison because her wicked masters could no longer make a financial profit from her bondage. They suffered a flogging and the stocks, but the final result was a miracle earthquake, the conversion of the jailer and his family, and the frightened cooperation of the political leaders of the city. All of this came from a group prayer meeting! The Book of Acts closes with another example of a group prayer meeting. Paul was on his way to Jerusalem. He knew that suffering awaited him there. He knew he would never see these dear Christians again in this world. How was he strengthened and supported for the ordeal that lay before him? By a group prayer meeting.

6. Through group prayer, God's children are strengthened for trials and even death.

Acts 20:17–38 gives a clear picture of this truth. Paul knelt down with them all. He needed the support of their prayers, even as Christ needed the support of His disciples' prayers in

Gethsemane, even as all of us who are Christians need the prayer support of our brothers and sisters in Christ. Group prayer is an essential part of the advance of the Kingdom of God on earth. It is a key factor in the great revival movement recounted in the Book of Acts. It has been a key factor in the great revivals of history. Let me share with you two examples.

THE CONVERSION OF REVIVALIST CHARLES FINNEY, AND THE REVIVAL THAT FOLLOWED

One of the most powerful revivals ever experienced in North America, was the revival in the early 1800s in which Charles Finney was involved. Mr. Finney had grown up with very little religious teaching of any kind. While studying and practicing law under the leadership of an attorney in a town called Adams, N.Y., he attended a Presbyterian church in the town. He could not make any sense of what he heard preached there, and as he studied the Bible for himself, he became more confused. There seemed to be contradictions between what he heard and what he read. There was a building, separate from the church building, where some of the people met for conferences and for weekly prayer meetings. Because God was at work in Mr. Finney's heart, he also attended those prayer meetings often. The people in those meetings were praying for revival and the conversion of unbelievers. They also prayed for God to pour out His Holy Spirit upon them, but none of their prayers seemed to be answered. This bothered Finney a great deal.

One evening as he sat in the prayer meeting, some of the people asked him if he would like them to pray for him. He told them no, because he did not see that God answered their prayers. He said,

> I suppose I need to be prayed for, for I am conscious that I am a sinner, but I do not see that it will do any good for you to pray for me, for you are continually asking, but you do not receive. You have been praying for a revival ever since I have been in Adams, and yet you do not have it. You have been praying for the Holy Spirit to descend upon you, and yet

complaining of your leanness. You have prayed enough since I have attended these meetings to have prayed the devil out of Adams if there is any virtue in your prayers. But here you are praying on, and complaining still.[5]

It is almost humorous to realize that their prayers for revival and Finney's conversion were about to be answered through the one accusing them.

Charles Finney continued to read the Bible and come under deeper and deeper conviction. Finally, one morning he went into the woods near town to pray, and after a terrible struggle with his pride was wonderfully converted. That same evening, he locked himself in the law office and went into the back room to pray. As he shut the door and turned around, it seemed to him that he met the Lord Jesus Christ face-to-face. He fell down at His feet and poured out his soul in prayer, weeping and covering the feet of Christ with his tears. After a long time, he went into the front office and made a fire in the fireplace. As he was about to take a seat by the fire, he received a mighty baptism of the Holy Spirit, without any expectation of it, and never having ever heard of such an experience. The Holy Spirit descended upon him and went through his body and soul. He had the impression of waves of liquid love, and the very breath of God. He felt like he was being fanned with great wings. He wept aloud and shouted out the unspeakable overflow of his heart. These waves of God's Spirit came over him and over him, until he cried out, "I shall die if these waves continue to pass over me, Lord I cannot bear any more!" Mr. Finney immediately gave up studying and practicing law. He said to a client who came to see him about a lawsuit, "I have a retainer from the Lord Jesus Christ to plead His cause and I cannot plead yours." Now Finney went looking for people to whom he could speak about their spiritual condition. It seemed that every person to whom he spoke soon after became a Christian. The next night after his conversion the news had spread through the whole village. The people automatically converged on the building where the prayer meetings were held, without any meeting being called. No one took charge of the gathering, so

Mr. Finney went forward and shared with them what God had done in his life. The result was a powerful moving of God's Spirit. Some rushed from the building and soon afterward were converted. These meetings continued for many weeks, spreading to other communities until the whole area was ablaze with a remarkable revival.

This revival launched Charles Finney into the long life of powerful revival ministry which touched all the northeastern part of the United States. It is reported that at least 50,000 were added to the churches of New England out of a population of 250,000. This revolutionized the religious and moral character of that society. What would happen to the society in which you and I live, if one fifth of them were soundly converted? All of this came from a group prayer meeting, which seemed as if it would never change anything or anyone, and continued through some of the most intense prayer meetings I have ever read about. Why should we find it hard to believe that God would repeat something similar in our communities if we would only get together and storm the gates of heaven with persistent prayer?

THE CANADIAN REVIVAL OF 1971

Group prayer meetings had gone on for two years since Duncan Campbell, the instrument God used in the Hebrides revival, had come through Saskatoon, Saskatchewan, Canada. While there, he said that God was going to bring revival in Canada, and that it would begin in Saskatoon. Rev. Bill McLeod was pastor of the Ebenezer Baptist Church in Saskatoon. God moved powerfully on his heart with a burden of prayer for revival. During the next two years, God took Bill to the death of self with Christ, and a newly spirit-filled life. That was not all. As he led his church in prayer for revival, the group prayer meetings increased in attendance until they equaled that of the Sunday morning service. At the same time, God was preparing the Sutera twins. Deep changes were taking place in their lives and ministry. Already, the flames of revival were beginning to burn in some of their meetings. Through a cancellation, God led them to Rives Junction, Michigan, to the Baptist church.

There, God came on the scene with such power that people were driving 100 miles to get to the meetings. That church was transformed! Those meetings interrupted the Suteras' schedule, and changed their whole approach to ministry. Shortly thereafter the Sutera Twins came to Ebenezer Church in Saskatoon for a short revival crusade. Now God brought together a prepared ministry with a prepared church, and a cloud burst of revival was the result. So powerful was the work of God's Spirit, that afterglows often went on all night. Fifty-nine churches in that area were touched by that revival. Over 3,000 lay teams went out to other communities to share what God was doing, and they seemed to take the revival with them.

That movement of God's Holy Spirit spread rapidly across the prairies, went all the way to the west coast, and even touched down in some parts of eastern Canada. That revival came across the border into the midwestern United States, and in 1972, moved into the Brown Street Alliance Church of Akron Ohio, where I was pastor. Without a crusade or an evangelist, God visited our congregation in supernatural power. Some who thought they were Christians discovered they were not, and were truly converted. The lives of many Christians were changed, and miracles of healing occurred. It is interesting to note that, in that church, there was a group who had been meeting in homes for two years, praying for the conversion of our unsaved children and loved ones. The story of that revival is still being written in the lives of hundreds of people all across North America and in other parts of the world. That is all the result of group prayer for revival!

CHAPTER EIGHT

The Steps of Repentance

If my people, who are called by my name,
will humble themselves and pray and seek my face
and turn from their wicked ways, *then will I hear*
from heaven and will forgive their sin
and will heal their land.

~ II Chronicles 7:14

Is it true as some Christians think, that the atrocious wickedness of unbelievers in our world is what hinders revival? **No, it is not!** In this verse of Scripture, God's people, who are called by His name, are called upon to **turn from their wicked ways**, so that God may forgive the sins of His people and then heal our land.

Do God's people have wicked ways? They must, or God would not call on them to turn from them. This verse does not say that they have wicked hearts, but wicked ways. A person then, may be truly born of God, saved by God's grace, and indwelt by the Holy Spirit, and still have in his life some wicked ways. What are the wicked ways in the lives of God's people in our day that are hindering revival?

I have been a pastor for over fifty years, and have been involved in revival ministries since 1972. Over those years, I have become familiar with the things that seem to hinder revival. I want to share with you what I consider to be the principle "wicked ways" in the lives of God's people, that I believe are hindering revival. They will not necessarily be in order of importance, since I am convinced that we must turn from them all if revival is to come. The first wicked way I want to consider is:

WORLDLINESS

Do not love the world or the things in the world. If anyone loves the world, the love of the Father is not in him. For all that is in the world—the lust of the flesh, the lust of the eyes, and the pride of life—is not of the Father but is of the world. And the world is passing away, and the lust of it; but he who does the will of God abides forever (I John 2:15–17, NKJV).

I grew up in a church setting where we were constantly exhorted to "not be worldly." In that group, those who were considered to be worldly were those who wore lipstick and possibly earrings, those who attended the theatre or the movies, those who danced, played cards, smoked, drank, attended ball games on Sunday, or ran with a non-Christian crowd. As children in a Christian home, we were allowed to play Bible games on Sunday, or possibly go for a walk, but nothing more. I complied with those standards and took it for granted that I was not "worldly." I am not implying that any of those practices I have listed above are all right for a Christian. Indeed, some of them are not! That, however, is not the point. Many years later, I discovered that such an artificial list did not really deal with the wicked way of worldliness at all. In fact I became aware that one could comply with all these standards and still be worldly.

Jesus never used the words "worldly," or "worldliness," but He had a great deal to say about the "WORLD." For instance, Jesus said, "I came into the WORLD, I am going out of the WORLD, I am not of this WORLD, and the WORLD hates Me."

Again, He said in John 15:18–19, and 17:13–18,

If the world hates you, keep in mind that it hated me first. If you belonged to the world, it would love you as its own. As it is, you do not belong to the world, but I have chosen you out of the world. That is why the world hates you. I am coming to you now, but I say these things while I am still in the world, so that they may have the full measure of my joy within them. I have given them your word and the world has hated them, for they are not of the world any more than I am of the world. My prayer is not that you take them out of the world but that you protect them from the evil one. They are not of the world, even as I am not of it. Sanctify them by the truth; your word is truth. As you sent me into the world, I have sent them into the world.

Jesus talked about the world hating Christians. Today, Christians in North America are not so much hated as they are ignored. Jesus taught that Christians do not belong to the world. Many Christians I know belong very much to the world. In fact, most of their time is spent in activities of the world, and running around making sure their children succeed in the activities of the world. Many Christians are totally preoccupied with the sports of the world, and push their children to excel there, even though that world reeks with every possible vice.

The Roman Church made the mistake of trying to obey this Scripture by withdrawing from the world into monasteries. Jesus made it clear that He did not mean that. He taught separation as distinct from segregation. We are not to go out of the world, but to live in it as shining lights distinct from the darkness.

Jesus compared our relationship with the world to His relationship with the world. Jesus loved the people of the world, and gave Himself to minister to those needs. He lived among the people of the world. He made a living as a carpenter. He was part of an earthly family. However, He refused to be caught up in the spirit of the world. He would not compromise with its evil, but constantly rebuked it, especially when He found it among those who professed to be children of God. When James and John wanted to burn up some persecutors, He said to them, "You do not know what spirit you are of." They were reacting to circumstances in the same way the world would react. If I want to know whether or not I am worldly, I should measure my way of life in this world with that of Jesus.

1. What is the "world"?

The "WORLD" is simply "this world" with all that is in it. This becomes very clear as we see how the "world" was talked about in Scripture. John 17:5, "And now, Father, glorify me in your presence with the glory I had with you before the world began."

He was in the world, and though the world was made through him, the world did not recognize him. He came to that which was his own, but his own did not receive him. Yet to all who received him, to those who believed in his name, he gave the right to become children of God—children born not of natural descent, nor of human decision or a husband's will, but born of God. The Word became flesh and made his dwelling among us. We have seen his glory, the glory of the One and Only, who came from the Father, full of grace and truth. (John 1:10–4).

It was just before the Passover Feast. Jesus knew that the time had come for him to leave this world and go to the Father. Having loved his own who were in the world, he now showed them the full extent of his love (John 13:1).

Jesus talked to His Father about the glory He had before the creation of the world. In this case it is evident that He is talking about this created earth and all that is in it. Again, in John 1, the writer is talking about this created world. Jesus came out of heaven into this created world, which He had made. At the Passover feast, Jesus was aware that His time had come to physically leave this created world. Everywhere, Scripture takes it for granted that the world is simply this created earth and everything that is in it. Our text talks about "ALL" that is in the world. We Christians get confused about this matter, because we try to come up with a list of activities or things that are, or are not worldly. It is our entire attitude toward the entire world about which God is concerned! In I Corinthians 7:31, Paul says, "...those who use the things of the world, as if not engrossed in them. For this world in its present form is passing away". We live in this world, and use the things of this world, and participate in many of the activities of this world, but our attitude toward all of that is different than the man or woman of the world. So we ask:

2. What is "worldliness"?

Worldliness is to love, or give priority to, the things or activities of this world rather than God and His Kingdom! Jesus said,

> "So do not worry, saying, 'What shall we eat?' or 'What shall we drink?' or 'What shall we wear?' For the pagans run after all these things, and your heavenly Father knows that you need them. But seek first his kingdom and his righteousness, and all these things will be given to you as well" (Matt. 6:31–33).

Jesus said that our heavenly Father knows we need things of this world to exist in this world. Paul taught that if we don't work, we should not eat. Jesus was not promoting laziness or disinterest in normal-life activities and labours. Both He and Paul were talking about attitudes and priorities. Christians ought to participate in all the normal activities of life with enthusiasm and diligence. The truth is, that the Christian's participation in the normal things of life should be superior to the ungodly, because he is free from the bondage of those things.

The 'typical American' male described in a demographic survey[1] is a twenty-seven-year-old who doesn't read so much as one book a year. Materialistic and satisfied with small pleasures, this individual finds theological disputations boring. Although he may attend church twenty-seven times a year, he is concerned with neither heaven nor hell. In fact, he has no interest whatsoever in immortality. His principal interests are football (in Canada, hockey), hunting, fishing and car-tinkering. Would you say such a man is worldly? Do you know any Christians like that? I know some who attend church about that often! Why don't we give ourselves a test?

Which Disturbs Me Most?

A soul lost in hell—or a scratch on my new car?
Missing church on Sunday—or missing a day's pay?
A sermon ten minutes too long—or a hockey game played overtime?
My Christian life not growing—or my garden not growing?
My Bible unopened—or the newspaper unread?
My service for God undone—or the housework not finished?
Missing a good Bible study—or missing a TV program?
The spiritual hunger of people around me—
or missing a meal to attend prayer meeting?
My tithes decreasing—or my income decreasing?
My children missing Sunday School—
or my children missing public school?
Which really disturbs me most?
AM I WORLDLY?[2]

Long ago, William Law warned Christians that,

> The world is now a greater enemy to the Christian than it was in apostolic times. It is a greater enemy, because it has greater power over Christians by its favours, riches, honours, rewards, and protection, than it had by the fire and fury of its persecutors. It is a more dangerous enemy, by having lost its appearance of enmity. Its outward profession of Christianity makes it no longer considered as an enemy, and therefore the people are easily persuaded to resign themselves up to be governed and directed by it.[3]

Let me add that we are now so desperately in need of a great revival, that the world no longer calls itself Christian, and is beginning to throw off the yoke of Christian morals and values once placed upon it by the influence of the great revivals of the past. Is it true then, that we Christians must be openly persecuted, before we will be willing to turn from our wicked way of worldliness? I hope and pray not. I pray that God will open our eyes, so that we will turn, repent, and live once more as strangers and pilgrims on our way to another world. God is more than willing to heal our land, but **we** must turn from our wicked ways!

When God said "love not the world," He then defined all that is in the world as, "the lust of the flesh, the lust of the eyes, and the pride of life." The desires of the natural man were given to us for our enjoyment, not our enslavement. If the fulfilling of any desire of my flesh is given priority, I am a lover of the world, since I am giving myself to the fulfilling of that desire. Sensuality is worldliness. The lust of the eyes is the desire to possess or bring under my control people, things, or activities. Adam and Eve were supposed to rule over the world as God's representatives, holding all things as His servants or stewards. Covetousness is idolatry, which seeks to dethrone God and put something else on that throne. If I hold anything for myself, I am worldly. I am to hold all I possess for God as His steward. Those who give to the work of God grudgingly are worldly. In the Canadian Revival of 1971, some Christians actually took the deed to their house, the keys to their car, and their bank books, and laid them out in the middle of a table. Then, gathering their family around the table, they prayed and gave everything to God.

The pride of life is the consuming desire for self exaltation, or self fulfillment. The entire "self-fulfillment" movement, whether in the Church or out of it, is worldly. It is "self-love." Only as the Christian is restored to the image of God in Christ can he be truly fulfilled!

Our text says that those who love the world, as defined above, **do not have the love of the Father in them!** That is, they are not manifesting God's kind of love toward this world. In revival, the love of God envelops us, transforms us, and flows out through us to those around us. If we really want revival, we must repent of our wicked ways of worldliness! Then God's love will be poured out on the church and our lost world.

3. What Is the solution for worldliness?

When Jesus prayed for His followers in John 17, His prayer was all about two worlds: this created world in which we now live, and the heavenly world from which Christ came, and to which He was about to return, and to which we also are headed. Please walk with me through this chapter as I pick out His statements about these two worlds.

> *Before the WORLD began—those you gave me out of the WORLD —I am not praying for the WORLD—I will remain no longer in the WORLD—but they are still in the WORLD—while I am still in the WORLD—the WORLD has hated them for they are not of the WORLD anymore than I am of the WORLD—I do not pray for you to take them out of the WORLD, but that you keep them from the evil—they are not of the WORLD, even as I am not of it—As you sent me into the WORLD, I have sent them into the WORLD—so that the WORLD may believe—complete unity to let the WORLD know—you loved me before the creation of the WORLD—the WORLD does not know you.*

Christ was from above (the heavenly world), we are from beneath (this present world). Christ was about to return to that other world. How can we get out of this world? "Flesh and blood cannot inherit the Kingdom of God." There are only two ways to leave this world—either by death or by translation. The way of death is offered to us even while we live, through the death and resurrection of Christ. Paul said,

> *I am crucified with Christ: nevertheless I live; yet not I, but Christ liveth in me: and the life which I now live in the flesh I live by the faith of the Son of God, who loved me, and gave himself for me. But God forbid that I should glory, save in the cross of our Lord Jesus Christ, by whom the world is crucified unto me, and I unto the world* (Gal. 2:20; 6:14, KJV).

When a man was crucified, he was through with the world.

He became dead to it. The price for revival is death on the cross! All Christians are glad to identify with Christ in His death as they understand that they were judged for their sin in the person of their substitute. It is a far different matter, though, when we see that God wants to make that work of the cross real in our lives in order to free us from sin and the world. Jesus said that the one who tries to save his life for himself will lose it, and the one who gives up his life for Christ will save it for eternity. A mere mental ascent will not do here. In agreeing with God about this matter, and surrendering ourselves up to the death of the cross, there will be real anguish. Jesus was on the cross six long hours. So you and I may need to go through a painful process, as the Holy Spirit helps us bring each aspect of our lives to God, and totally give up our life. This can only be done by faith. A faith that believes in that other world, and that dying with Christ is not too much to ask in order to begin to live and walk in the ways of that world now, looking forward to the day when we will arrive there. Abraham and his contemporaries had that kind of faith. We read in Hebrews 11:8–10,13–16,

> *By faith Abraham, when called to go to a place he would later receive as his inheritance, obeyed and went, even though he did not know where he was going. By faith he made his home in the promised land like a stranger in a foreign country; he lived in tents, as did Isaac and Jacob, who were heirs with him of the same promise. For he was looking forward to the city with foundations, whose architect and builder is God.*
> *All these people were still living by faith when they died. They did not receive the things promised; they only saw them and welcomed them from a distance. And they admitted that they were aliens and strangers on earth. People who say such things show that they are looking for a country of their own. If they had been thinking of the country they had left, they would have had opportunity to return. Instead, they were longing for a better country—a heavenly one. Therefore God is not ashamed to be called their God, for he has prepared a city for them.*

Bud Robinson, the well-known holiness preacher of the past generation, was taken to New York City by some friends. They showed him the sights of New York. That night in his prayers, he is reported to have said, "Lord I thank you for letting me see all the sights of New York. And I thank you most of all that I didn't see a thing that I wanted."

Someday, I will be taken out of this world, either by death or the return of Christ. How do I feel about that? Dr. H.A. Ironside tells the following story:

> I remember one night in Stockton, California; I was preaching about the coming of Jesus. As I was in prayer I was conscious of a woman getting up and going out, for in those days the skirts would swish whenever a lady walked. It seemed to me that this lady must have gone out in a hurry. When I finished my prayer and went to greet the friends at the door, I found a woman pacing back and forth in the lobby. The moment I came, she said to me, "How would you dare to pray like that—'Come Lord Jesus'? I don't want him to come. It would break in on all my plans. How dare you?" I said, "My dear young woman, Jesus is coming whether you want it or not." Oh, if you know him and love him, surely your heart says, "Come Lord Jesus!" What does your heart say?[4]

So, worldliness is one of the wicked ways from which God's people must turn if God is to be morally free to bring the revival we so desperately need. The second "wicked way" I want to discuss is:

POWERLESSNESS

Is it a wicked thing for a child of God to be powerless? What do you think—is it wicked, or just unfortunate? Is there any Christian who has the power he needs to serve God strictly within himself? If not, where can he get it? The Word of God says, "Once God has spoken; twice I have heard this: that power belongs to God" (Ps. 62:11, NASB). God is the source of all power. Is that power available to any Christian, or is

God a respecter of persons? Jesus said, "You will receive power when the Holy Spirit comes upon you" (Acts 1:8). He said again,

> *If you then, being evil, know how to give good gifts to your children, how much more will your heavenly Father give the Holy Spirit to those who ask him!* (Luke 11:13).

And then, hear Peter saying, "And we are witnesses of these things; and {so is} the Holy Spirit, whom God has given to those who obey Him" (Acts 5:32, NASB). Once more, notice the promises of God in this regard in Peter's sermon at Pentecost. In referring to the coming of the Holy Spirit upon them, he said,

> *But this is what was spoken by the prophet Joel: 'And it shall come to pass in the last days, says God, that I will pour out of My Spirit on all flesh; your sons and your daughters shall prophesy, your young men shall see visions, your old men shall dream dreams. And on My menservants and on My maidservants I will pour out My Spirit in those days; and they shall prophesy. Then Peter said to them, "Repent, and let every one of you be baptized in the name of Jesus Christ for the remission of sins; and you shall receive the gift of the Holy Spirit. For the promise is to you and to your children, and to all who are afar off, as many as the Lord our God will call* (Acts 2:16–18,38,39, NKJV).

These Scriptures seem to make it clear that the power of the Holy Spirit is available to all of God's children! Add to that the fact that God has said, "And do not get drunk with wine, for that is dissipation, but be filled with the Spirit" (Eph. 5:18, NASB). Now we have not only the possibility, but the clear command that we are to be filled with the Holy Spirit! And what is needed to bring revival? The power of God! And who is the only source of that power on earth? The Holy Spirit. And how is His power to be released in this dark and desperate world? Through the people of God. What do you think then? Is it, or is it not, exceedingly wicked for we, who are the people of God to be powerless? If it is wicked to live a life of drunkenness, then it is wicked to live a life of powerlessness, for both commands are in the same verse of Scripture! Now brother and sister, let us lay aside all of our theological arguments about how this takes place, and ask ourselves, "Am I a powerless Christian?"

If so, what am I going to do about it? What can I do about it? In his book *The Pursuit Of God*, Dr. A.W. Tozer said,

> Current evangelicalism has laid the altar and divided the sacrifice into parts, but now seems satisfied to count the stones and rearrange the pieces with never a care that there is not a sign of fire upon the top of lofty Carmel.[5]

Does your heart cry out with mine, "Lord, send the fire?" Evangelist D.L. Moody said,

> In some sense, and to some extent, the Holy Spirit dwells with every believer; but there is another gift, which may be called the gift of the Holy Spirit for service. This gift, it strikes me, is entirely distinct and separate from conversion and assurance. God has a great many Christians that have no power, and the reason is, they have not the gift of the Holy Ghost for service. God doesn't seem to work with them, and I believe it is because they have not sought this gift.[6]

So.... Now the question stands before us, "How can I experience this power of the Holy Spirit?"

HOW TO BE FILLED WITH THE HOLY SPIRIT

There are two basic things involved in being filled with the Holy Spirit: *1. The giving of the Holy Spirit by God*, and *2. The receiving of the Holy Spirit by man*. First then:

1. The Holy Spirit given by God.

It is not likely that I will receive the Holy Spirit unless I believe that God has given Him, or is willing to give Him to me. I will always be asking, but never receiving. God has given and will give the Holy

Spirit, because that is what God has promised. That promise was given through Joel, John the Baptist, and Jesus. Joel said,

> *'Even now,' declares the LORD, 'return to me with all your heart, with fasting and weeping and mourning.' Rend your heart and not your garments. Return to the LORD your God, for he is gracious and compassionate, slow to anger and abounding in love, and he relents from sending calamity. Who knows? He may turn and have pity and leave behind a blessing—grain offerings and drink offerings for the LORD your God. Blow the trumpet in Zion, declare a holy fast, call a sacred assembly. Gather the people, consecrate the assembly; bring together the elders, gather the children, those nursing at the breast. Let the bridegroom leave his room and the bride her chamber. Let the priests, who minister before the LORD, weep between the temple porch and the altar. Let them say, 'Spare your people, O LORD. Do not make your inheritance an object of scorn, a byword among the nations. Why should they say among the peoples, "Where is their God?"' Then the LORD will be jealous for his land and take pity on his people.' '...And afterward, I will pour out my Spirit on all people. Your sons and daughters will prophesy, your old men will dream dreams, your young men will see visions. Even on my servants, both men and women, I will pour out my Spirit in those days. And everyone who calls on the name of the LORD will be saved'* (Joel 2:12–18,28,29,32).

Here is this great promise in the Old Testament that the day would come when the Holy Spirit would be poured out on all of God's children, regardless of age, sex, or position. This giving of the Holy Spirit would bring healing to their land. What God's people should do to bring this about is clearly set forth. This call to prayer is given to leaders, laymen, young people, and even children. For whom is this promise given? Whoever else was included, we know it was given to the Church, for Peter said that what happened at Pentecost was the fulfillment of that promise by Joel. What a wonderful promise of Holy Spirit power for revival! Next there is John the Baptist. His promise is quoted in Matthew 3:11,12 in these words:

I baptize you with water for repentance. But after me will come one who is more powerful than I, whose sandals I am not fit to carry. He will baptize you with the Holy Spirit and with fire. His winnowing fork is in his hand, and he will clear his threshing floor, gathering his wheat into the barn and burning up the chaff with unquenchable fire.

This is the fire we need upon the sacrifice! On several occasions Jesus repeated the promise of His gift of the Holy Spirit:

On the last and greatest day of the Feast, Jesus stood and said in a loud voice, "If anyone is thirsty, let him come to me and drink. Whoever believes in me, as the Scripture has said, streams of living water will flow from within him." By this he meant the Spirit, whom those who believed in him were later to receive. Up to that time the Spirit had not been given, since Jesus had not yet been glorified (John 7:37–39).

And I will ask the Father, and he will give you another Counselor to be with you forever—the Spirit of truth. The world cannot accept him, because it neither sees him nor knows him. But you know him, for he lives with you and will be in you (John 14:16–17).

On one occasion, while he was eating with them, he gave them this command: "Do not leave Jerusalem, but wait for the gift my Father promised, which you have heard me speak about. For John baptized with water, but in a few days you will be baptized with the Holy Spirit" (Acts 1:4–5).

"But you will receive power when the Holy Spirit comes on you; and you will be my witnesses in Jerusalem, and in all Judea and Samaria, and to the ends of the earth" (Acts 1:8).

Again and again, God assured us that He would freely bestow the mighty power of the Holy Spirit upon His children in our day. What happened at Pentecost was the beginning of the fulfillment of that promise.

Now when the Day of Pentecost had fully come, they were all with one accord in one place. And suddenly there came a sound from heaven, as of a rushing mighty wind, and it filled the whole house where they were sitting. Then there appeared to them divided tongues, as of fire, and one sat upon each of them. And they were all filled with the Holy Spirit (Acts 2:1–4).

But this is what was spoken by the prophet Joel: 'And it shall come to pass in the last days, says God, that I will pour out of My Spirit on all flesh; your sons and your daughters shall prophesy, your young men shall see visions, your old men shall dream dreams. And on My menservants and on My maidservants I will pour out My Spirit in those days; and they shall prophesy' (Acts 2:16–18).

This Jesus God has raised up, of which we are all witnesses. "Therefore being exalted to the right hand of God, and having received from the Father the promise of the Holy Spirit, He poured out this which you now see and hear" (Acts 2:32–33).

Now when they heard this, they were cut to the heart, and said to Peter and the rest of the apostles, "Men and brethren, what shall we do?" Then Peter said to them, "Repent, and let every one of you be baptized in the name of Jesus Christ for the remission of sins; and you shall receive the gift of the Holy Spirit. For the promise is to you and to your children, and to all who are afar off, as many as the Lord our God will call" (Acts 2:37–39, NKJV).

The poet Faber describes this event in these dramatic words:

He comes! He comes! that mighty breath from
    heaven's eternal shores;
His uncreated freshness fills his bride as she adores.
Earth quakes before that rushing blast,
    heaven echoes back the sound,

And mightily that tempest wheels the Upper Room around.
One moment—and the Spirit hung o'er them
    with deep desire;
Then broke upon the heads of all in cloven tongues of fire.
What gifts he gave those chosen men past ages can desplay;
Nay more, their vigor still indwells the weakness of today.
The Spirit came into the church with his unfailing power;
He is the living heart that beats within her at this hour.[7]

The Holy Spirit has been given by God, and continues to be given by God to every believer at the moment of his new birth. Many Scriptures attest to this fact:

And you also were included in Christ when you heard the word of truth, the gospel of your salvation. Having believed, you were marked in him with a seal, the promised Holy Spirit, who is a deposit guaranteeing our inheritance until the redemption of those who are God's possession—to the praise of his glory (Eph. 1:13–14).

However, you are not in the flesh but in the Spirit, if indeed the Spirit of God dwells in you. But if anyone does not have the Spirit of Christ, he does not belong to Him (Rom. 8:9).

For all who are being led by the Spirit of God, these are sons of God. For you have not received a spirit of slavery leading to fear again, but you have received a spirit of adoption as sons by which we cry out, "Abba! Father!" The Spirit Himself bears witness with our spirit that we are children of God (Rom. 8:14–16, NASB).

All believers are indwelt by the Holy Spirit, but all believers are not filled with the Holy Spirit! And it is just that filling that makes all the difference when it comes to this matter of revival! At Pentecost, God says they were all filled with the Holy Spirit. Again in Acts 4:31, we read,

And when they had prayed, the place where they had gathered together was shaken, and they were all filled with the Holy Spirit, and {began} to speak the word of God with boldness (NASB).

Many of those present in this gathering had already been filled with the Holy Spirit at Pentecost. Now they experienced a new filling along with the others present who were already Christians, and indwelt by the Holy Spirit. This makes it obvious that being filled with the Holy Spirit is something distinct from the indwelling of the Holy Spirit that is the experience of every true Christian. In Ephesians 5:18, the command to be filled with the Holy Spirit is given to Christians, who have already been told in Ephesians 1:13 that they were sealed with the promised Holy Spirit when they believed. Here are two distinct workings of the Holy Spirit in the lives of those who are Christians.

Dr. James M. Gray, when expounding Romans 12:1, said,

> Have you noticed that this verse does not tell us to whom we should give our bodies? Jesus has a body. The Father is in heaven. Another has come to earth without a body. God could have made him a body. God gives you the honor of presenting your bodies to the Holy Spirit as his dwelling place on earth. If you have been washed in the blood, yours is a holy body, washed whiter than snow, and will be accepted by the Spirit when you give it. Will you do so now?[8]

All great soul-winners and revivalists have been filled with the Holy Spirit. This is true regardless of their particular theological background. Let me share with you a brief cross-section.

D.L. Moody was converted as a young man in the great prayer meeting revival of the 1800s. Mr. Moody had preached the gospel and built a great church in Chicago. The Chicago fire destroyed that church building, and Moody was trying to raise funds to build a new one. He was visiting in the east to secure funds, but his heart was hungry for more spiritual power. Here is his testimony in his own words:

> My heart was not in the work of begging. I was crying all the time that God would fill me with his Spirit. Well, one day in the city of New York. Oh what a day. I cannot describe it. I seldom

refer to it. It is almost too sacred an experience to name. Paul had an experience of which he never spoke for fourteen years. I can only say that God revealed himself to me, and I had such an experience of his love, that I had to ask him to stay his hand. I went to preaching again. The sermons were not different. I did not present any new truths, and yet hundreds were converted. I would not now be placed back where I was before that blessed experience, if you should give me all the world. It would be as the small dust of the balance.[9]

Dr. Scofield of the Scofield Bible conducted Moody's funeral. Here is what he said:

The secrets of Dwight L. Moody's power were; First in a definite experience of Christ's saving grace. He had passed out of death into life, and he knew it. Secondly, he believed in the Divine authority of the Scriptures. The Bible was to him the voice of God, and he made it resound as such in the consciences of men. Thirdly, he was baptized with the Holy Spirit, and he knew it. It was to him as definite an experience as his conversion.[10]

Billy Sunday won over a million souls to Christ in his great campaigns. In one crusade alone, in Omaha, Nebraska, in 1915, he preached three sermons from the following texts: "Have you received the Holy Ghost since you believed?" "But tarry in the city of Jerusalem until you be endued with power from on high." "But you shall receive power after that the Holy Ghost is come upon you." In that same meeting, he preached a sermon entitled, "The Revival At Pentecost." Every time Billy Sunday preached, he opened his Bible to one text of Scripture that declares, "The Spirit of the Lord God is upon me, because he has anointed me to preach." He laid his sermon notes upon that text, and preached with fire and power![11]

I have already given the testimony of the great revivalist Charles Finney in another place in this book, where he describes the mighty outpouring and filling of the Holy Spirit which was the power behind his ministry. Time would fail me to tell of George White-field, John Wesley, Charles Spurgeon, Evan Roberts, A.B. Simpson, Billy Graham, and a host of other great soul winners, who all testified to the fact that they were filled with the Holy Spirit as a work of God distinct from the regenerating work of the new birth, and the indwelling of the Spirit common to all true Christians.

Even the Lord Jesus Christ did not begin His great ministry until He was filled with the Holy Spirit, and this in spite of the fact that He was the sinless Son of God, conceived by the Holy Spirit, and must have been indwelt by the Holy Spirit from His conception!

Now we come to the second aspect of how to be filled with the Holy Spirit.

2. The receiving of the Holy Spirit by man

Everywhere in the Book of Acts, this filling with the Holy Spirit is described by the word "receive." In Acts 1:8, Jesus said you will receive the power of the Holy Spirit. In Acts 2:38, as Peter was preaching at Pentecost about this filling that had taken place, he told the crowd of deeply convicted people that they, too, could receive the gift of the Holy Spirit. In Acts 8:15,17, where Deacon Philip had led in a great revival, the coming of the Holy Spirit upon these new, baptized Christians was described as a receiving of the Holy Spirit. In Acts 19, where Paul instructed a small congregation of disciples who had heard only the preaching of John the Baptist, he asked them if they had received the Holy Spirit since they believed. Even before Pentecost, in John 20:22, we hear Jesus saying to His disciples, "Receive the Holy Spirit!"

But wait a minute—didn't you say that all Christians have received the Holy Spirit? No, I did not say that. I said that all Christians have been given the Holy Spirit by God, and that the Holy Spirit dwells within every Christian, but God giving the Holy Spirit is not the same as man receiving the Holy Spirit. One person gives, the other person must receive. At your conversion, who did you believe on, and who did you receive? Jesus Christ, of course! Just so! The focus of the sinner is on the person of Christ as Saviour, exactly where it should be. Jesus said in John 14:16,17,

> *And I will ask the Father, and He will give you another Helper, that He may be with you forever; {that is} the Spirit of truth, whom the world cannot receive, because it does not behold Him or know Him, {but} you know Him because He abides with you, and will be in you* (NASB).

It is clear from this Scripture that people of the world, sinners, cannot receive the Holy Spirit. They do not behold Him or know Him. They behold Christ crucified and fix their faith on Him and receive Him. But these disciples could receive the Holy Spirit. From man's side, there is a conscious receiving, but it is the receiving of Christ, not the Holy Spirit. From God's side, there is a giving of the Spirit of Christ, who is the Holy Spirit. If you are a Christian, God has given you the Holy Spirit, but have you received Him?

For most Christians, the Holy Spirit is only a guest in the house. He is not the owner, and is limited to certain rooms and activities which that Christian allows. Because of this, the Holy Spirit is constantly grieved, resisted and even quenched, so there is no fire, but the Christian life is cold and powerless. I ask you, is this an exaggeration or a sad fact? if I came to your house, you would probably invite me in. If I were preaching in your church, you might invite me to be a guest in your home while I was in the city, as many have. In trying to make me feel comfortable, you would say, "Now make yourself right at home!" You do not mean that at all! Suppose, the next morning when I come out to breakfast, I should say, "I don't like the colour of my bedroom, so this afternoon I have decided to paint it a different colour, and while I am at it, I think I will change the kitchen also." What would you do? You might laugh, hoping it was a joke. But when I brought home two gallons of paint and some brushes, you probably would sit me down and let me know that I am not "at home," but in someone else's house. Do you see what I mean? God has given you the Holy Spirit, but have you received Him as owner and ruler of your life? Or are you really still in command, and the Holy Spirit is a guest that you call on for help occasionally? You do appreciate His being there as long as He knows His place, and does not try to take over your life. He is a very important guest—but only a guest, after all.

All this raises the question, "**How do I receive Him?**" There were some other people who asked the same question. They were the people who heard Peter's sermon on the day of Pentecost. They said, "What shall we do?" Then Peter said to them,

> *Repent, and let every one of you be baptized in the name of Jesus Christ for the remission of sins; and you shall receive the gift of the Holy Spirit. For the promise is to you and to your children, and to all who are afar off, as many as the Lord our God will call* (Acts 2:38,39, NKJV).

There were three things they could do. They could "repent," they could "be baptized," and they could "receive the Holy Spirit." Repentance deals with sin and faith in Christ. Baptism deals with the death of self in identification with Christ in His death, burial, and resurrection. Receiving deals with surrender and faith. What are the things that hinder people from being filled with the Holy Spirit? *Sin, Self, and Unbelief!* Let us take a few minutes to consider each one.

SIN. In Acts 8, there is a story of a great revival. In that revival there was a man by the name of Simon who believed and was baptized. This, of course, was what was happening to most of the population in this city. What makes Simon's case different from others is what he had been before the revival. Let us look at the account in Acts 8:9–24:

> *Now for some time a man named Simon had practiced sorcery in the city and amazed all the people of Samaria. He boasted that he was someone great, and all the people, both high and low, gave*

him their attention and exclaimed, "This man is the divine power known as the Great Power." They followed him because he had amazed them for a long time with his magic. But when they believed Philip as he preached the good news of the kingdom of God and the name of Jesus Christ, they were baptized, both men and women. Simon himself believed and was baptized. And he followed Philip everywhere, astonished by the great signs and miracles he saw.

When the apostles in Jerusalem heard that Samaria had accepted the word of God, they sent Peter and John to them. When they arrived, they prayed for them that they might receive the Holy Spirit, because the Holy Spirit had not yet come upon any of them; they had simply been baptized into the name of the Lord Jesus. Then Peter and John placed their hands on them, and they received the Holy Spirit.

When Simon saw that the Spirit was given at the laying on of the apostles' hands, he offered them money and said, "Give me also this ability so that everyone on whom I lay my hands may receive the Holy Spirit."

Peter answered: "May your money perish with you, because you thought you could buy the gift of God with money! You have no part or share in this ministry, because your heart is not right before God. Repent of this wickedness and pray to the Lord. Perhaps he will forgive you for having such a thought in your heart. For I see that you are full of bitterness and captive to sin."

Then Simon answered, "Pray to the Lord for me so that nothing you have said may happen to me."

Here was a new believer, saved in the midst of a revival. He wanted the power of the Holy Spirit that he saw in the revival, manifested in his own life and ministry, but with the wrong motives. Peter said he could not have this power, because his heart was not right in God's sight. Simon was full of bitterness, and still in bondage to sin. Sin was a hindrance to the fullness of the Holy Spirit in his life. Peter told him to repent! If we want the power of the Holy Spirit in our lives so we can be like someone else, or be admired and thought to be spiritual, or so we can be a success in the ministry and have a large church, we will not be able to receive this fullness. In all revivals, there is an intense sense of the presence of God and his holiness. In that atmosphere there is deep conviction for sin, and thorough repentance. If we want the power of the Holy Spirit either personally or collectively, we would do well to deal thoroughly with sin in deep repentance and cleansing. Thank God, if we walk in the light, and confess our sins, God is faithful and just to forgive our sins, and the blood of Jesus Christ cleanses us from every sin! We Christians are temples of God on earth.

Do you not know that your body is a temple of the Holy Spirit, who is in you, whom you have received from God? You are not your own; you were bought at a price. Therefore honor God with your body (I Cor. 6:19–20).

There is an account in the Old Testament of the cleansing of the Temple of God, that pictures beautifully what many of us need to do about our temple, so that God may be free to fill us with His glory. You will find it in II Chronicles 29.

I don't believe the Temple, in Hezekiah's time, became closed overnight, but over a period of time. Through carelessness, worldliness, personal lusts, and disobedience to God, the junk collected. Some of the idols of the heathen were brought into the temple. The priesthood became unclean, and unfit to lead in worship. Finally, so much junk was lying around in the Outer Court that they couldn't offer the sacrifices. And if the priests came into the Holy Place, there was garbage, trash, and old idols stacked on everything, so they could not lay out the bread, light the candlestick, or burn incense. Even the Holy of Holies was filthy and unusable. No more spiritual activity was possible within that Temple! Finally, the doors were closed. The sacrifices and prayers were no longer offered. The light of testimony no longer shone. Needy people could no longer come to that Temple to meet with God.

I believe the same thing had happened in Jerusalem in Jesus' day, when He found it necessary to cleanse the Temple—which had not become filled with politics, dishonesty, and hypocrisy suddenly. That Temple had a full religious schedule, but without any power, for the glory of God had departed. It looked good. But in every way that mattered, it was as unclean as the Temple in Hezekiah's day. Then the Lord, whom they were pretending to seek, suddenly came to His Temple and demanded that it be cleansed!

The cleansing of the Temple by Hezekiah presents a pattern for us to follow. First they opened the doors. Then they carried out the trash. Then they reinstituted the sacrifices. They lit the lamp of testimony. They offered the incense of prayer. Finally, they consecrated the whole place to God, and His Glory filled the Temple again.

In revival, the Lord comes and insists that we cleanse our temples, both individually and corporately. All kinds of rubbish collects in our lives and in our churches. A small disobedience to God here, and little sin there. Things we don't think God is concerned about. We lay one thing over here in the corner by the altar. Something that isn't just right, but isn't too big, we put over there behind the laver. Then there is that thing that isn't really sinful, but has no place in a Christian life. We stack that on the table of shewbread. Then some other things collect—a little dishonesty, a little hypocrisy, a relationship with a Christian brother that isn't just right. And before we know it, our Christian life, slowly—slowly, not suddenly, not overnight, not immediately, but over a period of time—our Christian life becomes cluttered with all kinds of rubbish and junk! Some of it is unclean. Some of it is just in the way. We stumble over it. Every time we try to offer a sacrifice or a prayer to God, or let our light shine for Christ, we are hindered. There is no glory. There is no power. What do we need to do?

Since 1972, I have been involved in revival ministries. I have seen what God has done in many lives in revival. So many follow the same pattern as Hezekiah. First, they get the doors open, and start to get honest. They let the light of God shine in on the mess. He begins to search their inner life. They begin to pray and seek His face. They begin to offer up the sacrifices of a broken heart. Then as they submit and yield to God, He points out all the trash and filth that has collected in their lives. Then they begin a process of cleansing. They start to carry out the junk and garbage and idols. They even carry out those things that are not sinful, but are just in the way. For some people, it takes some time, even as it did in Hezekiah's day. Finally, they come to an end. Then the Holy Spirit of God moves in with power, and fills their life with His presence and glory. How many times I have seen their faces shine as the glory of God filled His temple!

Is that what you want for yourself and your church? Cleanse your temple and see what God will do! The second thing that hinders receiving the fullness of the Holy Spirit is:

SELF. Most Christians have had very limited teaching about baptism, and think of it only as a public testimony of their faith in Christ, or the other extreme of equating it with the new birth and believing in baptismal regeneration. Neither view does justice to the biblical doctrine. Romans 6 gives clear teaching on this matter. Here God is plainly saying that our old self was crucified with Christ! He asks, "Do you know that?" The next question is "Do you believe that?" And finally, "Will you agree with God on that score, and yield yourself up to the reality of that death and that life?" This is a teaching much deeper than merely a testimony. This accords with Jesus' teaching when He said,

215

And He summoned the crowd with His disciples, and said to them, "If anyone wishes to come after Me, he must deny himself, and take up his cross and follow Me. For whoever wishes to save his life will lose it, but whoever loses his life for My sake and the gospel's will save it. For what does it profit a man to gain the whole world, and forfeit his soul? For what will a man give in exchange for his soul?" (Mark 8:34–37, NASB).

Jesus taught that the way from the self-life to the Christ-life is through the cross. A person may be a Christian and still be trying to save his life for himself. He must give up his life so completely to Christ, that it is the same as dying and rising again!

If I insist on keeping self at the center of my life, it is impossible to put the Holy Spirit in full charge of my life. I cannot live for self and Christ at the same time. God cannot fill me with His Holy Spirit if I am full of self. If I truly want the power of a Spirit-filled life, I must be willing to attend my own funeral. The giving of self over to the death of the cross must be real. Dealing with sin may be painful, but bringing self to death will be much more painful. I truly believe that this refusal to let self die is the main hindrance to being filled with the Holy Spirit. The writings of Paul are filled with this truth. One of his most striking statements is found in Galatians 2:20, where he says,

I have been crucified with Christ; and it is no longer I who live, but Christ lives in me; and the life which I now live in the flesh I live by faith in the Son of God, who loved me and gave Himself up for me (NASB).

Two others are as follows:

For Christ's love compels us, because we are convinced that one died for all, and therefore all died. And he died for all, that those who live should no longer live for themselves but for him who died for them and was raised again (II Cor. 5:14–15).

Since, then, you have been raised with Christ, set your hearts on things above, where Christ is seated at the right hand of God. Set your minds on things above, not on earthly things. For you died, and your life is now hidden with Christ in God (Col. 3:1–3).

These Scriptures make it clear that in God's view we have been put to death in the person of Jesus Christ. We have been raised with Him and are now seated with Him at God's right hand in the highest heaven. In that death and resurrection we have been freed from sin, or self-centredness, or the self-life, which is the sin principle from which all sin springs. We are therefore no longer to live the self-life, but the Christ-life. We do this by agreeing with God by faith, and living in complete dependence on the life of Christ within us by the indwelling Holy Spirit. This is not sinlessness or perfectionism. It is the life of Christ being lived out through us by the Holy Spirit. This means a very real and practical renouncing of the self-life, and commitment to the Christ-life within us. To help us deal with this process, I have listed below some characteristics of the self-life. I invite you to go through the list slowly and prayerfully, and check those that seem to apply to your personal life.

__Self-will	__Self-indulgence
__Self-seeking	__Self-complacency
__Self-pity	__Self-exaltation
__Self-confidence	__Self-consciousness
__Self-depreciation	__Self-importance
__Self-vindication	__Self-preoccupation
__Self-choosing	__Self-pleasing
__Self-righteousness	__Self-preservation
__Self-fulfillment	__Self-love
__Self-satisfaction (pride)	__Self-advancement *(unholy ambition)*

(You may want to add some of your own that God points out to you.)

Here is a suggested funeral prayer for the self-life:

Dear Lord, I thank You for taking my sinful self-life to the cross. I thank you for dealing with it there in Your death and resurrection. I want to agree with You, Lord. I surrender my self up to the sentence of death You have already pronounced upon me. (Now take each part of the self-life you have checked or named above and pray this prayer sincerely and thoughtfully to the Lord Jesus Christ.)

Lord Jesus, I give up my Self-_____ to You. I renounce it, and refuse to live in it any more. In its place I take You, Lord Jesus, as my very life! Thank You, Lord Jesus. Amen.

This brings us to the third hindrance to being filled with the Holy Spirit:

UNBELIEF. God promised the Holy Spirit. God has given the Holy Spirit to us. Now we must in faith receive the Holy Spirit to fill every part of our lives. It is my firm conviction that if we are convinced that the Holy Spirit has already been given to us, and sin and self are dealt with thoroughly, we will not have any real problem with faith. It will be as simple to receive the one God has given to us, as it was to receive Christ. Our temple will be cleansed and vacated, and God will be quick to fill it at our invitation and full surrender.

David Brainerd experienced powerful revival among the American Indians. He tells how, on one Sunday night, he offered himself to God to be used only for His glory. He said, "It was raining and the roads were muddy; but the desire to surrender to God grew so strong, that I stopped my horse and kneeled down by the side of the road, and told God about it. I told him that my hands should work for him, my tongue speak for him, if he would only use me as his instrument; when suddenly the darkness of the night lit up, and I knew God had answered my prayer, and I felt that I was accepted into the inner circle of his will."

God's Word has promised that God will give the Holy Spirit to those who ask Him, and to those who obey Him. Peter said, "You shall receive the gift of the Holy Spirit." There comes a time when we have put away all known sin. We have offered up our lives in full surrender. Now God invites us to simply believe Him and receive the Holy Spirit.

Dr. F.B. Meyer was a man greatly used of God in the generation before this one. The power of God was obviously on his life! Here is his testimony:

"I left the prayer meeting and crept out into the lane away from town. As I walked I said, "O my God, if there is a man who needs the power of the Holy Ghost to rest upon him it is I; but I do not know how to receive him. I am too tired, too worn, too nervously down to agonize." A voice said to me, "As you took forgiveness from the hand of the dying Christ, take the Holy Ghost from the hand of the living Christ." I turned to Christ and said, "Lord, as I breath in this wiff of warm night air, so I breathe into every part of me thy blessed Spirit." I felt no hand laid upon my head, there was no lambent flame, there was no rushing sound from heaven; but by faith, without emotion, without excitement, I took, and took for the first time, and I have kept on taking ever since."[12]

May I share with you my own testimony? I was a young pastor preparing for my ordination. I had read the prescribed books, written the necessary doctrinal papers, and studied for the oral examination I would encounter. In a few days, my wife and I would be traveling to a conference grounds to attend our District Conference. There, if I passed all the tests, I would be ordained. There was one question I knew they would ask, that was bothering me. It would be a question about this matter of the fullness of the Holy Spirit. As I honestly faced this question,

I knew I was not filled with the Holy Spirit. I knew I was not going to lie about it. What would they say? I did not know. I wrestled with the matter in prayer, but got nowhere. My wife had gone to bed, as it was very late. Finally, about 2:00 a.m., I slipped into bed. The night was dark about me. I lay there, quietly thinking and praying about this problem. I longed for this filling of God's Spirit. Then it seemed a very quiet voice said, "Just as you received Christ, so you can receive the Holy Spirit." I answered, "Is it that simple?" God said, "It is that simple!" And so, lying there on my back with my wife asleep beside me, I silently responded. I said, "Alright then, I receive the Holy Spirit." Like Dr. Meyer, I saw no tongues of fire, nor did I hear or feel anything. But my friends, the Holy Spirit filled me for the first time, and has filled me afresh a number of times since.

This would be a good place to stop reading, and settle this matter with God. Will you do it? Why not begin with a thorough cleansing of your temple? Then go on to deal thoroughly with the self-life at the cross. When all is complete as far as you know, and your heart is at rest before God, then simply receive God's Holy Spirit. He will fill you! He has promised!

Now we come to the third wicked way from which God's people need to turn. Along with Worldliness and Powerlessness, we find the wicked way of:

PASSIVENESS

Are you shocked that I would call this a "wicked way?" Oh, but it is! In fact, it may be the most wicked of the three. In recent years, there has been a problem in Banff Park between tourists and grizzly bears. The bears have multiplied and there doesn't seem to be enough room for the bears and the people to stay out of each other's way. One afternoon, some tourists were coming down a trail in the woods. A short way from their trail was another trail. The two trails met in an open, grassed area. The problem was that a large grizzly bear was coming down the other trail, and neither could see the other. Both the people and the bear were so located on their separate trails, that they were going to meet each other where the two trails converged. In another area, near the hotel, was a group of people who were so located they could see both trails, and what was about to happen. These unsuspecting people were in serious danger! What was the reaction of those who could clearly see the danger? They got very excited. They started to shout, wave their arms, and point to the other area. They got the attention of the tourists on the trail, and waved their hands at them as if they were pushing them back. At first, the tourists just waved back. As they came closer, however, they could see these people were not just being friendly, but were trying to warn them of some kind of danger. Finally they were persuaded, stopped, and went back up the trail. Later they were very grateful that they had been saved from the danger of coming face-to-face with a large grizzly bear. What would you think of those people at the hotel if they had been passive? Did they have a right to be indifferent to the danger of other people? You say, "Certainly not! They did the right thing!"

All around us, thousands of people are wandering out into eternal darkness, and everlasting hell fire! Daily, our society grows more evil and more alienated from God. We say we believe they will be lost without Christ. We say we believe Christ is the only way of salvation. We say we believe that the gospel of Christ is the power of God unto salvation to everyone who believes. We say it is true that Christ has commanded us to preach the gospel to every creature. We say we wish God would bring a great revival that would save thousands of people and change our world. Yet, many of God's people go on living their private lives without any burden to pray, without any concern over their own powerlessness, and without any personal effort to win the lost around them to Christ. If that kind of a passive attitude of indifference is not wicked, what would you say it is? I wonder how many are truly willing to lay aside their personal comfort, and allow God to stir them up about revival and winning the lost?

Outside of the love of God, I do not know of anything more wonderful than the grace of God. Thank God for His wonderful grace! Oh how we Christians love to sing, teach and testify about the grace of God! And so we should! But—my Christian brother and sister, do not use the grace of God as a cloak to cover your indifference. Our dear Saviour had some very hard things to say about that attitude. We read in Revelation 3:15–16, "I know your deeds, that you are neither cold nor hot. I wish you were either one or the other! So, because you are lukewarm—neither hot nor cold—I am about to spit you out of my mouth." Then there are those who hide behind the doctrine of Election and Predestination. They say there is no reason to be so stirred up, because God will save those He has chosen, and we cannot change it one way or the other. And so they settle down in their comfortable state, and let the world around them go to hell with wicked indifference.

God will never make machines out of any of us. God's grace does not impose His will upon ours. God's challenge is, "Choose this day whom you will serve!" Everywhere, the Scriptures take it for granted that we must not be passive, but active in responding to God. Paul said, "I do not frustrate the grace of God." Passiveness will send the unbeliever to hell, because although he has heard the gospel, he does nothing about it. A passive attitude in the life of a Christian will make him immature, carnal, and part of the problem rather than part of the cure. No Christian has a right to sit around and say that revival and the winning of the lost is someone else's responsibility. We must respond to God and our lost world to the limit of our ability. That is **response-ability**. Christian, it is wicked for you to be passive about praying, giving, growing in Christ, being Spirit-filled, and winning the lost to Christ. God says we must turn from our wicked ways, if He is to heal our land. Am I willing to turn? Are you willing to turn? The Apostle Paul was certainly not passive! Listen to what God said to him in Acts 26:17–19:

'...I am sending you to them to open their eyes and turn them from darkness to light, and from the power of Satan to God, so

that they may receive forgiveness of sins and a place among those who are sanctified by faith in me.' "So then, King Agrippa, I was not disobedient to the vision from heaven".

We have already talked about prayer and our need for power, so I will not deal with that again here. But, let me ask you a very important question: **Are you a soul winner?** In Proverbs 11:30, God says. "He who wins souls is wise." Jesus said that the angels rejoice more over one soul that repents, than over ninety-nine justified persons who do not need to repent. During the revival at Brown Street Alliance Church in Akron, Ohio, in 1972, God gave me a new view of Psalm 126. The entire Psalm is a marvelous picture of revival. Look at these exciting words:

When the LORD turned again the captivity of Zion, we were like them that dream. Then was our mouth filled with laughter, and our tongue with singing: then said they among the heathen, The LORD has done great things for them. The LORD has done great things for us; whereof we are glad. Turn again our captivity, O LORD, as the streams in the south. They that sow in tears shall reap in joy. He that goes forth weeping, bearing precious seed, shall doubtless come again with rejoicing, bringing his sheaves with him.

Any church would love to have an experience like that! But *How?* Verse 6 gives us four simple steps. They are not easy steps, just simple! Here they are:

1. The GO in Soul Winning. "He who goes forth..."

The main reason Christians do not win souls, is simply because they do not get at it. They do not try. They do not GO! Christians who lead good lives do not necessarily win souls. Christians ought to lead good lives. But that in itself does not make them soul winners. There are thousands of Christians whose lives are exemplary in every way. Yet, most of them have never led a person to Christ. Some have been Christians ten, twenty, forty or fifty years, and have never won one soul. Why? They do not go! Christians who know their Bibles do not necessarily win souls. There are Sunday School teachers who have taught the Bible for forty years, but never led another person to Christ. There are even pastors, missionaries and denominational leaders who fit in that category!

I was senior pastor of a church where we were in need of a Minister of Personal Care. There was a man who had the qualifications we were looking for, but he was one of our missionaries. I heard that he was coming home for an extended leave because of a health problem in his immediate family. I wrote to him, asking if he would consider filling that position on our pastoral staff. I received a letter in reply, in which he stated that he would be interested in coming if we would promise to make him a soul winner while he was with us. I wrote back and said, "Yes, I guarantee it!" And we kept our promise! I expect every pastor on our staff to be a soul winner, regardless of what his ministry may be.

When Dr. Kennedy, of Ft. Lauderdale, Florida, was a young pastor, he struggled with this problem. He said he could not win souls because of a "back problem." Yes. He said the problem was a big yellow stripe down the middle of his back. Today, he is the founder and leader of Evangelism Explosion, which reaches around the world in soul winning.

So—I can read my Bible every day, memorize large portions of it, understand all the main doctrines, and even teach or preach it to others, and still never lead others to Christ. Why? Because I don't do what Jesus said and GO!

Christians who are faithful to the Church do not necessarily win souls. Some dear Christians are at church every time the door is open. They give their money, serve wherever asked, attend the business meetings, back their pastor, and support the program of the church on all sides. They are wonderful people. Every church needs many more like them. Yet, they have never led an unbeliever to Christ. Why? The main reason is because they just don't get at it. They do not GO! Christians who win souls are those who **obey** God, and GO forth, and make an honest effort to bring lost people to Jesus Christ!

DO YOU KNOW ANY NON-CHRISTIANS? Can you think of anyone by name right now, that you are actively trying to bring to Christ? If not, why not?

During the Civil War in the United States, a southern farmer named Jim was drafted into the Confederate Army. He could not read, therefore he did not know the drill manual. He couldn't make sense out of the bugle calls or the various ways to march. Nevertheless—he brought his squirrel rifle, and he could shoot. His regiment engaged the enemy, but were greatly outnumbered, so retreat was sounded. The regiment regrouped, but could not find Jim. The others thought he was surely captured or dead. While they were discussing his fate, they saw two figures coming toward them through the woods. When they got closer, it became obvious that it was Jim with a Yankee prisoner. They all crowded around him with great excitement, asking, "Where'd you get him Jim, where'd you get him?" Jim looked around angrily and replied, **"Go out and get one for yourself, the woods are full of them!"**

Our churches are often like that. Someone leads an unbeliever to Christ and we are all so amazed. But our woods are filled with non-Christians! We need to obey God and GO after them.

This brings us to the second step in soul winning:

2. The BROKENNESS in Soul Winning— "He who goes forth weeping."

This speaks to me of compassion, intercessory prayer, burden, really caring about lost sinners. **Jesus** wept over Jerusalem because they were lost. **Paul** reminded the church in Ephesus that, "by the space of three years I ceased not to warn everyone night and day with **tears!**" **Jeremiah** said, "Oh that my head were waters, and my eyes a fountain of **tears**, that I might weep day and night for the slain of the daughter of my people."

How different that sounds from the indifference and passiveness of the average Christian in our churches. But, someone says, "I don't have this concern." Listen, go forth in obedience, and sincerely and actively attempt to win the lost to Christ. Keep at it. I promise you that eventually you will come to brokenness over the desperate condition of those who are lost! Even now, hundreds of thousands of souls a day are dropping into eternal hell! I will never be stirred until I really **see** them. When Jesus **saw** the multitudes like sheep without a shepherd, he was **moved** with **compassion** over their desperate plight. **GO! Look! Lift up your eyes!**

An evangelist was staying in the home of a church family while conducting a soul-winning crusade in that church. There were two teenage boys in that home who were not attending the meetings. One day, the mother of the home asked the evangelist if he would pray for her unsaved boys. He replied, "No, I will not." She looked at him, astonished, and asked why not. Again, he replied, "Your eyes are dry." She stared at him and went away quietly. That night, she ate no supper. Late into the night, the evangelist could hear her praying down the hall in her bedroom. He awoke a number of times in the night to hear her muffled groans and tears. The next morning, she looked haggard but determined. She ate no breakfast, lunch or supper, but after serving the others, went away to continue praying. That night in the crusade, two teenage boys walked the aisle to receive Christ as their Saviour and Lord!

What a question this poses to my heart! Where are **my** tears? **Why are my eyes so dry?** How is it that I can cry over silly novels or TV programs that are not real, but have no tears for the most terrible reality in the universe—the everlasting separation of eternal souls from God, and their unending torment in a devil's hell? How can I be so passive when they are dying? Why am I not at least concerned for God's glory if I do not care about the people around me? His name is blasphemed by their rebellion and hatred against Him. Why do I not speak up for God? Oh, brother and sister, plead with God to break your heart!

If we go with a broken heart, what else do we need? We need:

3. The WORD OF GOD In Soul Winning— "bearing precious seed."

Jesus said, "The seed is the Word." **Peter** tells us that we are, "Born again, not of corruptible seed, but … through the Word of God which lives and abides forever" (I Pet. 1:23, NKJV). Again, the writer to the Hebrews reminds us that the Word of God is alive and powerful and sharper than any two-edged sword, piercing even to the dividing of soul and spirit … and is a discerner of the thoughts and motives of the heart (Heb. 4:12). **Jeremiah** quoted God as saying, "Is not my Word like as a fire … and like a hammer that breaks the rock in pieces?" (Jer. 23:29).

When we go out to win the lost to Jesus Christ, we must in some way take them the Word of God. This precious seed must be planted in their hearts if they are to be born again. Many Christians who sincerely believe the Word of God for themselves, seem to lack faith in its power when it comes to witnessing for Christ. Sometimes they say, "But what is the use of giving them Scripture if they do not believe it is the Word of God?" Let me ask you this; Suppose you lived in the old days when men used swords to fight one another. And suppose you were in a duel in which your life was at stake. And suppose you had in your hand a sword of the finest Damascus steel, sharp as a razor. And suppose your adversary mocked you, and said, "I don't believe your sword is sharp enough to cut butter." What would you do? Would you drop your sword, or would you give him a skillful thrust and let the sword speak for itself? My friends, the power of God's Word is not affected in any way by what others think about it! Even while the unbeliever is saying he doesn't believe it, it is cutting him to the very heart! For many years I conducted evangelistic home Bible studies in which we allowed the Bible to answer every question. We made no effort to defend its validity. We never argued about doctrine. We simply gave them the Word of God and let them wrestle with it for themselves. What happened? We saw people come to Christ continually by the scores, and they were our most solid converts!

One Sunday morning while I was pastor of Hillsdale Alliance Church in Regina, Saskatchewan, Canada, I was standing at the main entrance to our sanctuary before the early service. Four men approached, and in broken English, asked if they could attend the service. I assured them that they were welcome, and invited them in. It turned out that they were Chinese scholars from the university nearby. One of our men, who had a Bible study in his home, came to them immediately, introduced himself, and invited them to sit with him. After the service was over, he invited them to come to his Bible study. They came. None of them had ever seen a Bible before. Some of them were working on their doctorates. All they knew was communism. These four invited others. Soon, they filled a row across the center section of our sanctuary. Within two years, fourteen of these Chinese scholars were born again through the study of the Word of God!

Let me ask you this, "DO YOU HAVE A PLAN?" Do you have some method by which you present the gospel to unbelievers? There are many good methods available. Here are four, all of which I have used at some time or other: "The Four Spiritual Laws," "Evangelism Explosion," "Evangelistic Home Bible Studies" and many forms of "Friendship Evangelism." What is your method? You say, "I don't have any." Why not?

One afternoon Mr Sankey, who worked with D.L. Moody, was speaking on "Soul Winning." He shared with his audience the method he used at that time. After the session he was approached by a man who, in the course of their conversation, said he didn't like Mr. Sankey's method of soul winning. Mr. Sankey said, "I don't like it very well myself. What is yours? "Well," the man stammered, "I, uh—well I—that is—I guess I don't have one." "Well then," said Mr. Sankey, "I like mine better than yours." End of conversation!

Sometimes I go through periods in my Christian life when I get careless about this. I get so busy serving God, that I neglect this absolutely essential service to God. Then God will do something to get my attention to what is happening. Let me share with you two such occasions. They both took place while I was pastor at Hillsdale Alliance Church in Regina. I am changing the names of the people involved to preserve their privacy.

There was a doctor in the church who was a gynecologist and a surgeon. His oldest child and only girl died with leukemia. She was only seventeen, but a committed Christian, and a beautiful and gifted girl. During her illness, a member of the Cancer Society came to visit her. This woman had recovered from cancer, and was there to encourage this girl. It turned out that the girl and her mother encouraged the visitor instead. The visitor was Dolly Kawalchuk, the wife of Larry Kawalchuk, an attorney in the city. It so happened that they lived only five houses from us, but we had never met them. They were lovely people, but were not Christians.

When this teenage girl died, her parents invited the Kawalchuks to the funeral. They were overwhelmed with the service and message from God's Word. They had never seen or heard anything like this. Dolly asked if they could come to church with the doctor and his wife, and so they did. Within two months, Dolly received Christ as her Saviour. Larry made no move in that direction, but they continued to attend church regularly for the next two years.

One day, in my prayer time, God spoke to me about Larry Kawalchuk. I responded to God by saying that surely one of the men must have talked to Larry by now. But God would not let me off the hook. I felt rebuked that this man had attended our church for two years and I did not know his spiritual condition. I called Larry on the phone, and asked him if I could take him out one night that week for a steak dinner, He was delighted, and asked me what was the occasion. I told him frankly that I wanted to talk to him about his relationship with God. He said he would like that.

I drove by, picked him up, and we went to dinner. After we had eaten, I asked him over coffee if he had yet received Christ as his Saviour. He said, "No." I asked him if there was any reason why he did not want to become a Christian. Again, he said, "No." I asked him if he understood the gospel. He said, "Yes." I asked him if he would like to receive Christ right now, tonight. He responded that he would, but suggested we do it somewhere else. I paid for the dinner, and we drove back to his house and parked in the driveway. There in the car, Larry prayed very sincerely, inviting Christ into his life. Then I prayed. He could hardly wait to rush into his house and tell Dolly that he had become a Christian. That couple continues to live for the Lord in that church.

The other incident has to do with a man who owned a real estate company. Marvin Cramer and his wife were invited to attend one of our Christmas musicals. They came. At those occasions, we always gave people an opportunity to pray to receive Christ. There was a card they could fill out, giving us an account of their response. Marvin's wife filled out the card, indicating that she had prayed to receive Christ. The next Sunday, they showed up in church, and continued to attend every Sunday. The first Sunday they came, they paused at the door going out, and invited my wife and me to go to lunch with them. We went, and had a good time getting acquainted. After that, they repeated this invitation two more times, quite close together. I wondered why they were doing this, and suddenly God got my attention. This man wanted to talk to me about Christ! What was the matter with me?

So, I called him up and invited him to lunch with me during the week. He accepted with enthusiasm. We met at my favorite place, where the food was good, and the non-smoking section was under a glass arch where you felt like you were sitting out in the sun. We ate, and I explained the gospel to him carefully, telling him what he needed to do to receive Christ. I asked if he wanted to do that. He replied that he did. I suggested we go out to my car and pray together. He wondered why we should go outside.

He asked if it was alright if he prayed right there and now. I agreed. And so he prayed out loud, with everyone around us able to hear every word. Marvin was soundly converted. Since that time he has had two businesses fail, and gone through a heart attack. Through it all, the Lord has been his strength, and he has remained faithful to God. The last time I saw him, he had started a new business which was a success.

So let me ask you again; what is your plan for winning souls? This brings us to the fourth step in winning souls:

4. The RESULTS in Soul Winning—
"He shall doubtless come again with rejoicing bringing his sheaves with him."

THE RESULTS ARE ABSOLUTELY ASSURED! We must expect results and ask people to make a commitment. We will not win everyone to whom we witness—maybe not even most of them. But we will win some! God has promised it. A farmer always plants more seed than he expects to grow. The wise man said, in Ecclesiastes 11:1–2:

Cast your bread upon the waters, for after many days you will find it again. Give portions to seven, yes to eight, for you do not know what disaster may come upon the land.

Whoever watches the wind will not plant; whoever looks at the clouds will not reap (Eccl. 11:4).

Sow your seed in the morning, and at evening let not your hands be idle, for you do not know which will succeed, whether this or that, or whether both will do equally well (Eccl. 11:6).

Isn't that Scripture clear? God says go out and sow the seed. Share the gospel with those around you in love and faith, and leave the results with God. And there will be results! In Jesus' parable of the farmer sowing the seed, only one out of four brought forth good fruit. We will not win them all. But—if I go forth obediently, if I allow my heart to become involved, if I give out the Word of God, if I keep at it, **I will without any doubt get a harvest!** Oh, what joy! Jesus said in the parable of the lost son, "Rejoice with me!" That is what will happen if we Christians turn from our wicked way of passiveness and indifference. God will forgive us. The revival we long for will come. God will heal our land!

On that historic night in 1904, when God used Evan Roberts to launch the great revival in Wales, the matter of witnessing was one of the commitments he asked of those seventeen people who stayed to hear what he had to say. Let me give you his challenge again: "I have a message for you from God. You must confess any known sin to God, and put any wrong done to man right. Second, you must put away any doubtful habit. Third, you must obey the Spirit promptly. **Finally, you must confess your faith in Christ publicly.**" By ten o'clock, all seventeen had responded, and the revival was on! These Christians turned from their passive ways, and decided to become active for God. That was one of the conditions of that great revival, which went around the world. It was a time of revival for God's people, it is true, but it was, far beyond that, a great gathering in of the lost into the Kingdom of God.

In the great revivals under the leadership of Charles Finney, the two outstanding emphases were prayer and personal soul winning. In his autobiography, he wrote about his ministry in New York City:

> When I first went to Chatham Street Chapel, I informed the brethren that I did not wish to fill up the house with Christians from other churches, as my object was to gather from the world. I wanted to secure the conversion of the ungodly to the utmost possible extent. We therefore gave ourselves to labor for that class of persons, and by the blessing of God, with good success. Conversions were multiplied so much that our church soon became so large, that we sent off

another group of believers to form another church. When I left New York we had seven churches thus begun, **whose members were laboring with all their might to secure the salvation of souls.**[13]

My dear friends, that is what is on the heart of God! May He be pleased to put that same burden on my heart and yours! So we see, that God is more than ready to forgive His people and heal our land, if we will only turn from our wicked ways of *Worldliness, Powerlessness*, and *Passiveness*. Whatever God says to you—DO IT!

CHAPTER NINE

The Steps of Healing

If my people, who are called by my name,
will humble themselves and pray and seek my face
and turn from their wicked ways, then will I hear
*from heaven and **will forgive their sin***
*and **will heal their land.***

~ II Chronicles 7:14

God wants to cleanse and heal our land! This of course, is only possible as the people of our land are cleansed and healed. This verse makes it clear that all this depends on what happens in the lives of the people of God, both individually and collectively. As God's people humble themselves, pray, and turn from their wicked ways, God will forgive their sins. They will be cleansed, separated from the world, filled with God's Holy Spirit, and actively seeking to win the lost to Christ. Some of these changes in our lives may take place quickly, even dramatically. Other necessary changes we will find to be a process. A process of healing will need to take place before, during and after the revival that is coming. In this chapter I want to deal with three areas of healing that will require a process. I want to begin with the first one, which is the basic concept on which the other two will be built. It is the question of living my Christian life by "Faith Or Feeling."

If I live by faith, I am walking in the Spirit.
If I live by my feelings, I am walking in the flesh.
The Word of God raises this question in these words,

But I say, walk by the Spirit, and you will not carry out the desire of the flesh. For the flesh sets its desire against the Spirit, and the Spirit against the flesh; for these are in opposition to one another, so that you may not do the things that you please. Now those who belong to Christ Jesus have crucified the flesh with its passions and desires. If we live by the Spirit, let us also walk by the Spirit (Gal. 5:16,17,24,25 NASB).

As we live the Christian life, every moment, in all we think, do, and say, we are either walking in the Spirit or the flesh. We either act in accordance with our feelings or we act in accordance with God's Word by faith. I do not mean that our feelings are always in conflict with our faith, for indeed, sometimes they are together. The question is, what is the basic motivation of my actions?

We live in a day when a favorite bumper sticker reads, "If It Feels Good, Do It!" One day, my wife and I were on a trip. I was driving and she was looking for something in a magazine. In the process she came across a page of advertisements for needlepoint. There were both pictures and mottos. She called my attention to one motto which fits the philosophy of our day. It read, "When the rush is over, I am going to have a nervous breakdown. I worked for it. I owe it to myself, and no one is going to cheat me out of it." **That** is living by one's feelings!

Unfortunately, Christians have also been encouraged to believe that living the Christian life will always feel good. When revival comes, the fountains of the deep are always broken up. Deep conviction of sin, thorough repentance, and total surrender to God will bring to most people an unusual emotional upheaval. Tears, inward pain, abounding joy, and deep peace will often be experienced. Great tenderness of heart and feelings on the surface are common in revival. These emotional outpourings may continue for many days, weeks or even months. I have heard people say, in revival, that they felt as if they were walking around knee-deep in love! This emotional state will produce singing like you will never hear in any other setting until you get to heaven. All this is wonderful! We wish it could go on forever! We cannot however, live at this emotional pitch for the rest of our lives. Charles Finney has said that the emotional excitement in a genuine revival is so great that the physical frame could not stand it indefinitely. Eventually, we all must go back to our regular lives in the market place, the farm, the school and the home. There, we will find many reasons for our feelings to be affected. Those feelings may change suddenly or slowly. At that point, we need to understand how our feelings function or we will become discouraged and defeated. Along with that understanding, we need some guidance as to how to walk by faith rather than our feelings. The purpose of this chapter is to supply that understanding and guidance.

I want to begin by making some very important statements about our emotions. If you get an understanding of these concepts, it will help you with all the rest. Here they are.

1. Emotions are neither good nor evil. They are amoral. That is they have no moral quality. By themselves, our feelings are neither holy nor unholy. Our emotions were created by God and are part of what we are. Anger as a feeling is not sinful. We read in Ephesians 4:26, "Be angry, and {yet} do not sin; do not let the sun go down on your anger" (NASB).

Even Jesus felt anger, for we read in Mark 3:4–5,

> *Is it lawful on the Sabbath to do good or to do harm, to save a life or to kill?" But they kept silent. And after looking around at them with anger, grieved at their hardness of heart, He said to the man, "Stretch out your hand." And he stretched it out, and his hand was restored* (NASB).

From these Scriptures, it is clear that the feeling of anger is not in itself sinful. It is how we handle our feeling of anger that will determine whether or not our feeling becomes an occasion for good or evil.

2. The reason emotions are neither good nor evil, is because they are involuntary. Your emotions are automatic reactions that occur without your direct control. You cannot decide to feel angry or joyful strictly as a decision of the will. You can control your feelings indirectly by what you choose to **think, say, or do.** Nothing in our lives has moral quality unless it involves a decision of the will. Because our feelings are involuntary, they are not good or evil in themselves.

3. Things that happen to us affect our feelings. Good news may make us feel joyful. Bad news may make us feel sad. In neither case is there good or evil in how we feel. We react automatically to the situation.

4. Our physical condition can affect how we feel emotionally. Tiredness or rest, sickness or health can produce feelings of various kinds. Indeed, some sickness can produce deep depression, and good health may produce a feeling of well-being. In neither case do such feelings indicate a spiritual state of good or evil.

5. The spiritual state of a person is determined by his relationship to God, and not by how he feels. If the will is fully surrendered to God, and fully committed to trust in God, that person is right with God. How he feels about that, or anything else, does not affect that relationship. Many Christians (and some non-Christians) are determining their spiritual state from their feelings, rather than from the Word of God. Some people who are obviously living in blatant disobedience to the Word of God will tell you that they must be pleasing to God because they feel fine. Others who are living in careful obedience to God's Word as far as they know, are concerned about their spiritual state because they do not feel close to God. Christians must learn to determine their spiritual state by the Word of God rather than by their feelings. This is always true, but it is especially true during and after revival.

I have had many experiences which have confirmed the validity of what I am saying. When I was a pastor in Akron, Ohio, there was a Christian woman in our church whose husband was an unbeliever and an alcoholic. One of the Elders and I visited in that home, and asked the husband if we could share the gospel with him. He said no. The Elder, who had been an alcoholic before his conversion, tried another approach. He told the man that he had been an alcoholic for twenty-two years. He asked if the man would like to hear how he quit drinking. Immediately, the man was interested and said yes. As my friend gave his testimony, he carefully wove the gospel into the story. The man listened intently. When he finished, the elder asked the man if he would like to receive Christ as his Saviour. The man said no, that he was not interested. We prayed and left.

A number of months later, this lady informed me that her husband was sick and in the hospital. I went to see him. I found his wife and two daughters in the waiting room. The two girls were home for a visit from California. They had been part of the hippy scene, but were both saved in the "Jesus People" revival. As soon as they were introduced to me, one of them said, "We are going to stay here and pray, while you go in and lead our father to Christ." This statement bothered me, for I felt very discouraged about this man, and didn't really expect him to respond that easily. I tried to avoid the issue, but they wouldn't let me. One of the girls repeated the statement again. I went in, sat down by the bed, and as soon as possible tried to talk to the man about his need of Christ. He stopped me, and reminded me that he was not interested. I thought, "I was right." Suddenly, he said to me, "Do you think Christ is coming back soon?" I said that was possible, and we discussed the return of Christ for a few minutes. I tried to turn this to the fact that he needed to get ready, but it didn't work. I gave up!

Then I said something that I really did not mean. I said, "Why don't we have a word of prayer together, and then I will be going." What I really meant was, "I am going to pray while you listen, and then I will be going." He didn't know that. We bowed our heads and I said, "Dear Lord." He immediately said, "Dear Lord." I said, "I am a sinner." He said, "I am a sinner." Phrase by phrase I led him through a sinner's prayer. When we finished and raised our heads, I asked, "Did you receive Christ?" He replied, "Of course!"

That man was totally transformed! All his profanity left, and he never took another drink of alcohol. He read the New Testament through in two weeks. He went home, lived a Christian life, and five months later, on Easter Sunday afternoon, went to be with the Lord while taking a nap.

Is it possible to lead someone to Christ when you don't feel like it? Can the Holy Spirit fill and use me when I don't feel spiritual? Can I be right with God and have His power resting upon my life when my feelings are all negative? Yes to all of the above!

What do the Scriptures say? Let us look at some Bible men who understood the difference between the fleshly experience of their feelings, and the spiritual experience of faith.

The Apostle Paul: What do you think about the Apostle Paul? Was he godly? Was he filled with the Holy Spirit? Was his life pleasing to God? Did he always feel great? No! Please notice with me Paul's feelings in two of his letters:

> We do not want you to be uninformed, brothers, about the hardships we suffered in the province of Asia. We were under great pressure, far beyond our ability to endure, so that we despaired even of life. Indeed, in our hearts we felt the sentence of death. But this happened that we might not rely on ourselves but on God, who raises the dead. He has delivered us from such a deadly peril, and he will deliver us. On him we have set our hope that he will continue to deliver us (II Cor. 1:8–10).

> I speak the truth in Christ—I am not lying, my conscience confirms it in the Holy Spirit—I have great sorrow and unceasing anguish in my heart. For I could wish that I myself were cursed and cut off from Christ for the sake of my brothers, those of my own race (Rom. 9:1–3).

Paul had experienced great revivals and had a personal walk with God experienced by few men in this world. Paul also suffered many hardships, and almost intolerable pressures. His emotions reacted like everyone else's emotions. He said the pressures were actually more than he could bear, so much so that he thought he was going to die. In his letter to the church in Rome, he said that he experienced great sorrow and constant anguish over the lost condition of his fellow Jews. How did he survive? He said he already had the sentence of death within himself. "Those who are Christ's have crucified the flesh with its passions and desires" (Gal. 5:24). Paul had given his flesh over to the death of the cross, and did not measure his spiritual reality by his feelings! He said that his conscience confirmed his true state by the witness of the Holy Spirit, not by the witness of his feelings.

The Prophet Jeremiah: What shall we say of the Prophet Jeremiah? Don't you think he was one of the greatest men of God in the history of Israel? He was so full of the Holy Spirit that at one time he said,

> *But if I say "I will not mention him or speak any more in his name,"*
> *his word is in my heart like a fire, a fire shut up in my bones. I am*
> *weary of holding it in; indeed, I cannot* (Jer. 20:9).

What were the feelings of this godly man? We have them in Jeremiah 8:20–9:1—

> *"The harvest is past, the summer has ended, and we are not saved."*
> *Since my people are crushed, I am crushed; I mourn, and horror*
> *grips me. Is there no balm in Gilead? Is there no physician there?*
> *Why then is there no healing for the wound of my people? Oh, that*
> *my head were a spring of water and my eyes a fountain of tears! I*
> *would weep day and night for the slain of my people.*

Oh, how this man was torn apart by his emotions! He said, "I am crushed, I mourn, horror grips me... I would weep day and night." None of these feelings changed his relationship to God, or the power of his anointed life and ministry. Jeremiah took twenty-three years to write his great book. It was the work of his life. There was one hand-written copy. When the king read the manuscript, he had it burned page by page. Did Jeremiah give up and take his life? Never!

He simply began again, and wrote it all over again. That is why it is in the Bible. Jeremiah did not measure his spiritual condition by his feelings, but walked by faith in God's Word!

The Lord Jesus Christ: And what shall we say of our Saviour? God said, "This is My beloved Son in whom I am well pleased." He

241

was spotless and perfect. The Holy Spirit was given to Him without measure. Was He always full of laughter and wonderful feelings? Certainly not. The Scriptures tell us that,

> *During the days of Jesus' life on earth, he offered up prayers and petitions with loud cries and tears to the one who could save him from death, and he was heard because of his reverent submission. Although he was a son, he learned obedience from what he suffered, and, once made perfect, he became the source of eternal salvation for all who obey him* (Heb. 5:7–9).

It is likely that this passage refers to Jesus' struggle in the garden right before His crucifixion. Please look with me at this account, and you will see feelings that go beyond our imagination. You will find this account in three of the Gospels: Matt 26:36–39, Luke 22:41–44 and Mark 14:33–42.

Please note with me the words used to describe Jesus' emotional anguish—"sorrowful and troubled," (Mark says "deeply distressed"), "overwhelmed with sorrow to the point of death," "in anguish," His sweat was "like blood falling down to the ground". Isaiah states He was a man of sorrows, and acquainted with grief. Here is human feelings stretched to the uttermost limits! Through all this, did Jesus have victory? Yes He did! How? He prayed, "Not my will, but Thine be done." The will of Jesus was totally surrendered to the will of His Father. That is perfect spiritual victory! During the next few hours, Jesus walked through the betrayal, the trial, the flogging, the crucifixion and death for sinners in perfect spiritual victory. That is the truth we must see if we are to pay the price for revival, be sustained through revival, and live in victory after revival.

6. **The feelings that often accompany spiritual experience are a result rather than a cause.** Genuine spiritual experience may cause reactions in the person involved in the experience that are felt in the emotions or even the body. This may be true whether the cause is from God or demons. Those feelings may be pleasant or unpleasant. The demonized boy in Mark 9 was affected severely in mind and body by a spiri-

tual experience. In that case, the effect was destructive. Both John, in Revelation 1, and Daniel, in Daniel 10, went through spiritual experiences that affected them emotionally and physically. Even though those experiences were unpleasant—even frightening—they were not destructive, since they were the result of a gracious experience with God.

We live in a world where people are greatly preoccupied with "experiences." This fad has invaded the Church. There are few areas in church life today where there is greater confusion than in this area. Jesus gave us a two-point formula for judging spiritual experiences. In John 4:23–24, Jesus said,

> *Yet a time is coming and has now come when the true worshippers will worship the Father in spirit and truth, for they are the kind of worshippers the Father seeks. God is spirit, and his worshippers must worship in spirit and in truth.*

It is not enough to worship in spirit, we must be careful to worship in truth. Why? Because there are many spirits in the world! God has commanded us to test the spirits. God is a Spirit. Angels are spirits, both God's angels and those angels working with Satan. There are evil spirits, and even human beings have a spirit. Then there are emotional and physical experiences which we think are spiritual, but they are not.

With all these possibilities we need to obey God and test all things! All spiritual experiences, and the feelings that may accompany them, must be measured by God's Word. Isaiah 8:20 states, "To the law and to the testimony! If they do not speak according to this Word, they have no light in them!"

A common mistake made by many sincere Christians, is to try to reproduce a genuine spiritual experience by reproducing the emotional or physical effects. Let me explain what I mean. A person is in a situation where he honestly responds to the truth of God's Word and the working of the Holy Spirit. He believes, obeys, and surrenders to God. God does a genuine work in his life. In that process he reacts to what God is doing with strong feelings. He may shout for joy, weep, laugh or clap his hands. If he is overwhelmed by deep conviction for sin, or the fear of God (which often happens in revival), he may be unable to sit or stand, and may fall on the floor. Because his experience with God at that time is genuine, the results of that experience are beneficial. Now he wants someone else to have that same beneficial experience with God. So he encourages that person to clap his hands, shout, laugh or fall on the floor. He may even do those things himself, hoping to reproduce the same feelings, and thereby the same experience with God. But that is all backward! He is seeking the effects rather than the cause. We must not seek experiences! We must seek God! If we seek God according to His Word, we will experience God according to God's will, and our own nature.

There are some who will struggle with what I am saying, because they know what happened to them was a true experience. That is, it really did happen! If a person has an experience of any kind, it is a true experience. The question is not then, "Did he have a true experience?" The question is, "What experience did he truly have?" Was it a biblical experience? If not, then it was not an experience of truth, but of error. Is it possible for a genuine Christian to be deceived? Yes it is. He can be deceived by his own human nature. He can be deceived by other people. He can be deceived by Satan or evil spirits. God says we are deceived if we are only hearers and not doers of the Word of God. God says that the man who claims to be without sin is deceived. God says we are deceived if we claim to be pious and cannot control our tongue. Satan is a liar and the father of lies. His chief weapon is deceit. Revival is a time when the Kingdom of God is making great advances. It is also a time when Satan will fight back. He will do everything he can to discredit what God is doing, and to defeat those who have truly been changed by God's power.

Sometimes very sincere Christians have a difficult time discerning the difference between the voice of the Holy Spirit and the voices of evil spirits. For this reason I am including here a chart I put together that has been a help to many.

TEST THE SPIRITS

Dear friends, do not believe every spirit, but test the spirits to see whether they are from God, because many false prophets have gone out into the world (I John 4:1).

Ephesians 4:27, "And do not give the devil a foothold."
Evil Spirits seek to gain ground, or a foothold in a life by deceit.

HOW?

1. By false doctrine—doctrines of demons.

2. By false peace—the deceitfulness of sin—seared conscience.

3. By false guidance—as angels of light—counterfeiting the voice of God.

4. By false guilt—a vague and unreasonable sense of guilt.

5. By false visions and experiences that claim to be from God.

6. By temptations to be rebellious—continued willful yielding to the voice of evil spirits which leads to demonic control and bondage.

HOW CAN I DISTINGUISH BETWEEN THE VOICE OF EVIL SPIRITS AND THE VOICE OF GOD?

Evil Spirits	The Holy Spirit
1. They make us self-conscious or spirit-conscious.	Makes us God-conscious or Christ-conscious.
2. They seek to dominate through feelings and experiences, emotional and physical.	Leads by the Word, a still small voice, circumstances and godly advisers.
3. They accuse through morbid introspection and vague accusations—heaviness.	Convicts clearly of specific sin!

Evil Spirits	The Holy Spirit
4. They are clamorous—seek to hurry us—force us through fear.	Leads us quietly and gently and reasonably.
5. They are inconsistent and changing—seeking to confuse and discredit.	Consistent, steady and unchanging.
6. They are harsh, binding, enslaving. Seek absolute control.	Loving—the Spirit of Liberty and freedom.
7. They seek to make us passive that they render us useless or control us.	Active—co-operation with God.

So—revival is a time of great blessings and great dangers. God is mightily at work among us, but so is Satan. We are not ignorant of his devices. He can appear to be an angel of light. As we seek to bring ourselves into the place where God is morally free to pour out His Spirit upon us, let us be careful not to seek feelings, or depend on feelings, but to seek the face of God, and obey His Word. When God does move in revival power, and we or others may react emotionally or physically, let us be careful not to get our eyes on those experiences, but keep our eyes on God and His Word. Finally, when the wave of revival has diminished, let us not be defeated by trying to regain the feelings of the past, but let us fix our eyes on the Lord and walk by faith in His Word, rather than by our feelings.

Jesus said, "The spirit (our human spirit) is willing, but the flesh is weak." If we are not careful the desires of our hearts (our inner spirit) will be defeated by the flesh. We will find ourselves walking by our feelings rather than by faith. When Peter failed the Lord during Jesus' trial, it was not because he did not have a sincere heart's desire to be true to Christ. His statement that he was ready to die for Christ was genuine. His spirit was indeed willing, but his flesh was weak. Peter shed bitter tears over his failure, and so have some of us done likewise over ours. An incident from the life of a small boy illustrates it well.

This small boy lived in the slum district of a large city. His parents were dead, and he could not remember them. He had been passed around among the relatives, who were all poverty-stricken. He was a burden to them and had never known what it is to be loved.

The time came when he was old enough to go to school. He was sent because it was the law. He started in first grade, and fortunately got a teacher who loved children, and loved to teach them. She took an interest in this boy, who seemed so lonely and unloved. She washed his dirty face, and found some extra clothes for him. She even shared some food at lunch time. Best of all, she helped him learn. And did he learn! He ate up knowledge like he did food, as if he were starved. The result was predictable. He became a top student, and fell madly in love with his teacher. He would have done anything in the world for her. He would have given her anything, but he had nothing to give. So he worked hard and brought joy to her heart by his good grades. However, in the back of his mind he always cherished the thought that some day he would be able to give her a gift.

Then one day his chance came. He was on the way to school, when he saw a large navel orange lying in the ditch. He picked it up, wiped it off on his shirt, and saw that it was in perfect condition. Immediately the thought came—I have a gift for my teacher! How thrilled he was! He began to skip along, shining the orange on his shirt, and thinking how she would look when he gave her the orange.

Now, you have to realize that he had never tasted an orange. He couldn't help but wonder how it would taste. Then he got an idea. He would take his pencil and put a small hole in the top where the stem had been, and see what would happen. Immediately a small bubble of orange juice came out of the hole. He licked it off. He had never tasted anything so good in all his life! How thrilled his teacher would be! Another bubble came up and he licked it also. He kept skipping along thinking of how wonderful it would be to give the orange to his teacher, and licking the juice as it came out. Finally the juice stopped coming. He discovered that more would come if he squeezed the orange just a little. So he continued on his way, squeezing, sucking, and thinking about the wonderful gift he had for the woman he loved! His hands were dirty as usual, so now the orange was sticky and muddy, too.

Presently he arrived at the school. He rushed into his school room and with great delight held out to the woman he loved, a dirty, shrunken mess that had been a beautiful orange! The smile on his face faded as he saw what he had done. He burst into tears and rushed outside, where his teacher found him sobbing as if his heart would break. He had discovered, what you and I have discovered—that the desires of the flesh can rob us of the desires of our hearts! The spirit is willing, but the flesh is weak.

One more thing before we leave this subject. I am not in any sense promoting a Christianity void of emotion. We ought to feel deeply about what God is doing in our lives. We need reality in our experience with God. We should come to know God in a deeply personal way. A cold formal Christianity is not the experience of the people in the New Testament, or those involved in revival in history. The completing of the Scriptures and the passing of the apostles should not change that. If anything, my experience should be more real than theirs! What I am saying, is that those wonderful experiences and feelings must not be mistaken for true spiritual experience with God.

LOVE, HUMAN AND DIVINE

As we continue to look at the healing process involved in revival we come to another area where we will need to learn to walk by faith rather than our feelings. We will need to learn how to walk in the Spirit rather than in the flesh. This is the all-important area of love.

Earlier in this chapter, I told how I had heard people in the midst of revival saying, "I feel like I am walking around knee-deep in love!" Why would they feel that way? First, because God's manifest presence is so intense, and "God is love!" Second, because people are getting right with each other, and that creates an atmosphere of warmth and love. This is all very wonderful. Eventually however, everyone must go back into their own surroundings, where the intensity of that atmosphere may not be so evident. What then? Do we stop loving others because things do not feel the same? Of course not! That is the reason for dealing with this subject next in our chapter on the healing process.

Now, I want to ask a question. Who do you love? You may say, "I love God." Do you love anybody else besides God? You answer, "My spouse and family." Alright, so you love your husband or your wife, and your family. You love your children. You love Uncle Pete and Aunt Susie. Do you love your pastor? I hope so. So, we're talking about these people that we love. And then I hear someone suddenly say, "Well, you know, I really love my new Ford pick-up." Ah yes, is that right? And then some lady says, "I just love my new KitchenAid dishwasher." Then, "You know, I really love barbecued chicken." "I'll tell you what, I love to play hockey!" Or "I love to fish." Do you understand these kinds of things? We do that all the time, don't we? We use the word "love" like that continually. We say we love God, we love our husband or wife, our children, our friends, other people in the church, and we say we love our pick-up, we love our dishwasher, or we love certain kinds of food, or certain kinds of activities. We use the word "love" that way constantly. How do I know I love these persons, these things, these activities. If I were to discuss that with you for a little bit, you would say something like this, "Well, I really like it a lot." Or, "I enjoy it." or "It's fun for me, it gives me pleasure" or "I like to be with that person." What am I really saying about love? **I'm saying that love is a feeling.** Certain people make me **feel** that way. I like to be with some people because of the way they make me feel. I don't like to be with some other people because of the way they make me feel. Is that right? You see, human love, (and that's what we're talking about, natural human love that has nothing to do with God's love), natural human love is a feeling. In fact, natural human love is a feeling I have based on something in the person or the thing or the activity that I love. Something about that person or that activity or that thing affects me a certain way and makes me feel a certain way and therefore I say I love it. It is a feeling. You say, "What's wrong with that?" There's nothing wrong with that. That's fine, that's the way God made us as creatures of feeling. And our natural human love is a feeling. In fact, I'm glad that we have it. It makes life fun. It makes life full of spice and excitement. If we didn't have it, life would be blah. But we have this ability to feel towards people or things or activities, and we call it love.

Love is a feeling. Can I show you that from the Bible? Yes, I can. I want you to see this is true. This is expressed in the Song of Solomon, Chapter 4.

Read verses 1 to 7 about Solomon's love for his bride. This is the Word of God. This is inspired by the Holy Spirit. Solomon is talking about his love for his bride, and he is talking about natural human affection. Everything he says has to do with her. He loves her because of what she is, because of how she acts, how she walks, how she talks, how she looks. He loves her because of what is in her. What is in her makes him feel loving toward her. He says, "There is no flaw in you." What is he saying? Everything he is saying is what she is, and how she looks, and how she acts. And he says, I love you. Do you see that his natural human affection is based on things in her. That is very important!

Now, how does she respond? Look at the Song of Solomon, Chapter 5 and verses 8 to 16. She says, "He is altogether lovely." Now, again, she is speaking about her love for him, but everything she is saying is about him. It's the things in him that affect her and make her love him. That's natural human affection.

I still remember the first time I saw my wife. Do you remember the first time you saw your wife, or your husband? I was a freshman at Bible college and I went into the room of a friend of mine, and there was a picture on his dresser of a beautiful Kentucky gal with golden hair and big brown eyes. I said to him, "Wow, who is that?" and he said, "Down boy, that's my girlfriend!" She was not at our school yet. She went to another Bible college for a while. Finally, in my senior year, she got transferred to my school. I still remember the first time I saw her in the flesh. She was better than the picture. It was just great! I liked everything about her. Do you understand what I'm talking about? I fell in love! I wrote love poems. I was *really* in love. I liked the way she walked, I liked the way she talked, I liked the way she tossed her hair, and I liked the way she laughed. I liked everything about her. To me, she was altogether lovely. She was perfect. And I loved her because of all the things about her. That's fine. That's good. That's the way God created us. There's nothing wrong with that as far as it goes. It just doesn't go far enough. That's the problem. Because of human sin, and because of our fallenness, and because of our imperfections, our natural human love is not adequate for the world in which we live and the pressures under which we live. And if my love is based solely on what is in the other person, what will happen to my love if the other person is not what I thought, or if the other person changes? Everyone changes in some way if they live long enough. There's no way you can avoid that. Once in a while, my wife fusses at me and says, you told me I would never get old. And that's true. But, you see, we change. You may think that boy or girl is perfect now, but I've got news for you, they're not going to stay exactly like that. And some people change dramatically, don't they? Not just in their looks, not just because we get older, not just because we get wrinkles or something. Some people change in their character. Some people change in the way they act. When we first meet them and know them, they seem to love us, and then afterwards, they change in the way they treat us. There are people reading this with broken hearts because of that. And then what happens to our love?

One day, I was reading the *Readers' Digest* and I came across something that shocked me. It was a story about Leola Mae Harmon. She was a U.S. Air Force nurse, 23 years old, strikingly beautiful, married to a handsome Air Force lieutenant. Both were stationed in Alaska on the same station. On her way to work in the surgery section of the hospital one afternoon, at about 2:00 p.m., she came up over a hill on the highway in her Volkswagen Bug. A tractor-trailer truck was coming towards her on her side of the road. Just before they hit head-on, she saw the driver slumped over the wheel. She thought she was dead. She was floating in a sea of whiteness. It was cold all about her. She thought, *this is what death feels like*. And then she heard a voice close by say, "I wonder if she's alive?" She raised her head out of the snow bank where she was lying and left two-thirds of her face in the snow. She was snatched up and rushed to the hospital, where emergency personnel frantically tried to stop the bleeding and save her life. Someone notified her husband, who worked on the base. He came rushing into that emergency room, walked over and looked down at what had been his wife, turned around without a word and walked out of that room and out of her life permanently. "Well," you say, "that's extreme." Yes, it is. Things don't normally happen like that, but it does explain to us what we're talking about. The love that is based solely on the other person has limits. And, therefore, we need a love that is totally different than that kind of love. What we need, is the love of God. We need divine love.

Divine love is exactly opposite from human affection. Natural human love is a feeling I have based on things in the other person. Divine love, however, is not a feeling at all. Divine love is an action, and is not based on anything in the other person. It is based on something in the lover, rather than the beloved. It is based on something in me, rather than something in the other person. A brother in Christ whose life God changed in revival used to stand and face a large congregation and say, "There's nothing you can do to keep me from loving you." That is because the love is based in him, not in the other people to whom he is speaking.

What is this divine love and what is it like? God's Word says, "Let us not love with words or tongue, but with actions and in truth." You see, action is the issue. I want you to look with me in the Bible for God's definition of love, in John 3:16. It is really one of the greatest definitions of divine love in the Bible. "For God so loved the world, that ..." Now you know something's coming. That what? Next is coming either a definition or an illustration or a description of God's love. What is coming is going to define it for us. What is next? "God so loved the world that He gave…"! Isn't *that* interesting. It doesn't say God so loved the world that He felt. "Well," you say, "doesn't God feel toward us?" Yes, He does. He has great compassion for us. His heart is broken for us. But, whenever the Bible talks about God's love for us, it never talks about feeling, it always talks about action. God so loved that He gave … What did He give? "His only begotten Son…" And who is that? That is Jesus. Who really is Jesus, anyway? He is God. Do you believe He is God manifested in the flesh? He is the second person of the divine trinity. God of very God, eternal God, the everlasting Word who came down, focused Himself in a woman's womb and was born into this world with a human nature. But, He is God Himself. And who did God give? He gave Himself! Now do you see the definition of divine love?

Let me give it to you. It could change your life. I'm going to give you a simple definition from John 3:16 and from many other Scriptures. "Divine love is to give myself to another person's legitimate need." I didn't say their wants. Their wants may not be right or proper, but to their legitimate needs.

Divine love is to give myself to another person's legitimate needs. Isn't that what God did? We were lost sinners, helpless and hopeless and damned without God and without hope in the world. God came into our world and gave Himself to our legitimate needs.

That means not only to give myself to the other person's legitimate need—it means to give myself, whether I feel like it or not. Do you know you can love someone you don't like? "How can you love someone you don't like?" Because you can give yourself to their legitimate need even if you don't like them. You say, "Isn't that hypocrisy?" No, it is not. It is obedience to God. It's giving myself. It is asking God to live His life through me. That truth changed my whole life. It changed my whole preaching ministry as a pastor. There have been people in churches I pastored that I didn't like! Do you think that's possible? It's even more possible that there have been people in my churches who didn't like me!

How do you love someone you don't like? Just don't worry about whether you like them or not. Forget that. Commit that to God. That's just your feelings. Don't believe the world's lies! In Jesus' name, give yourself to the legitimate needs of that other person. Do it for Jesus' sake, by faith, give yourself to the legitimate needs of that person. Do you know what can happen then? God can change your feelings. He can enable you to like the person, whom you didn't like, if you love them with God's kind of love, because feelings follow actions!

It means to do it whether I feel like it or not, and whether they do it back or not. Our Scripture text said, "Herein is love, not that we loved God ... but that He loved us and sent His son to be the sacrifice for our sins." God gave Himself to us when we didn't love Him. Let me ask you, has God given Himself for people that will never love Him? Absolutely! Because He shed His blood for the sins of the whole world. Christ died for all men. He died for those who will hear about it, will know about it, will turn their backs on God, will walk away from Him and go to hell and never respond to the love of God. He loves them anyway and gave Himself for them. He didn't wait for them to respond—He just gave. That's divine love.

God wants to teach us that we can give ourselves to the legitimate needs of others, whether we feel like it or not and whether they respond or not. Didn't God feel like giving Himself for me? No. He had compassion on us, His heart was broken for us, but when He knelt in the Garden of Gethsemane, He cried out and said, "Oh My Father, if it be possible, let this cup pass away from me." He did not feel like going to Calvary, He did not feel like dying for us, He just did it! And that's God's kind of love. That's the kind of love God wants us to demonstrate. But now the question arises—who should I love? Why, everyone, of course. No! I cannot love everyone. I don't know everyone, and I can only love people I know. I should love people with real names and addresses. But God knows everybody, and loves them. And God doesn't love people as a mass of humanity, God loves people individually, one at a time, with names and addresses. How do I know that? Because the Bible says it. Jesus loved people that way. "Now, Jesus loved Martha and her sister and Lazarus," as the Scriptures say. And we know where they lived; in Bethlehem. Real people with names and addresses. "He was leaning on Jesus' bosom, one of His disciples whom Jesus loved." That was John. Of the rich young ruler, it says "Jesus beholding him loved him." The Bible has gone to great lengths to show us that God loves each human being individually as a real living person with a name and an address. He knows all about us and He loves us as individuals. God is saying to you and me, we are to love the people in our lives, the people we know, the people around us, the people in our families, the people that are our neighbours, the people we work with, the people in the church, the people with names and addresses that we know. They are the ones to whom we are to give ourselves, in the name of Jesus.

How can I practice divine love? I want to give you three ways. **First, I cannot do it unless I take self to the cross.** My friends, God has pronounced the end of all flesh. He says, "The end of all flesh has come before me." When Jesus died on the cross, in God's mind, we died there in the person of Christ. Paul the Apostle says,

I have been crucified with Christ, nevertheless, I live, yet not I but Christ lives in me, and the life that I now live in the flesh I live by the faith of the Son of God, who loved me and gave Himself for me.

He says again, "Do you not know that as many of you as were baptized into Jesus Christ were baptized into his death?" In fact, that is what the word "baptism" means. It comes from the Greek word *baptismo,* which means to be buried.

When you go down in the water and come back up, you're saying I have been buried with Christ in baptism and resurrected with Him and seated with Him at His right hand. And then Paul says, in that same chapter, "Reckon ye also yourselves to be dead indeed unto sin but alive unto God through Jesus Christ the Lord." We can't love other people with divine love as long as we are filled with self-love. You can be a Christian and be self-centered, with the self that has to have its own way, to be loved, to be treated properly and be preserved. We must take that to the cross and agree with God that it can die with Christ and that we can deny self, pick up the cross and follow Him. Only when we turn away from self-love as the center of our being can God begin to show us how to love other people with divine love.

The second thing is, we can love divinely by the strength and power of the indwelling Holy Spirit. The Word of God says that, "God's love is shed abroad in our hearts by the Holy Spirit, who was given unto us." Yes, the spirit of God comes to live within us and that is God Himself, who is love. Therefore, when we yield to the Holy Spirit and ask Him to fill us and take over our lives, then He strengthens us in our inner man and makes it possible for us to love divinely. And only God, in the fullness of His Holy Spirit, can do that.

We've already talked about the third thing at some length. **We need to choose to give ourselves to the legitimate needs of those in our lives.** How do we do it?

One time a husband came to see his pastor because he realized that he did not love his wife the way he should. After he had shared this problem with his pastor, he asked what he could do. The pastor took him to Ephesians 5 where God says, "husbands, love your wives, even as Christ also loved the church and gave Himself for it." "Oh," he said, "Pastor that's too high a standard. I could never love my wife like that." The pastor said, "Well, let's lower the standard a little bit, then. Jesus said to love your neighbour as yourself and your wife is your closest neighbour, so you should love your wife as yourself." He said, "Pastor, I couldn't do that. I could never measure up to that standard." The pastor said, "In that case we'll lower the standard a little bit more. Jesus said, love your enemies." Please look at that verse with me. It's from Matthew 5:44 and it has a formula for love. "But I say unto you, love your enemies," and here's how, there are three ways. "Bless them that curse you, do good to them that hate you, and pray for them that spitefully use you and persecute you."

Bless them with your mouth, do good to them with your life, and pray for them and not against them. Brother and sister, this will work. We have a tendency to talk against those people we need to love, and to actually curse them with our mouth. I don't mean we use bad language, but we have a tendency to tear them down, tell them how they mistreated us and hurt us. God wants us to bless them. Sometimes we have a tendency to hurt them with our words. Out of the same mouth proceeds blessing and cursing. This ought not to be. God says bless them with your mouth. Say good about them, to them. Next, ask God to show you some way to do good to them. That is, in some way give yourself to their legitimate needs in a practical way. Finally, pray for them. Begin to pray for them on a daily basis. Don't pray for God to judge them or catch up with them or stop them. I've heard some interesting prayers in my time. But pray for God to bless them and to meet their needs.

Frank, a friend of mine, is a wonderful Christian! When he was a very young Christian, there was a restaurant in Akron, Ohio, where we had what we called a common table. Anyone could sit there. We had discipling going on every lunch hour. Five days a week, it took me two hours for my lunch. We had a great time. Frank was one of those who came in there whenever he could for discipling. One day he said, "Pastor, I've really got a problem."

I asked, "What's the problem, Frank?"

He said, "Well, you know I'm a salesman for a large chemical company here, and there's a new salesman who moved into our area from another company. He is going over my territory and calling on my customers. He is telling lies about me and our products, and he's stealing accounts from me. I don't know what to do."

I said, "Frank, you're going to have to love him."

He said, "What?"

I said, "You're going to have to love him."

"Well," he said, "how am I going to do that?"

So I opened my New Testament to Matthew 5:44, and read it to him. I said, "There it is. You've got to bless him with your mouth, do good to him with your life and pray for him."

"Oh," he said, "how am I going to do that?"

I said, "When you come home at night after a hard day's work, you sit down at the dinner table with your wife and children and you're making the dinner hour miserable as you tell all the bad things about this man. Every night you've been fussing and fuming about him."

He said, "Have you been talking to Gladys?"

I said, "No, she hasn't said a word to me. I just know what you're doing."

He said, "That *is* what I'm doing."

I said, "Alright, you need to come home every night and start saying good things about him."

He said, "There isn't a good thing you could say about him."

I said, "You could say he's a good salesman." He grumbled. I said, "You ask God—He'll help you say some good things. Start talking good about that man and then do something good for him."

He said, "What could I do?"

I said, "Why don't you take him out for lunch and share the gospel with him?"

He said, "You're kidding!"

I said, "No, I'm serious. Call him. Invite him out to lunch, and share the gospel with him. You know how to share the gospel."

He said, "Boy, you're serious!"

I said, "No, God is serious. He means business."

He said, "All right. What next?"

I said, "Start to pray for him on a daily basis. Don't pray against him. You've probably been asking God to get rid of him. Don't do that. Start to pray for God to bless him, to bless his marriage, his kids, his family, his home, his health and his business."

He said, "If God blesses his business anymore, I'll be out of business."

I said, "No, God knows more about the chemical business than you do. Just trust God and do what you're supposed to." So he went out and I didn't see Frank for a while. Then he came back in one day all excited.

He said, "Hey, it worked!"

I said, "Tell me, what happened."

He said, "Well, I started doing what you said and for the first week or so, nothing happened. Some of the things just got worse and worse. He stole a major account from me. I just figured that a little bit more and I was finished. But I want to tell you what happened. I kept doing it. I took him out to dinner and I shared the gospel with him. He was astonished. He didn't receive Christ, but he listened."

I said, "Good. Are you praying for him?"

He said, "Yes, every day. But this is what I've got to tell you. This past week, I have done more business than I have done in the last two months all put together!"

I said, "I told you God knew more about the chemical business than you did."

He said, "You can't believe what's been happening. Accounts that I haven't called upon in years, people I just quit calling because they never gave me their orders, they've been calling me and asking me if I would come by and see them."

I said, "Frank, God knows how to work when we find out how to love."

I must share with you one more incident, because it comes right home where we live. I had a young lady call me one day. She said, "Pastor, I have a friend of mine who doesn't come to our church, but they are Christians. They are in real trouble and she wants to know if she can talk to you."

I said, "Sure" I made an appointment with the young lady.

She came in, sat down, and cried for a little bit. Then she said, "I have to tell you what's happening to me. I was married and loved my husband and we had two little girls. My husband got into an affair with someone at the office and left me. He divorced me and married the other woman, leaving me with the two little girls. After a few years, I met a young man who had a similar experience. The woman he loved had left him and married someone else and left him with two little boys. We fell in love. We got married and we thought we'd be happy and have a wonderful home with four lovely children. Then, somebody invited us to a home Bible study and we both got saved. We're in church now and we love the Lord. We want to have a Christian home, but everything's going wrong. I've always thought that I could love any child—I always loved my two little girls and I didn't think I'd have any problem with those two boys, but I can't seem to love those two little boys."

I said, "What's the matter?"

She said, "Well, the oldest boy remembers his mother very well and he screams at me, kicks me, hits me with his fist and shouts 'You're not my mother! I don't have to do as you say and I hate you.' I'm finding that, inside of me, I'm becoming full of resentment and anger toward him. I'm afraid I'm going to get violent with him. The younger boy is starting to copy his older brother and do the same things, and I find that I don't have any mother's love in my heart for them. I'm angry and full of frustration. My husband and I are beginning to quarrel over it, because they are his children. I don't know what I'm going to do."

I said, "Well, to begin with, God doesn't require you to love those two little boys like you love your own two little girls."

She said, "What?"

I said, "God doesn't require you to love those two little boys with a mother's love at this point."

She said, "What does He require?"

I said, "He just requires you to love them with divine love."

She said, "What's that?" And, so, we spent about an hour and I explained it to her. Finally, I gave her an assignment. I said, "This is what you're to do. Once a day, you are to take each one of those children separately—the girls, too, as well as the boys—into a room. Shut the door, get down on your knees, take the child in your arms, hug the child, kiss the child, and say, 'Mommy loves you.' You are to do this once a day with all four children."

She said, "Won't I be a hypocrite?"

I said, "No, because you're not going to love with human love, you're going to love with divine love. If it will help you, just say 'in Jesus' name.' But, you do it." She said she would do it. I set up an appointment for a week later.

One week later, she came into my office with her face shining. She said, "It worked!"

I said, "Wonderful. Tell me."

She said, "I've been doing what you said. Thursday night I was giving the youngest boy a bath. You know how little guys are when you take them out of the tub, all wet and you have them wrapped in the towel. I started kissing his wet shoulders, and all at once, he threw both of his wet arms around my neck. He hugged me so tight he almost choked me, and said, 'Mommy, I love you'."

I said, "What happened to your feelings?"

She said, "I had all the feeling for him I wanted. And then, today at noon, the older boy came running into the house from school. I heard him slam the front door. He came running through the house to the kitchen. All the way through he was shouting, 'Mommy, Mommy, Mommy'. He ran into the kitchen, threw his arms around me, put his face up against me, and said, 'Mommy, I love you'."

And I said, "What about your feelings?"

She said, "I have all the feelings that I will ever need." She had discovered that the world is wrong, totally wrong, when they tell us that if we get our feelings straightened out, our behaviour will straighten out. No—God says to get your behaviour straightened out, and your feelings will straighten out. God can heal our feelings. She found what hundreds of others have found, that human love could be born out of divine love. And that's God's message to us. We must give ourselves to the legitimate needs of those around us, and God will renew our hearts and give us human love to go with it.

THE RENEWING OF THE MIND

The farther we go in the healing process of revival, the more evident it becomes that our thought life is a major area that must be renewed. I will go so far as to say, that if our thought life is not renewed our revival will not last! This is not only true for an individual, but is also true for a congregation. There must be some change in the attitudes and beliefs of a congregation for that group of people to even experience revival at all. Of course, this means a change in the thinking of the individuals who make up that congregation. To come to grips with this issue I want you to look at some very important passages of Scripture with me. Please read Romans 12:1–2, and Ephesians 4:17–24.

Many Christians have memorized Romans 12:1. I have no idea when I first memorized it. I was brought up in a Christian home and was in Church, Sunday School and Youth groups. Somewhere in all that process, I memorized Romans 12:1 and have been able to quote it as long as I can remember quoting Scripture. I did not *learn* Romans

12:2. As the years have gone by and God has worked in my own life and in the lives of others, I have discovered that, if possible, the second verse is more important than the first. And, so, that verse is my text for this subject. It says, "Be transformed by the renewing your mind."

I have never met a true Christian, who did not have down in his heart, a desire to live and walk in the perfect will of God. I have met many Christians who are not doing it, and who know they are not doing it. They may be even in despair because they are not doing it. Maybe their life is full of defeat and sin and problems. They are not living and walking in the perfect will of God, and their heart is full of agony and pain because of it. Sometimes that desire to please God has been covered up by years of failure, things of the world, and all kinds of things that are displeasing to God. Nevertheless, down underneath it all if the person is truly born of God, there is that desire to live and walk in the perfect will of God.

I know if you are a Christian, I am speaking to your heart. But as I speak to your heart, I wonder what your response is. Many Christians know in their heart that this situation exists, yet they go on and on in the same way of defeat. Why? There is certainly more than one reason. But one of the greatest ones, and one of the most important ones, and the one I want to talk about, is because they have never learned how to have their minds renewed. God's Word says that our life is transformed by the renewing of our mind. I'm going to say again that without the renewing of the mind, the life is never transformed! We may be saved, we may be born of God, we may be wanting to live the Christian life, but we never quite make it unless the mind has been renewed.

How does the mind work? God's Word has a great deal to say about the mind. I'm not going to say anything at all that comes out of the behaviour sciences. Everything I say will come out of the Word of God. God made us and He knows how we function. We need to learn how to trust Him and His precious Word.

How does the mind function, and why is it that we cannot control our minds? As we were out there in the world living a life of sin, our minds became filled with all kinds of sinful thought patterns.

Those thought patterns became very deep, and they hold us in very strong bondage. When we come to Christ He has set us free. We have been redeemed. Christ has come to live in our hearts by the Holy Spirit, and yet many discover that their minds are still in bondage.

I want to illustrate this with a story about a man who committed a serious crime and was sentenced to life in prison. After many years of good behaviour, however, he came before the parole board. They looked at everything and decided that he could be released from prison.He had been there many, many years. His whole life had become shaped by the prison life. He got up at the same time every morning, ate at the same time, worked at the same time, went to bed at the same time, wore the same kind of clothes, walked in the same places, and exercised the same. Everything had become routine—his whole life, year after year after year. Now came the time for him to be released. The gate swung open and he walked out. They shut it behind him with a clang, and he stood on the sidewalk a free man. There was a guard walking up on the wall. Over the years he had come to know the guards and they had become friends. The guard called down and said, "Hey, Jack."

"Yes, John."

"Jack, tell me. What's it like to be free?"

He stood there, thought for a moment, and said, "I'm not sure yet. I'll tell you later." He went on, walking down the street towards the boarding house that had been prepared for him. His friends had helped him to get a job and a place to live. When he got to the boarding house, he went down into the basement, and looked around until he found a glass bottle that had a long, thin neck. He put it up on a shelf, saying, "I'm going to find out what it's like to be free." So, every day as he went to work and went about his life activities, he looked for small pieces of wire. Wherever he found one that could go in the bottle, he would pick it up, bring it home, go down to the basement, and drop it down in the bottle. Some of the pieces of wire were straight and stiff, some were soft and curly, some were stringy, some were thick, some were thin, some had rubber on them, some were bare. All kinds of wire. And he kept dropping these little pieces of wire into the bottle. After a while, you can picture what would happen. The bottle began to fill up. It got more and more full until the wire began to get packed tight inside. Finally, he had to push the pieces of wire down into the bottle. He kept pushing and forcing them in. Of course, as they went in they became all intertwined with one another, and they became packed in there more and more tightly. He kept that up as the months went by, until finally, that bottle was so full of wire he could not force one more piece of wire into the bottle. It had been many months. This wire had been imprisoned in that bottle for a long time. He said, "Now, I'm going to see what it's like to be free." So, he laid the bottle down on the floor, took a hammer and, with one blow, shattered the glass into many pieces. Now the wire was free. Or, was it? Some of the pieces of wire jumped right out onto the floor immediately, totally free, just like they were before. But, the vast majority of those pieces of wire were still in the shape of their imprisonment. In fact, the cluster was so much in the shape of the bottle that you could have set it up on its bottom and it would have stood up. Even though, technically, the wires were absolutely free, the reality was that that wire kept the shape of its old bondage. In order to set it free, it was necessary to disentangle each wire, strand by strand. And so, that is how the mind works. When the mind gets into bondage, the Lord may set us free, but unless He performs a miracle of healing on our brains and our deep emotional life, we will find that some of those thought patterns are still there. Those patterns of lust, fear, unbelief, bitterness, and anger may still be there. There are all kinds of thought patterns that have been developed in our lives, and we may find, that even though our freedom in Christ is real, in our personal experience, we are not always free. We are still in bondage. You understand what I'm talking about, don't you?

I didn't have any long life out in the world. I was brought up in a Christian home. I received Christ when I was seven, was preaching when I was seventeen, and I was a pastor of my first church when I was twenty-two. You don't get into too much trouble that way. But I was a sinner, and needed a Saviour. During my first years, I had been in a little country schoolhouse where we had to walk two-and-a-half miles to school for six classes and one teacher. We had very few books. I think we had two shelves of books for a library. I had an insatiable desire to read. So, when I got to high school we were bussed into the city. I went into this high school and walked into the library. Ohhh! There were rows and rows and rows of books. I came to the fiction section and I went absolutely crazy. I went down those rows of books. I started reading, reading, reading—I read everything that came to hand. Even though I was a Christian, and I knew what was right and what was wrong, it never dawned on me that the things that I put into my mind could actually affect my life. Over the years, I filled my mind with all kinds of material that came out of books and magazines. Finally there were TV programs, and on and on. I found myself, as a pastor, born of God, called to preach, trying to lead a congregation, but with a mind that was still in bondage, and that needed to be set free. That's what I want to talk about, because it can happen to us even after we become Christians. If we live many years in the world and in sin before we become Christians, it can be even more difficult. Without the mind being renewed, there is no way there can be complete victory and power and blessing in the Christian life.

There are two words we need to look at in Romans 12:2. The word **transformed** and the word **conformed**. The word **transformed** divides into two pieces—"trans" and "formed." "Trans" means to be changed, and "formed" means shape. So, we're talking about being changed in shape. I don't mean the shape of our bodies. We're talking about the shape of our Christian lives. What God wants to do is take us who have been in sin and change us into the image of Jesus Christ. We need to be renewed in knowledge after the image of Him who created us. God wants to restore us to the image of God, which has been lost. When He talks about being transformed, He's talking about the shape of our lives being totally changed so that our life is reformed, reshaped, in the image of Jesus Christ, our Lord and Saviour. Isn't that what we want? Isn't that what every Christian wants? He wants to be like Christ. And that's what God wants to do for us. So, He says we need to be transformed, but that it can only be done by the renewing of the mind. The reason that so many Christians have such a struggle in getting their life reshaped, and made in the image of Christ, is because their mind has not been renewed.

Why is the mind so important? The mind is so important because everyone thinks. "Oh," you say, "I know some people who don't think." No, you don't. You don't know anybody that doesn't think, they just think differently than you do. But they think. Everybody thinks. I was a pastor in Tuscaloosa, Alabama for a number of years. They have a mental hospital there with 7,000 patients in it. I went to visit someone in my church there one time, and didn't think about picking up a pass at the desk. I just walked in, but I should have gotten a pass, because I couldn't get out. I went to the elevator, all dressed up in my suit and tie, and said, "I'm Reverend Sipley from the Tuscaloosa Alliance Church."

And they said, "Pardon us sir, but there's a lot of people here who think like that." They said, "We even have the president of the United States." And so I had a little difficulty, but eventually I got out.

Yes, we all think. We just think differently. Another thing about our minds is, we think all the time, 24 hours a day. My friends, I want you to know that everything you put into your mind will affect your life, not occasionally, but 24 hours a day, 365 days a year, every year, from now on. Everything that is in your mind will affect and shape your life. That mind keeps functioning when you're asleep. That's why we dream, because the mind functions, all the time. Another thing about the mind that is very important, is that we can do anything in our thoughts. You can go anywhere and do anything in your thoughts. I can stop and think, and in just a moment I can see the Alliance Church in the heart of Tokyo where I preached to three different congregations in one day. I can stop and think, and I can see a little church in Brazil where I preached in a revival crusade. I can still see the demon-possessed man coming down the aisle toward the pulpit while I was preaching.

You see, you can do that in your mind. You can go anywhere, you can do anything in your thoughts. I wonder how many things you have done in your thought life this week that you would be ashamed of if the rest of us were to know? I know I'm speaking to your condition. I really want to help you more than anything in the world. I know what it means to have a mind that is in bondage and hindering me from the blessing of God in my life. And I know what it means to have God set my mind free so that I could serve Him with the mind He has given me. I tell you, God can take a very ordinary mind and He can make it what He wants it to be, if we give it to Him.

The mind is important because what you think will shape your life. As he thinketh in his heart, so is he, says the Word of God. Be not deceived, God is not mocked. For whatsoever a man soweth, that shall he also reap. He that sows to the flesh, will of the flesh reap corruption. He that sows to the spirit, will of the spirit reap life everlasting. What we put into our minds is what we will get out. Garbage in, garbage out.

The mind is very much like a computer. No, that's not right. The computer is like the mind. The human brain is the original. It is part of God's creation. It makes any computer look like nothing. But we see in the computer a picture of what happens in the mind. When I resigned from the church in Regina, I had to get a computer, because suddenly I didn't have all that stuff in the office, and the secretaries to help. So, I had to learn to use the computer. It's a wonderful thing, you know. One day, before I had finished at the church, our minister of music, who was the computer expert in the office, came in. I was complaining to him and I said, "Floyd, the trouble with this computer is, it just won't do what I tell it to do!"

He looked at me with his very friendly smile and said, "Pastor, it does exactly what you tell it to do." And that is what it does. What you put in is what you get out. If you put into that computer that two and two make five, then every time you ask it a mathematical question, you get a wrong answer.

The mind is important because it will absolutely shape your life. It is impossible to live a victorious Christian life and have a mind that is still in bondage to sin. It cannot be done! God has so created us that the mind will absolutely shape our lives. So, it needs to be renewed. I can just imagine someone reading this and saying, "But Brother Sipley, you don't realize *it's not my fault*. I mean, a lot of the things that are in my mind were put in my mind when I was a child. You don't understand the kind of a childhood I had. You had a good childhood with a Christian home, but you don't know how I grew up with all of the filth, sin, insanity, immorality, impurity and violence that was pumped into my mind as a child. Even as a young person, before I ever came to God, there was a lot out there, for which I was not to blame! It was done by other people, and is still a matter of bondage to my mind." Yes, I know that's true. I know it's a very painful and hurtful thing, and my heart goes out to you in compassion. I've heard the stories over and over. But, I do want to say something to you. After you read this chapter, you alone will be responsible for your mind, because you will know how to have it renewed, and it will be up to you to do it.

There was a little boy that was helping his mother. He was down in the basement sweeping the floor. He swept under the sofa in the basement and a mouse ran out. It so happened that the mouse's hole was under there, but the mouse ran out the wrong way, and the little boy was between the mouse and the sofa. So, the mouse ran across the room. The boy chased it. He hit it with the broom, but it was still running. It ran over into the corner and couldn't escape. He hit it again. It ran out into the middle of the room. He caught up with it and hit it again. It couldn't run anymore, so he took the broom and beat that mouse to death. It was what you call overkill. He killed it about five times. When he got through it was a sight! It was smashed and bloody and mangled and horrible. But, he was very proud of what he had done for his mother. So, he grabbed the mouse by the tail and went running up the stairs. When he got to the top of the stairs and the kitchen, he could look straight through into the living room. He could see his mother sitting in a chair there. He ran through the house and into the living room, shouting, "Mother! Mother! look what I've got— look at this mouse. It was down in the basement. I was sweeping the floor, and it ran out from under the sofa. I hit it but it wasn't dead, so I hit it again, and it still wasn't dead, and then… " and then he saw the preacher sitting in the living room. The preacher had come to call on his mother and he didn't realize it. He looked at the preacher, and he looked at his mother, and he looked at the mouse. He said, "and then... and then... the Lord called him home!" The old blaming game. It's not my fault! I'm not to blame for what's in my mind. It's my parents' fault. It's my wife's fault or it's Satan's fault, or it's even God's fault, because, I've asked God to take it away and He won't do it. But God doesn't wish to damage your brain, my friend. God has given us a way to get our minds renewed.

I want to help you understand that way. But first, we need to look at our second word—**conformed**. That word divides into two parts also. The front half is "con," the back half is "formed." "Con" means "like," and "formed," again, means "shaped." So this means "to be shaped like." God says do not be shaped like the world, but have your life reshaped in the image of Christ, by the renewing of your mind. How do we get a life shaped like the world? Our lives become shaped like the world by thinking the thoughts of the world after it. This is true. If we constantly fill our minds with the thoughts of the world, with the entertainment of the world, with the philosophy of the world, with the writings of the world, with their whole view of the world, if we constantly pour that into our minds, then our lives will be shaped like the world. And God says, don't be shaped like the world. Your life is to be reshaped in the image of Christ. How will that happen? To begin with, we must stop thinking the thoughts of the world!

My friend, the first step to having your mind renewed, is to change all the input into your mind. That is something you can do by God's grace. You need to go through your life from one end to the other and change all the input into your mind. You say, "Well my goodness, if I should do that, I'd have to almost stop watching television!" Hmmm... Yes. There isn't much, is there? A few things. I'm not even sure the news is fit to watch anymore. I watch it because I want to know what's going on in the world, so I'm wise to the times. Sometimes, I get so sick of it that my wife will say, "Aren't you going to watch the news tonight?" and I will say, "No, I've had it right up to here. I can't stand any more of their trouble. I've just got to go to bed tonight without it." My friends, when God finally got through to me on this issue, I went through my life. I went through my library. I had me a book burning! "Oh!" You say, "That sounds like the witches in Salem or something!" No, it doesn't. It sounds like the Book of Acts, Chapter 19. That's what it sounds like. In Acts 19, they had a great revival. In that revival, the newly-converted people brought their books and there were about fifty thousand dollars worth of books. That's a lot of books. And they burned them! Here is what it says,

> *Many of those who believed now came and openly confessed their evil deeds. A number who had practiced sorcery brought their books together and burned them publicly. When they calculated the value of the books, the total came to fifty thousand drachmas. In this way the word of the Lord spread widely and grew in power* (Acts 19:18–20).

So, I had a book burning. I went through my library and went through all the magazines. I went through anything I had that was literature. We had a steel barrel out in the back yard. I didn't want to give the books to anybody else. I went through and I burned them. I went though my television viewing and I said to myself, "Alright, it doesn't matter if you never watch television again, you are not going to watch anything that will put the unclean thoughts of the world into your mind." I just cleaned it out. Well, there wasn't much left. I went through my life and totally cleaned up the input. If you're not willing to do that, there isn't anything else I have to say to you that will do you any good. That's the first step. You must clean up the input into your mind. You must get rid of all the garbage that's going into your mind. You may have to do that with music, too. I'm not going to quibble about it. I'm just going to say it flatly. Music full of filth, obscenity, rebellion, and immorality of every kind is not for the Christian mind!

I want you to know that music has a very powerful influence on the mind. If you are determined to listen to that stuff, it is going to shape your life. You know, David said, "He has brought me up out of a pit of noise and set my feet upon a rock and established my goings and he put a new song in my mouth, even praise unto our God." We need to get some new music into our minds and hearts and praise God. So we must clean up all the input into our minds.

The Word of God is very clear on this point. One example is in Psalm 1. It begins like this: "Blessed is the man who does not walk in the counsel of the ungodly." In my generation, thousands of Christians brought up their children by Dr. Spock. They left their Bible closed on the top shelf. We do not need the world to give us advice. We do not need the world to tell us how to live. We do not need the world to tell us how to get our emotions straightened out. They have it all backward. They think if we get our emotions all straightened out our behaviour will change. That never works. God says, if you change your behaviour, your emotions will straighten out. It's exactly opposite. Blessed is the man who does not walk in the counsel of the ungodly. We need to clean up all the input into our minds.

The second thing is, we need to fill our minds with the thoughts of God. Do you want to be like Him? Do you want to be like Christ? How can you do it? By thinking His thoughts after Him. Do you want to be shaped like Him? What do you think will shape your life? If you fill your mind with the things of God, if you fill your mind with the Word of God, if you fill your mind with the beliefs of God, the thoughts of God, you will become godly. If your books are Christian, your programs are Christian, your music is Christian, your conversation is Christian, and your thought life is occupied with the things of God, you will see your life begin to change shape. You say, "Why did the older Christians spend so much time reading the Word of God?" Because the Word of God absolutely changed their lives. Jesus said, "Sanctify them by your truth. Your word is truth." They were changed by filling their minds with the Word of God. We need to change all the input, get rid of the thoughts of the world, and fill our minds with the things of God. As we do it, our lives will begin to change.

Philippians 4:8 says,

Whatsoever things are pure, whatsoever things are true, whatsoever things are lovely, whatsoever things that are of good report, if there be any praise if there be any virtue, think on these things.

We have the mind of Christ available to us. Let this mind be in you which was also in Christ Jesus. The Word of God is full of this doctrine. We simply must fill our minds with the thoughts of God so we will become like him.

I want to deal with one more thing or some of you won't get free. Some of you are reading this book and saying, "Well, I have recognized this long ago. I've recognized that my mind was in bondage. I've asked God to forgive me. I asked God to take the bondage out of my mind and set me free. He hasn't done it and I don't know what to do. I'll be going along, minding my own business, trying to live the Christian life, and suddenly something will trigger that old sinful thought pattern in my mind, and before I know it, my mind is down that old track again, clickety-clack. Away my mind goes down the track of that sinful thought pattern. I suddenly stop and realize what I'm doing and I'm defeated again." What you are dealing with there is a habit. You are dealing with a habit of the mind.

Habits are good things. If we couldn't form habits, you'd still be trying to get dressed this morning. But, you just do it automatically. Did you ever see a baby trying to learn to eat? I was watching the baby of one of our Assistant Pastors. She was a perfect example—she put it right in her hair. It was very interesting. You have a little baby, sitting up there in a highchair. You put some baby food in front of him. The baby takes a spoon and sticks it in the food, and he makes a pass at his mouth. It goes right in his hair. Now he's a little frustrated. He sticks it in again and makes another pass, and it goes down the front of him. Now he's getting angry. So, his mother helps him, and he gets half of it in his mouth. Right? That's how it works. What are they trying to do? They're trying to form a habit. You don't have that problem at all. I mean, you could sit there and just put it right in. You don't even have to look or aim or anything. It goes in so easy. And you could talk a mile a minute and put it in. Habits. You see, they are good things. They are wonderful things, if they are good habits. What if they are sinful habits? That is different. My friends, sinful thought patterns are habits. They are habits that must be changed.

I need to explain something to you that is very important for victory. If you have faced up to your sinful thought life, and have confessed it to God as sin—if you have asked Him to forgive you and cleanse you and set you free, He knows you want to be free, and God accepts what you have said and done as a reality. The next time that your mind automatically starts running down that track, that old sinful thought pattern, you are just doing something automatically by habit, and you never sin automatically. You only sin by choice of the will. So, when your mind starts to automatically run down that track into that sinful pattern of thinking, you are not sinning at that point, you're only being tempted. Your mind will only go so far and a little voice will say, "Uh, uh, you're doing it again." At that point, you have a choice to make. At that point, you have not sinned because you have already confessed and renounced it. It is just a habit. It is not a choice of your will, but now you have a choice to make. As soon as you are conscious of what you are thinking, you stop and face it. If you confess it as sin, you will not get victory. The devil will hold you in bondage. Do not confess it as sin at that point. At that point, you stop and say, no, I refuse to think that thought, in Jesus' name. I'm going to think the thoughts of God. Thank You, Lord, for the victory. Then you turn your thoughts to the things of God. Do you understand that? Temptation is not sin! And you have to deal with this in that way, or you will not get victory. But if you face the fact that you have only been tempted and you are going to stop it right there, you have not sinned. If you choose to continue that thought pattern, after you are totally aware of it, then you begin to sin. Then you must confess it as sin.

You say, "Well, I've done that. I've done it, and I've tried to turn away from that sinful thought pattern, but it came right back. I tried to turn away again. I said, no, I'm not going to think that, and it came right back." Now, if it comes back in that way, you're not only dealing with a habit, you're dealing with the devil. You are dealing with demonic pressure. And you need to deal with it like Jesus did. Do you remember when Jesus was tempted? He fasted 40 days and 40 nights. Afterwards, He was hungry. The devil came to Him and said, "If you are the Son of God, command that these stones be made bread." Jesus said, "It is written man shall not live by bread alone by every word that proceeds out of the mouth of God." The devil came right back again, took Him up on the pinnacle of the Temple and said, "If you're the Son of God, cast yourself down, for it is written He shall give His angels charge over you and they shall bear you up in their hands, lest you dash your foot against a stone." Jesus said, "It is written again you shall not put the Lord your God to the test." Satan took Him up to a high mountain and showed Him all the kingdoms of the world, and their glory, and He said, "All this will I give you if you will fall down and worship for me, for it is mine and I give it to whosoever I will." (You liar! It is not yours, it is God's!) Then Jesus said something you and I need to get. He said, "Satan, Go away, for it is written, you are to worship the Lord your God, and Him only shall you serve." What did Jesus do? Jesus took a passage of Scripture that applied to His particular temptation, and He used that for protection from the attack of Satan.

Let me illustrate to you how this works. Suppose that I have a serious problem with impure thoughts. Those thought patterns have been developed over the years and they are very powerful and very strong. They hold my mind in bondage. I'm constantly finding myself going back to it and it defeats me. But I have confessed it to God, I have asked His forgiveness, have renounced it and I don't want it. God knows that. I'm going along minding my own business, and all at once, something triggers those old thought patterns, just like pushing a button on a computer. And there my mind goes, down that track, thinking those unpure, lustful thoughts again. And all at once I'm aware of it, and I stop, and I say, "No, I'm not going to think that. I have renounced that, and I thank You, Lord for the victory. You have kept me from sinning. I renounce that. I will not think it." You try to turn your mind away and it comes right back. And you try to turn your mind away and it comes right back. Now, what you do is just what Jesus did. You see, one of the names of the devil is Lord of the Flies. Did you ever have a sticky fly bother you in the summer? You shoo him away and he buzzes right back. You shoo him away and he comes right back. Yes, that's what Satan is like. What do you do? Well, you turn on him as if you could see him standing there. Now, if other people are around I wouldn't do this out loud if I were you. I have done it out loud, but I usually do it silently. You turn on Satan and you say (and you can say it silently), *"Satan* (and you're addressing him directly, don't ask God to do it—you do it), *Satan, in Jesus' name* (make sure you use Jesus' name), *Satan, in Jesus' name, you go away for it is written…"* and then pick a little passage of Scripture that applies directly to your temptation. In this instance I would pick Philippians 4:8, just one little phrase: "Whatsoever things are pure, think on these things." So, you turn to Satan and you say, *"Satan, in Jesus' name, you go away, for it is written, 'Whatsoever things are pure, think on these things'. Therefore, Satan, in Jesus' name, you go away."*

Will that work? **It will work!** It is the authority and name of Jesus and it will work! When Jesus said that to the devil, he left! And the angels came and ministered unto Him. If you are having trouble getting him to leave, you just come back and say it two or three times, but I tell you what, Satan will leave. The next time that thought pattern starts in your mind, it won't go nearly as far before you will catch it. The next time, it won't go anywhere near as far before you catch it. After a while, it will be gone from your mind completely, and you will never be bothered with it again. I want you to know God set my mind free over forty years ago, or I wouldn't be writing this book. It's a wonderful thing to have a mind set free by God from bondage. It's a marvelous thing! You can't imagine if you haven't been set free. I want to tell you, this is the way to freedom.

Someone says, "That's not my problem, I have worry and fear." Alright, Philippians 4 is still a good place. Philippians 4:6,7 says,

Be anxious for nothing, but in everything by prayer and supplication with thanksgiving let your request be made known unto God and the peace of God that passes all understanding will keep your hearts and minds in Christ Jesus.

That's a good one, isn't it? Well, then, what would you do? When the old worry patterns come back again, you stop, you say no, and if they come right back again, you turn to Satan and you say, "Satan, in Jesus' name, you go away, for it is written, 'Be anxious for nothing, but in everything by prayer and supplication, let your requests be made known unto God and the peace of God...'" and you quote the Scripture to him and you say, "Therefore, Satan, in Jesus' name, you go away." And he will flee. The Bible says, "Resist the devil and he will flee from you." And God wants us to learn how to do it.

I want to tell you, you can have a mind that is free, renewed, full of God. What will happen is that your life will be transformed. Your *whole* life will be transformed. Maybe not overnight, but it will be transformed and made into the image of Jesus Christ. This is one of the very important healing processes that must take place if the revival in my life and in yours is to last.

CHAPTER TEN

A Challenge to the Leaders of God's People

As I bring this book to a close, I want to end by throwing down a challenge to the leaders of God's people. It is the challenge of a real life lived in this world. To open the story of this life, we will look at the first chapter of Nehemiah, then we will take a look at godly leadership that brings revival to a city. This is a message that I have a certain reluctance in presenting, because as far as I am concerned, it's a message above all things directed to me. Certainly, I believe it's a message to many of you, but I cannot avoid the finger of God pointing directly at me. I have to face the things that I'm going to say with great seriousness, and I want you to know that these truths make me tremble before God. I tremble with the possibility that God would want to bring revival to a city like mine, and somehow I wouldn't be what I should be that He could do that. A terrible thought! I can't stand to think of it, but the possibility is there and, so, it's very serious for me. As a basis for this challenge let us turn to Nehemiah 1:1–11.

To be cupbearer to the king in that day did not mean that you simply tasted the wine before he drank it so he wouldn't get poisoned. That, of course, may be where the custom first originated, but at this point, the cupbearer held a position of great political power, at the right hand of the sovereign, whoever he was, and a position in government. That was the position of Nehemiah in this foreign land, with a pagan king. He was right at the apex of power and wealth and influence. That is our introduction to this great man of God.

I want us to think now about the kind of godly leadership that God needs and wants in order to revive a city. Daniel Webster, the great statesman of other years, was once asked, "Mr. Webster, what is the most sobering, searching thought that ever entered your mind?" Without hesitation, the staunch statesman replied, "My personal accountability to God." Some day, sooner or later, I will stand in the unhindered presence of God, face to face, and give an account to Him. That's serious isn't it? And, any place of leadership we may hold makes it more serious.

The Apostle James stated that teachers of God's Word will give a more strict accounting to God than others (James 3:1). God has warned us, in II Corinthians 10:12, that losing ourselves in the crowd and measuring our lives by those around us is not wise.

I came across a story which possibly represents what many of us, in our day—even Christians who love the Lord—have a tendency to do. An Arab sheik once gave a banquet for his son and invited his friends to share his hospitality, all of them wealthy and powerful men. His one request was that each guest bring a small skin of wine as a contribution to the feast. On the appointed day, when the skins were emptied, it was found, to the mortification of host and guest alike, that they all contained water. Each guest had reasoned that since everyone else would bring wine, he might be able to make a substitution and not be detected.

We sometimes—as God's people, in the midst of His people in the church—say, "Well, everyone else will do the job. Everyone else will pray. Everyone else will give. Everyone else will serve God and be faithful. My little unfaithfulness won't be noticed." And then the whole pot's full of water, because we're not the only ones. How serious! How sad!

So everyone of us shall give account of himself to God, not to others. We're too quick to give account *of* others. One of the things revival does for us is to bring us so close to God, so much face-to-face with Him, that we forget to nit-pick about other Christians. Because everyone of us will give account of himself.

There are all kinds of leaders. Of course, there are pastors like myself whose place of leadership means it is very serious as to what kind of men we are. Then there are elders in the church. There are deacons, leaders of God's people, men who serve on the governing board of the church and give direction and guidance to the people of God. What kind of people they are, is extremely important. There are teachers in the Sunday School. Whether we teach ladies' Bible studies or whether we are a care group leader, it is serious. Whether we serve on committees in the church, or we are on the youth leadership committee with our young people or are youth sponsors, whether we are leaders with the boys' brigade or the girls' organization, or whatever it is, it is deadly serious! On and on it goes. Maybe we are "just parents" ... *Just parents?* **That is the most important leadership place in the world!** That is because the primary unit in God's economy is the home. That's the first unit. Parents are to be godly leaders, because that's the most important leadership place there is.

So, I haven't covered it all, but I want to get us thinking about what a terrible and wonderful thing it is to be a leader in the service of God. What a tragedy it is to fail in that place and bring shame and disgrace on the cause of Christ. I have prayed, many times, *Oh God, do not let me bring shame upon Your people. Take me to heaven and get me out of the way.*

Nehemiah is one of the Bible's most striking examples of godly leadership. This isn't some pretty story that was put in the Bible to inspire us. This is real history. Please look with me at a few characteristics that mark this man, that speak very strongly to me, and I trust will speak to you.

First of all, Nehemiah was a man of intense spirituality. The primary distinguishing factor of this man was his relationship with God—it marked his life totally. What I want to do very quickly is give you a fast walk through the Book of Nehemiah, starting with Chapter 1, Verse 4. I am going to bring out phrase after phrase to show the primary issue in this man's life—his relationship to God.

Here we go. Chapter 1, Verse 4, "he fasted and prayed before the God of heaven." That's the Almighty God, the God who sits on His throne, that we worship as we sing. The majestic God of the Universe. That's the one he prayed to. And in Verse 5, he said, "Oh Lord, God of Heaven, the Great and Terrible God." Do you think of God as the Great and Terrible God? When I think that when I stand before God, I will have no other recourse, it makes me very serious! He's final. There's nobody else to turn to. What He decides about me is final. He is absolute, and this is the God that he is praying to. The Great and Terrible God. Verse 11, "Oh Lord, I beseech Thee." Chapter 2, Verse 4, "so I prayed to the God of Heaven." Verse 8, "the good hand of my God was upon me." Verse 12, "what my God had put in my heart." Verse 18, "I told them of the hand of my God which was upon me." Verse 20, "The God of Heaven, he will prosper us." Chapter 4, Verse 4, "Hear, O our God, for we are despised." Verse 9, "Nevertheless, we made our prayer unto God." Verse 14, "be not afraid of them, remember the Lord, which is great and terrifying." Verse 15, "and God brought their counsel to nothing." Verse 20, "our God shall fight for us." Chapter 5, Verse 9, "shouldn't you walk in the fear of our God?" He's asking a question. Verse 13, "God will shake out every man from his house. All the congregation said Amen and praised the Lord." Verse 15, "I did not do it, because of the fear of God." There are a lot of things we ought not to do because of the fear of God. You see, his life was just saturated with this. Verse 19 of Chapter 5, "think upon me my God, for good, according to all that I have done for this people." I found myself praying that lately. Chapter 6, Verse 9, "now, therefore, O God, strengthen us." Verse 12, "I perceived that God had not sent him." You know, sometimes people come nattering to us and we perceive immediately that God didn't send them. And sometimes we want to know who sent them. It wasn't God.

Chapter 6, Verse 14, "My God, think upon Tobia and Sanbalat." Verse 16, "all our enemies were much cast down for they perceived that this work was wrought of our God." You see that, his mind is full of this. Chapter 7, Verse 5, "and my God put it into my heart." Chapter 13, Verse 9, "I commanded and they cleansed the House of God." Verse 11, "I contented with the rulers and said, why is the House of God forsaken." Verse 14, "remember me, O my God." Verse 22, "remember me, O my God." Verse 27, "shall we transgress against our God." Verse 29, "remember them, O my God." Verse 31, last verse in the book, "remember me, O my God, for good."

This man was saturated with God! See, what made him the leader—it was his intense spirituality, his relationship with God. God filled his thoughts, God filled his life, God was his strength, God was his love, God was his passion. Whatever he did, he did it for God. If he had courage, it was because he trusted in God. Every decision he made was based on his fear of God. And God was there as his vision and his power and his strength and his excitement as his grace and his wisdom and everything he needed. This man walked with God! What a challenge it is to my heart!

It can be very disconcerting to know the Bible well. I have saturated my life with this book from the time I was a little child, and I know so much in it that's not in me. Do any of you know what I'm talking about? I look at the intense spirituality of this man, whom God used to bring revival to an entire city that continued for hundreds of years. And I think, Oh God, who can You use in this city? Can You use me, at all?

Nehemiah was a man of compassion. He wept and mourned before God. He was a man of prayer. He fasted and prayed before God. He was a man of faith. He said, God will prosper us. He was a man of humility. He said, we have sinned, I and my father's house have sinned, with the rest of the people of Israel. He was a man of The Word. He said, remember Your Word, Oh God. So this man was intensely spiritual.

Woodrow Wilson was a great Christian leader of the United States years ago. A man high in political position, but a man who walked also with God, which was very unusual. He was a sincere Christian, not one that took it on his lips only. He spoke these words about preachers and they are worthy of careful consideration for all who are leaders in the work of God. It's interesting to have a man in his position say the following:

> "When I hear some of the things which young men say to men by way of putting the arguments to themselves for going to the ministry, I think they are talking of another profession. Their motive is to do something. You do not have to be anything in particular to be a lawyer; I know, because I've been one for years. You do not have to be anything in particular except maybe a kind hearted man to be a physician. You do not have to be anything, or undergo any strong spiritual change in order to be a merchant. The only profession which consists in being something is the ministry of our Lord and Saviour. And it does not consist of anything else."[1]

I am a prophet, and left to my own devices, I would be a flaming prophet—and very impractical. It's taken years for God to make me practical. The visionary says, "Call down fire from heaven, Lord, and burn them up!" When I started out in the ministry, that was my attitude. Of course, God knocked me flat before He got that out of me. But this man was not only a great man of God, with his intense relationship with God, but he was a man of careful practicality. He was very careful in laying his plans. Very careful about all the details of God's work. In Chapter 3, he devised the system of every family working in their neighbourhood. It's a beautiful, basic plan for revival. And then, in Chapter 4, he devised the scheme of working and warring. I call that the ministry of "The Sword and the Trowel." This was a very practical man. You don't have to leave your brains outside to be a spiritual person. To be a leader that God can honour, you don't have to quit thinking. God wants to take our minds and our gifts, cleanse them in Jesus' precious blood and fill us with the Spirit of God to set them ablaze for Him. Jesus was intensely practical, and the apostles also. All you have to do is study it and you see it. When He fed the crowds with a small portion—a boy's lunch—of fish and bread, He said to the disciples, have the people sit down in groups of fifty. Get it organized. Then He said, everybody take some of the bread and fish, break it and start to pass it out, and God will multiply it. Afterward, He said, collect up what's left—and there were twelve baskets left over. I don't know if they gave one of those big baskets to the little boy to take home or not. If they did, his mother got a shock. Very organized. When Jesus was going to send them out, He sent them out two-by-two and then, later, he sent out another seventy, two-by-two, and gave them careful instructions. He was always very practical. So, godly leadership means not only to be intensely spiritual, but it means to be intensely practical, to think and plan carefully, sensibly and reasonably in the work of God.

Dr. Adam Clark, the great commentator who wrote a commentary on the entire Bible, was a slow worker. That may encourage some of us. He could only produce his wealth of literary treasures by long and patient toil. He therefore made it his custom to rise early every morning. A young preacher, anxious to emulate the distinguished doctor, asked him one day how he managed it; I mean, getting up early in the morning. He said, "Do you pray about it?"

"No," the doctor quietly answered, "I get up." I love that! You don't have to pray about that, all you have to do is set the clock.

D.L. Moody was very much like that. An intensely spiritual man who led great prayer meetings out on the hillside of Moody Bible College. He was intensely spiritual, but he was very practical. They used to tell how once he came upon a group of wealthy American Christians who were having a prayer meeting that God would remove the debt of $500.00 on their church building. "Gentlemen," said Mr. Moody, in his incisive way, "I don't think if I were you that I would trouble the Lord about that matter." What did he mean? He meant, just take a collection here and it's all taken care of. You don't have to pray about that. Just go ahead and give it. You've got it—give it! That's practical.

D.L. Moody was on one of his journeys across the Atlantic Ocean. He was going to hold one of his great crusades in Europe. There was a fire in the hold of the ship. Those were the days when there weren't water pumps to put out fires. So the crew and some volunteers stood in line to pass buckets of water to throw on the fire. They had a bucket brigade. A friend who was part of Mr. Moody's evangelistic group came to him (very spiritual), and said, "Mr. Moody, let us go to the other end of the ship and engage in prayer." Mr. Moody answered, "No, sir, we will stand right here and pass buckets and pray hard all the time." Isn't that good? Very practical!

When Temple Hall in London was built, the masters of the bench ordered a handsome clock to be placed there with an appropriate motto on the face of it. For many days, the skillful mechanic waited for the motto, until, becoming impatient, he made his way to the benchers' chambers and walked right in on them, and pressed for the needed words. One of the masters, becoming angry, rose up and said to the mechanic, "Go about your business!" And there the words are until today. Go about your business! What a good thing to put on the face of a big clock!

There are times when we pray and talk spiritually, and yet God is just wanting us to do some common sense things. Just practical, common sense things, and He gives us the wisdom to do them. To be godly leaders, we need to be practical people.

Nehemiah was a man of inward vision. Look with me, please, at Chapter 2, Verse 12, and Chapter 7, Verse 5. He had just arrived, and was looking over the scene of Jerusalem. In Verse 11, he says,

I went to Jerusalem and after staying there three days, I set out during the night with a few men. I had not told anyone what my God had put in my heart to do for Jerusalem.

Now the city was large and spacious, but there were few people in it and the houses had not yet been rebuilt, so my God put it into my heart to assemble the nobles, the officials, and the common people for registration by family.

Throughout the Book of Nehemiah, many comments bring this strongly into focus. Nehemiah was a man of inward vision. He was a man who inwardly, in his heart, could see what God might do. How God needs to help us with that. He walked around that city and it was a terrible scene. We walk around our city and we get disturbed. Don't we? I do! We see all the sin and the wickedness and the corruption and on and on, you know. I don't need to recount it. You know it's all there. And we can get so discouraged. If this man hadn't had a vision in his heart of what God could do, he'd have never accomplished a thing. The walls were broken down, the gates were burned. The houses hadn't even been rebuilt. People were living in shacks and tents and crumbling buildings. It was a mess! The worship in the Temple had come to a standstill and the priesthood were compromisers and the people had intermarried with the pagans and, oh, read this book. It was a disaster! And yet, this man had a vision in his heart. He would not allow what he could see to dim the vision that God had put in his heart for the city of Jerusalem. In spite of all of the reality of the need and the desolation, the vision of God in his heart was a rebuilt city, a rebuilt wall, a reinstituted Temple worship, the houses built, families living there, everything going on, a City of God; and he had a vision in his heart. And nothing could change it.

My friends, if we're going to be godly leaders, whether it's for our homes or whether it's some other position in the Church of Jesus Christ, we have to have a vision in our hearts of what God can do and keep our eyes upon that vision.

Nehemiah was a man of deep conviction and undaunted courage. We need some conviction. We need to believe some things! And we need to believe them strongly! Now, I don't mean to be born with your mind made up and you can't change. That's not what I'm talking about. We need to be always open to the Word of God and to changing our thinking when we need to, but we need to get some deep convictions established on the things of God where we will not compromise with the world and with sin. This man had deep convictions. Look with me at Chapter 2, Verse 20, "I answered them by saying, the

God of Heaven will give us success." Now, they said, let's help you and he said, I don't want your help; you're ungodly, we don't need your help; the God of Heaven will give us success. He had convictions about what God would do. In Chapter 4, Verse 20, he says at the end of the verse, "…our God will fight for us." Not only will our God give us success, but our God will fight for us!

Let me tell you something about Christian leadership that I learned, years ago, from an older man in the Lord: Don't ever defend yourself. If you do, you'll just have yourself for your defence. Let God defend you. And then you'll have God for your defence." That's fantastic! I want you to know that if you are a servant of the most High God, He can take care of your case.

Look at Chapter 5, Verse 9, talking to the leaders of the people of God. Nehemiah confronts them with these words:

What you are doing is not right. Shouldn't you walk in the fear of our God to avoid the reproach of our gentile enemies? I, my brothers and my men are also lending the people money and grain, but let the exacting of usury stop.

They were charging their brothers interest, who were poor and couldn't pay it. "Give back to them immediately their fields, vineyards, olive groves and houses, also the usury you are charging them, the 100th part of the money, grain, new wine and oil. Give it back now!" And they obeyed. They also agreed to not demand anything from them. Here was a godly leader with convictions. There are times when some of those who are leaders of the people of God do things that are wrong. We need godly leaders with the courage to confront them and say, "that's wrong, you can't do that." That's the kind of man who brings revival to a city.

Look at what it says in Verse 12:

…then I summoned the priests and made the nobles and the officials take an oath to do what they had promised. And I also shook out the folds in my robe and said, in this way, may God shake out of His house and possessions every man who does not keep this

promise. So may such a man be shaken out and emptied. At this, the Lord and the people did what they had promised.

Oh, this was a man of convictions! Please look at Chapter 6, Verse 3, Chapter 13, Verses 7–12, 17–21, 23–28. That whole chapter is fantastic, about a man with convictions.

In a school examination, the examiner put the question, "What is false doctrine?" Up went a little boy's hand and there came this answer, "It's when the doctor gives the wrong stuff to the people who are sick." Well, that's pretty good.

George Whitefield was one of the greatest evangelists that ever lived, who preached, sometimes to crowds of up to 30,000 and 40,000 people outdoors, with a voice that could be heard like a bell. Thousands were converted! He was a great revivalist in the seventeenth and eighteenth century. He was also a great gospel preacher. What he said is this, "I love those that thunder out the Word. The Christian world is in a deep sleep and nothing but a loud voice can awaken it out of its sleep."

Nehemiah was a man of undaunted courage. There's a difference between courage and arrogance, courage and harshness, and between unkindness and having convictions. The courage of your convictions doesn't mean to be ugly or unkind, or condemning, or judgmental, or any of those things. It doesn't mean to be critical and mean. That's not what God wants in godly leaders. But, it does mean to have the courage to stand for the things of God against all opposition. Just remember—one man and God are a majority!

In these days, we need to have courage. This man did some unusual things. He was not only a spiritual leader, but a civil leader, of a civil government. Some of the leaders had compromised, had oppressed their brothers and dishonoured God, He grabbed some of them by their beards, and plucked out their beards and slapped their faces! He got pretty strong.

We have lived in North America for many years in a society which has been marked and influenced by Christian values. We have become very protected and comfortable in our Christianity. We have arrived at a time when God needs leaders who are intensely spiritual, very practical, and have an inner vision of what God desires. Men who have convictions and the courage to stand for the principles of God, and hold true until God comes onto the scene with tremendous power and brings revival. God is looking for men, women, and young people, who will become godly leaders, that He might bring revival to our city.

John and Charles Wesley and George Whitfield lived at the same time, worked together, and led the great revival in those days that changed the whole civilized world of that day. John Wesley said,

> "Give me one hundred men who fear nothing but sin and desire nothing but God, and I care not a straw whether they be clergy or laymen. Such alone will shake the gates of Hell and set up the kingdom of Heaven on Earth."[2]

That's quite a statement! Not Scripture, but said by a great man of God. May God give us such leaders in our day.

David Matthews lived in Wales, and was converted in the Welsh Revival of 1904–1905. The result was that he became an evangelist and traveled around the world in revival ministries. I want to end this book with a paragraph from the beginning of his book, *I Saw The Welsh Revival*:

> "Divine movements have their birthplace in the heart of Deity. But whenever God predisposes the inauguration of a period of blessing intended for the uplift of humanity, his Church in particular, multitudes of his chosen ones throughout the earth, become mysteriously burdened with the birth-pangs of a new era. Intercessions are stained with the crimson of a splendid agony. Undoubtedly, at such a time, God's people pass through their Gethsemane. Throughout the world there are now many thousands of devout Christians yearning passionately for a great spiritual awakening, convinced that only a mighty effusion of the Holy Spirit among the tormented nations can produce the turning point in the history of this distracted planet."[3]

That statement could certainly have been written for our day. I pray those intercessions will increase, until our loving God sees fit to pour upon us such a mighty cataclysm of His Holy Spirit, that the results will not only equal those of the Welsh Revival, but will exceed them beyond our imagination!

APPENDIX A

Forgiveness, Confession and Restitution

by Ralph Sutera

I John 1:9   *If we confess our sins, he is faithful and just to forgive us our sins, and to cleanse us from all unrighteousness.*

James 5:16   *Confess your faults one to another, and pray one for another, that ye may be healed. The effectual fervent prayer of a righteous man availeth much.*

Acts 24:16   *And herein do I exercise myself, to have always a conscience void of offence toward God, and toward men.*

What would make people do such things as place $100.00 in the church offering plate making restitution for a 50-year-old unpaid dentist bill, pay the grocer 99 cents for an unpaid bag of potatoes taken two years previously, return a Master's Degree from University for cheating on examinations, or write to the Prime Minister of Canada enclosing a cheque for unpaid back federal income taxes? ...What makes a person say, "I am having such a wonderful time making things right with God and with others that I can hardly wait for the Lord to reveal something else that needs to be made right! "…It can be explained in NO OTHER WAY except than people who are obsessed by a genuine desire to be TRANSPARENTLY HONEST and TRULY RIGHT with God and before men! They understand clearly that no unconfessed sins or unrighted wrongs are put under the Blood of Christ.

DOES THE BIBLE SAY ANYTHING ABOUT THIS? How far must one go in making restitution? Should a person ask forgiveness and confess sins publicly? To whom should such confession be made, if at all? What about sins committed BEFORE conversion to Christ or things I do not even remember? IS THIS ALL NECESSARY or is that going too far?

One thing is certain! No one can ever hope to experience the fullness of the "peace of God RULING" his heart until these things are made right with God and fellow man. The HORIZONTAL relationship between others must be right, as well as the VERTICAL dimension between God and Man. ONLY as one makes this "horizontal" dimension right is he revealing the true nature of the experience between himself and God.

When the Holy Spirit deals with us, we are made very sensitive to His will and to the wrongs committed against others. There is also an awareness that inward peace results only when such things are dealt with properly. Why talk about having peace WITH GOD if there is not the accompanying PEACE OF GOD ruling your heart and life? (Col. 3:15).

FIRST OF ALL, true forgiveness of sin begins with a deep recognition and godly sorrow over the fact that we have sinned PRIMARILY AGAINST GOD and in His sight! Without true confession and forsaking of sin before God, as revealed in I John 1:0, all confessions and restitution attempts to make right with OTHERS are nothing but "man-made" strivings to bring about what GOD ALONE can do through us. Such will produce the ill-effects that alone can result from humanly-motivated, self-centered efforts to achieve personal justification and vindication. Unless we deal with GOD concerning SIN and SELF in true forgiveness, cleansing and deliverance, there can be NO LASTING restitution between people.

He that covereth his sins shall not prosper: but whoso confesseth and forsaketh them shall have mercy. Happy is the man that feareth alway: but he that hardeneth his heart shall fall into mischief (Prov. 28:13–14).

Notice the heart-cry of the Psalmist David:

Have mercy upon me, O God, according to thy lovingkindness: according unto the multitude of thy tender mercies blot out my transgressions. Wash me thoroughly from mine iniquity, and cleanse me from my sin. For I acknowledge my transgressions: and my sin is ever before me. AGAINST THEE, THEE ONLY, HAVE I SINNED, and done this evil in thy sight: that thou mightest be justified when thou speakest, and be clear when thou judgest! (Ps. 51:1–4).

In the Disciples' Prayer, Jesus reminds us to pray to be forgiven in the same manner "as we forgive our debtors" (Matt. 6:12). Jesus answered St. Peter to forgive one who sinned against him "until seventy times seven" (Matt. 18:21–22). Interestingly, these Verses immediately follow one of the most oft-quoted prayer promises, "For where two or three are gathered together in my name, there am I in the midst of them." Could Christ be saying that there must be honest dealing with confession and forgiveness before we can truly CLAIM His presence for answers to prayer...?

Most of all, the worst damage is done when we live never willing to say, "I'm SORRY and will you PLEASE FORGIVE ME," and accept the same completely from others.

Dealing with confession of sins is a very sensitive matter and must be handled delicately, discreetly, and prayerfully, lest the individuals as well as the cause of Christ be adversely affected. Some simple principles must be followed in the matter of confession. A clear understanding of the KINDS of sins committed will make such a difference. Satan loves to magnify and "glorify" sin. He will do that whenever he can, sometimes to the damaging of marriages, friendships, etc., by indiscreet, unscriptural handling of this potentially glorious exercise in Christian grace.

Your confession MUST ALWAYS BE AND NEEDS ONLY BE as broad as the offense! Never forget this! ...It is therefore necessary to understand the difference between PRIVATE, PUBLIC, and PERSONAL SINS....

PRIVATE SINS...

PRIVATE SINS are when we are at fault, we have offended our brother or our brother is at fault having offended us. In St. Matthew 5:23—24, Christ admonishes us to "leave our gift at the altar" and go first to be reconciled to the brother if WE KNOW HE HAS "ought against us." We are to go to him directly for reconciliation first, and then with clear conscience offer our "gifts" to God, representing service for Him to accept. Interestingly enough, Christ reverses this in Mark 11:25 when he talks about when "we have ought against any" ...That is, my brother has offended me and is at fault. What is my attitude and reaction to be? It is wrong to offend another; but it is also wrong to TAKE OFFENSE! I must have a forgiving spirit toward my offending brother or I cannot expect God to hear and answer my prayers. Christ also refers to the problem of an aggravated offense on the part of one brother against another in Matt. 18:15—18, giving the steps to be taken for such reconciliation. So, PRIVATE or secret sin is to be taken care of PRIVATELY....

PUBLIC SINS...

PUBLIC SINS are when our sin is public, involving or affecting a church congregation, entire group of people, several in a group, an entire family, etc. When it becomes "public" sinning, confession needs to and must be made in public, seeking the forgiveness and restoration of the entire group involved. As one's heart is open and ready to obey, God will give discretion and sound judgment in these matters.

PERSONAL SINS...

PERSONAL SINS have to do with one's own personal sins, committed in the flesh-life and thought-life. Certainly, to harbour unclean lustful habits or thoughts is a sin against God (Matt.

5:27–30). These fiery darts of Satan (Eph. 6:16). may flash through one's mind, but it becomes sin when they are harboured and cherished. This is an area of great danger. Perhaps you have had bad thoughts or even lustful sinful thoughts and feelings about another person. ONLY if you've actually done something to that individual or someone has been directly involved, go to the person involved. But if it has only taken place in YOUR thought-life, it is a sin against God, not against the other person. DON'T DISOBEY GOD in this matter. Confessing such thoughts CREATES other problems. Deal with the right source! One must deal with God on a personal basis concerning any personal fleshly habits. Confession of sin that relates to problems of "personal morality and uncleanness" should not be shared publicly. USE WISDOM!

Thus, if you sinned against God alone, confess to Him alone. If you've sinned against your husband or wife, confess to husband or wife. If you've sinned against another person, go directly to that person. If you've sinned against the whole church, group, or family, go to that church, group, or family and make confession and restitution accordingly. Your confession must always be as broad as your offense. If you are to find full deliverance and reality with God, it CAN NEVER BE LESS BROAD than the scope of your offense! In personal confession and restitution, if at all possible deal "person-to-person" rather than by letter. Though anxious to be "open" in our spirit toward others, do so only as it relates to your "full" restitution, in no way injuring lives or defaming the cause of Jesus Christ. If you have any question about proper action to be taken, consult your spiritual leader before acting. When scriptural principles are followed, no one is offended and the cause of Christ is not adversely affected. GOD IS GLORIFIED!

So little is said about "**restitution**," but **the Bible is not silent on this most important subject.** The word comes from two Latin words meaning "to replace or restore." Restitution is clearly seen in the action of Jacob toward Esau (Gen. 32–39), and vividly illustrated in the story of Jesus and Zacchaeus (Luke 19:1–10). His desire to make things right was SO GREAT that "fourfold" was not too much for him to consider. He simply was anxious to DO ANYTHING to truly be right with his fellow man when he came face to face with Jesus Christ.

It was impossible for the dying thief, who had neither time nor opportunity to do the same in his DYING condition. The Holy Spirit deals faithfully with each individual where he is, and He has given both time and opportunity for YOU to begin to "set your house in order...."

So many professing Christians go through life with such doubt in their hearts, lacking a definite assurance of their salvation because of things in their lives that MUST be righted! The soul will never experience satisfying assurance until all the conditions for that assurance are met. Most complaints of "not having faith" or "not being able to believe" are really just saying, "I WON'T OBEY!" An unwilling spirit to set all things right produces a "problem" in believing. When one implicitly obeys God, he finds little trouble believing. No one needs to force himself to believe. It is as natural as breathing when once a person is willing to OBEY GOD!

Under the old Jewish economy, restitution was practiced because it was COMMANDED by God. "Then it shall be because he hath sinned, and is guilty, that he shall restore that which he took violently away, or the thing which he hath deceitfully gotten, or that which was delivered him to keep, or the lost thing which he found, or all that about which he hath sworn falsely; he shall even restore it in the principal, and shall add the fifth part more thereto, and give it unto him whom it appertaineth, in the day of his trespass offering..." (Lev. 6:4–5. Read also Ex. 22:1–15). Proverbs 6:31 says: "But if he (thief) be found, he shall restore sevenfold: he shall give all the substance of his house." Though not quoted as the pattern for THIS DISPENSATION, these passages show the place given to complete restitution for being right with God in the Old Testament!

People sometimes say, "I don't need to make right what I have wronged before I was converted." If an unconverted man did not make restitution before he came to Christ, he will be willing in his heart and anxious to do so at that time. The Holy Spirit will be faithful in reminding him of the things that he must make right. His obedience to the voice of the Holy Spirit will determine the QUALITY of inner peace and FULL ASSURANCE of forgiveness in his life. We will make full restitution in everything God reveals to us as we are able. When the Spirit of God reveals matters, we must act in obedience or walk in defeat! If the laws on the statue books of all lands cry out to man asking him to make things right or suffer the penalty of those laws, HOW MUCH MORE should God's law demand HONEST AND FULL OBEDIENCE in order to have spiritual victory!

Often people are perplexed about not being able to find the "wronged" party. In such cases, prayerfully consider making payment into the Lord's treasury, with full understanding to make right with the party if found later. Read Numbers 5:5–8 for an Old Testament example. In areas where the New Testament does not clearly indicate a pattern, the overall PRINCIPLES of Scripture can be followed. In doing so, we are giving God the BENEFIT of the doubt! As we seek His will in these matters, God will also give direction as to His desire. In EACH case, OBEY HIS VOICE!

Believers are to "rejoice evermore" (I Thess. 5:16), and not have any doubt about their salvation (Rom. 14:23b; I John. 5:11–13). There are no "rejoicing doubters"! If unconfessed, unforsaken wrongs and sins are harboured in your life, it is clear why you WILL HAVE doubts! Deal honestly before God and man in straightening out the past and kneel at the foot of the Cross in true repentance and obedience. God will give assurance of forgiveness and victory that is beyond words! If doubts return, they are caused by neglect of spiritual duty, unforsaken sins committed, or failure to WALK THE DAILY COMMITTED, SPIRIT-CONTROLLED LIFE! Search your heart....

If in doubt about restitution, VOTE WITH GOD and give Him the "benefit of your doubt." If your Christian life is lived in terms of the "maximum" rather than the "minimum," your obedience to scriptural principles will be the greatest delight of your life! THE GLORY OF GOD will be your biggest obsession! "Whether therefore ye eat, or drink, or whatsoever ye do, do all to the glory of God" (I Cor. 10:31). Study the following references prayerfully as well: II Corinthians 8:21; Ephesians 4:23–32; I Timothy 1:5,19; 3:9, and Hebrews 13:18.

Guidelines for Sharing in Public

Ps. 29:2a; 35:18; 89:1; 105:1-3,5;
107:2,8; 109:30; 111:1-4

1. Sharing Must Exalt Christ—Not Magnify Experiences

Sharing is not a can-you-top-this affair by telling the most super-spectacular experience, but to exalt Christ and bring glory to God. Those with no spectacular things to share have a testimony just as important as others. A greater testimony is to have been spared from what many have experienced (I Chron. 16:27–29; Ps. 34:3; 40:16; I Cor. 1:29–31).

Relate just enough of what happened to you as introduction to the significant thing that resulted in you. What God has done in you as a result of your response is more important than the experience itself. That is what brings glory to *His* name! God is not pleased when you glory in experience rather than in Him (Ps. 21:13; 22:22–23; 71:8, 15–16, 24a; 107:31–32; Is. 49:3; 63:7; Eph. 1:12; II Thess. 1:12).

2. Sharing Is to Edify the Church

Whatever does not build up the entire body should not be spoken. Sharing is joyful—not recounting morbid or unnecessary details (Ps. 40:10; 107:22; I Cor. 1:4–6; Gal. 1:23–34; Eph. 4:29).

3. Sharing Is Not for Questionable Doctrinal Distinctives

If sharing degenerates into doctrinal distinctives unique only to certain people, it will destroy the climate necessary for Christ exalting expression (Rom. 15:5–6; Eph. 4:2–6, 11–16; Phil. 2:2–3, 13–14).

4. Sharing Is Not to Degrade Personalities or Reflect on Anyone's Character

Relate specifically how God met your need without harmful mention of others, even if they were involved (Eph. 4:29–32; Col. 3:12–13; I Pet. 3:8; II Pet. 1:7).

5. Sharing Is Not for Confession of Personal or Private Matters

Matters of personal morality or things to be settled with individuals privately should not be discussed. Expression of thanks can be given without details that could injure others (Ps. 51:3–4; Prov. 16:20–24, 27–28; Eph. 5:12).

6. Sharing Does Not Make People "Holier" than Others

Those speaking are not primarily examples of having arrived spiritually nor are beyond areas of defeat. Public testimony merely suggests a person has opened his heart in positive response to God. Any time he disagrees with God he is walking in defeat in that area. He must make it right, whether or not he shares in public (I Cor. 10:11–13; Gal. 6:3–4, 12; Phil. 3:12–14; I Tim 6:11–12).

7. Be Specific

Unless asked, sharing is not the time for a life story, conversion testimony or previous dealings with God. Stick to the point of what God is doing right now (Ps. 66:16, 20; 105:1–2,5; 126:1-3).

8. Sharing Provides an Opportunity to Express Needs

Glowing testimonies of others should not stop you from expressing deep need or burden. True sharing is not only for people on the glory road of blessing but also to express needs. Minister to these whenever the situation is right to do so (II Cor. 9:14; Gal. 6:2; Eph. 6:18–19; Col. 4:2–3; 4:12; I Tim. 2:1, 2b).

9. No one Monopolizes the Time

Sharing means you give others an opportunity. Don't rob them of the privilege you desire yourself. Be a good listener (Rom. 12:3–5, 10, 16; 15:5–6; Gal. 5:25–26; Eph. 5:21; Phil. 2:2–4).

10. Speak Up So All Can Hear

No one can be edified if he cannot hear. Sharing is vital to the service. Therefore, do not hinder listeners from being blessed (Ps. 81:1; 109:30).

11. Submit to the One in Charge

Meaningful sharing needs a leader. He is responsible to maintain the right climate for all to be blessed and edified. Do not take personal offense if he assists you in getting started or in concluding. If unwilling to submit to the one in charge, do not share (Rom. 12:4–5,10, 16c; Eph. r: 3;5:21; I Thess. 5:12–14; Heb. 13:17).

Reconciliation Guidelines

by Ralph Sutera

Matt. 5:23,24, 6:12, 18:21,
Acts 24:16, 1 Tim. 1:5,19

1. Reconciliation must always be a blessing, never a curse or a burden: What God commands you to do will always end in a blessing. It should not be attempted until you are certain it will bless. TIMING is important. DON'T RUSH RECKLESSLY. We are to EDIFY each other.

2. Reconciliation results in love: It should cause more love for each other than ever before. FULL JOY comes when reconciliation is proper and complete.

3. Reconciliation is a matter of obedience: Don't sin by disobedience and expect God's blessing. Reconciliation evidences to man that a transaction has already been made with God. Be committed to making reconciliation when needed, in GOD'S TIMING.

4. Reconciliation should wait for God to prepare the way: He provides the circumstances to be reconciled. In some situations there is NO DOUBT or question about immediate action. In others GOD needs to take the initiative. Begin by RESTING the case with God. Pray, "Lord, I am personally willing to make reconciliation and will ALLOW THEE to take the initiative in preparing the way." When He does, ACT accordingly. It is just as important that the Lord prepare the other party to receive you, as it is your being willing to go to him. As you are prayerfully tuned to God, He will make it clear. The reception may not always be to YOUR LIKING, but when you move in God's way, it will be the way HE planned to bring about HIS results in HIS timing.

5. Reconciliation provides an opportunity to minister: Often the other party is in need of a bridge over which to cross from his self-centredness into positive obedience to God. Your example and making the move in his direction may free him to honestly face his own need in a way he has desired, but has not been able to fulfill. In some cases merely your moving toward him, "preaches" a powerful and convicting message to his soul, though THAT IS NOT your motivation in going.

6. Reconciliation is always unilateral, always one-sided: Never look for the other person to take the blame, or even share the blame. Reconciliation is specifically a matter of settling MY wrong. It deals only with MY BLAME, MY WRONGNESS in a given matter, and MUST NEVER be related to implicating anyone else in my wrong. It deals with the attitudes of MY own heart that even allow the situation to remain. By understanding MY SOLE RESPONSIBILITY to make reconciliation, I can move straight to the issue and avoid the snare of thinking that I must first establish a delicate "treaty" with the other party. God's work in another life is HIS business, though Satan will tempt me to share God's responsibility. Therefore, leave the other party with God. Do YOUR part. Be assured that if God asks you to do it, He will not only create the circumstances, but HE will also provide the RESOURCES for you to carry it out.

7. Reconciliation is never "IF": It is never preceded by the statement, "IF I have offended you," or "IF I have hurt you." The "Please forgive me IF I have been an offense"-type reconciliation will NEVER SETTLE ANYTHING, or produce the results God desires. If reconciliation deals with MY blame, then it must be that I HAVE offended, hurt, or allowed a bitterness to remain. It then should be, "Please forgive me. I am sorry and ask forgiveness."

8. Reconciliation never guarantees or presumes a right response: At the point you ask forgiveness, you are not responsible or guaranteed a positive, right response. Commit that to God.

9. Reconciliation must always be as broad as the offense, but never need be any broader than the offense: Deal with God alone about private sins of the mind and body. These should never be included in reconciliation. When the other party KNOWS NOTHING about it, DEAL ONLY WITH GOD. Never say, "I have had some bad thoughts about you," or "I RESENTED YOU," or "I have had lustful thoughts toward you and I want you to forgive me." Go to the other party ONLY WHEN he clearly knows about the situation. If you have shared these thoughts or feelings with a third party, let that party know you have made this right with God. GO NO FURTHER UNDER ANY CIRCUMSTANCES. Some have created thoughts in the other person's mind that were not there previously, and "created" a further problem, resulting in continued bitterness and resentment. Private lustful thoughts expressed to the other party could generate these same thoughts in his mind, and precipitate a sinful, immoral relationship. BE VERY CAREFUL.

Though private sins, some people feel strongly that they must say something to the person, EVEN THOUGH it is not necessary, and he knows nothing about it. If you are strongly compelled that this is necessary, always be POSITIVE, speak in LOVE, EDIFY, and make TANGIBLE EXPRESSIONS that confirm your love. Never say, "I am sorry for resenting you, please forgive me." Say something like this, "I just want you to know that God has put so much love in my heart for you, that I have never loved you more than I do right now. There have been times I SHOULD HAVE loved you more, but I thank God for giving me so much love for you now." Follow with tangible acts of kindness that confirm your love. Build him up and bless his life.

Personal sins affecting you and another person must be dealt with on a PERSONAL level alone. Public sins affecting a larger group or an entire church need to be made right on whatever level of people it affects. Always be AS BROAD AS THE OFFENSE, but not any broader.

10. Reconciliation is for the Glory of God: Reconciliation brings glory to God ONLY WHEN it exalts what Christ has done, rather than MAGNIFYING the situation itself. In the light of everything else discussed, personal testimony can be given. It then is not a matter of "hanging out dirty linen in public," but rather an expression of praise to God's glory in deliverance. Others then rejoice by your testimony in that God has performed a MIRACLE, rather than in your elaborating on all the details. ONLY WHEN the glory goes to Jesus will people be blessed and the church edified.

IMPORTANT FINAL WORDS

1. On matters of PERSONAL MORALITY (immorality), BE SURE to consult your minister or another reliable spiritual adviser BEFORE acting in any direction.

2. Never pressure a person to respond. If he is unwilling to forgive, ask him to contact you when he is ready.

3. If the sin occurred BEFORE conversion, deal with whatever THE HOLY SPIRIT REVEALS and IMPRESSES on you. Act only as HE reveals.

4. Aside from matters of PERSONAL MORALITY (immorality), the general rule is to deal person-to-person. If impossible, telephone. Letters should be a last resort.

5. If you have ANY QUESTION about the what, when, how, or EVEN IF reconciliation should be made, CONSULT YOUR MINISTER or reliable spiritual adviser. Don't wish when it is TOO LATE that you had gotten the right advice. You cannot always recover the damage.

Notes

Chapter 2: The Foundation of Scripture

[1] Charles Finney. *Revival Lectures* (Old Tappan, NJ: Fleming H. Revell Company), pp. 5, 6, 7.

Chapter 3: The Foundation of Doctrine

[1] Dr. John R. Rice, *We Can Have Revival Now* (Wheaton, IL: Sword of the Lord Publishers, 1950), pp. 71, 76, 77.

Chapter 4: The Foundation of History

[1] Rice, *We Can Have Revival Now*, p. 78.

[2] Craig Brian Larson, ed., *Illustrations for Preaching and Teaching* (Grand Rapids, MI: Baker Book House, 1993), p. 184.

[3] *Ibid*, p. 159.

Chapter 5: The Foundation of Church History

[1] Robert Hall Glover, *The Progress of Worldwide Missions* (New York, NY: Harper and Brothers Publishers, 1939), p. 44, 45.

[2] *Ibid.*

[3] *Ibid.*

[4] James Burns, *Revivals, Their Laws And Their Leaders* (Grand Rapids, MI: Baker Book House, 1960. Originally published London, England: Hodder and Stoughton, 1909), pp. 78, 79.

[5] *Ibid.*, p. 90.

[6] *Ibid.*, pp. 91, 92.

[7] *Ibid.*, pp. 162, 163.

[8] *Ibid.*, pp. 176, 177.

[9] *Ibid.*, p. 182.

[10] *Ibid.*, p. 188.

[11] *Ibid.*, pp. 190, 191.

[12] *Ibid.*, p. 288.

[13] *Ibid.*

[14] Arnold A. Dallimore, *The Life of George Whitefield, Volume I* (Santa Ana, CA: Cornerstone Books, 1979), p. 73.

[15] *Ibid.*, p. 77.

[16] Burns, *Revivals, Their Laws And Their Leaders*, p. 300.

[17] *Ibid.*, p. 299.

[18] *Ibid.*, p. 301.

[19] *Ibid.*, p. 308.

[20] Dr. John R. Rice, *The Power of Pentecost* (Wheaton, IL: Sword of the Lord Publishers, 1949), pp. 404, 405.

[21] Dr. J. Edwin Orr, "The Role of Prayer in Spiritual Awakening," Address given at a 1976 Concert of Prayer in the United States. Printed form taken from video transcript produced by Keynote Communications, copyright © Campus Crusade for Christ, p. 4.

[22] *Ibid.*, p. 5.

[23] *Ibid.*, pp. 5, 6, 7, 8.

[24] Helen Wessel, ed., *An Autobiography of Charles Finney* (Minneapolis, MN: Bethany House Publishers, 1977), p. 82.

[25] Author's paraphrase from Charles Finney, *Revival Lectures* (Old Tappan, NJ: Fleming H. Revell Company), pp. 219, 220.

[26] Dr. Orr, "The Role of Prayer" 1976 Address transcript, p. 6.

Chapter 6.: The Step of Humbling Ourselves

[1] A.T. Robertson, "From the Bible Today," reprinted by Walter B. Knight in *3000 Illustrations for Christian Service* (Grand Rapids, MI: Wm. B. Eerdman Publishers, 1949), p. 366.

[2] "Bible School Journal" reprinted by Paul Lee Tan in *Encyclopedia of 7700 Illustrations* (Rockville, MD: Assurance Publishers, © 1979; 7th printing, 1984), p. 458.

[3] William Edward Biederwolf, "The Man Who Said He Would," reprinted by Walter B. Knight in *3000 Illustrations for Christian Service*, p. 292.

Chapter 7: The Step of Prayer

[1] Lord Byron, "The Destruction of Sennacherib," *Norton Anthology of Poetry*, Third edition, Alexander W. Allison, ed. (W.W. Norton and Company,), pp. 588, 589.

[2] "God's Revivalist" reprinted by Walter B. Knight in *Knight's Masterbook of New Illustrations* (Grand Rapids: Wm. B. Eerdman Publishers, ©1956; 3rd printing 1961), p. 458.

[3] Dr. S.D. Gordon, *Quiet Talks On Prayer* (New York, NY: Grosset & Dunlap; © 1904 Fleming H. Revell).

[4] Dr. J. Sidlow Baxter, sermon delivered at a C&MA Annual Council. Reprinted in *The Alliance Life* (Colorado Springs, CO: Christian and Missionary Alliance), 1970.

[5] Helen Wessel, ed., *An Autobiography of Charles Finney*, p. 11.

Chapter 8: The Steps of Repentance

[1] United Press Survey, cited by Walter B. Knight, *Knight's Masterbook of New Illustrations*, p. 1638, #7516.

[2] Adapted by author from Paul Lee Tan, *Encyclopedia of 7700 Illustrations*, p. 1639, #7524.

[3] Tan, *Encyclopedia of 7700 Illustrations*, p. 1640, #7528.

[4] Knight, *Knight's Masterbook of New Illustrations,* pp. 603, 604.

[5] Dr. A.W. Tozer, *The Pursuit Of God* (Harrisburg, PA: Christian Publications, 1948), p. 8.

[6] Rice, *The Power of Pentecost,* p. 394.

[7] Frederick William Faber, "Pentecost," *The Christian Book of Mystical Verse,* compiled by A.W. Tozer (Harrisburg, PA: Christian Publications Inc., 1963), p. 27.

[8] Knight, "His Temple," *3000 Illustrations for Christian Service,* p. 351.

[9] Tan, "Moody's Experience," *Encyclopedia of 7700 Illustrations,* p. 555, #2230.

[10] Rice, *The Power of Pentecost,* p. 395.

[11] *Ibid.,* pp. 402, 403.

[12] Dr. F.B. Meyer, "The Overcomer," *Knight's Masterbook of New Illustrations* p. 287.

[13] Helen Wessel, ed., *An Autobiography of Charles Finney,* p. 173.

Chapter 9: The Steps of Healing

[1] Leola Mae Harmon, "Why Me, God?" *Reader's Digest,* October, 1976.

Chapter 10: A Challenge to the Leaders of God's People

[1] Knight, *3000 Illustrations for Christian Service,* p. 522.

[2] Tan, *Encyclopedia of 7700 Illustrations,* p. 1155, #5083.

[3] David Matthews, *I Saw the Welsh Revival* (Jasper, AR: Endtimes Handmaidens Inc.), Introduction.

Selected Bibliography

Baxter, Dr. J. Sidlow. "The Alliance Witness." *The Alliance Life* (Colorado Springs, CO: Christian and Missionary Alliance).

Burns, James. *Revivals, Their Laws And Their Leaders.* (Grand Rapids, MI: Baker Book House, 1960. Originally published London, England: Hodder and Stoughton, 1909).

Robert Hall Glover. *The Progress of Worldwide Missions* (New York, NY: Harper and Brothers Publishers, 1939).

Gordon, Dr. S.D. *Quiet Talks On Prayer* (New York, NY: Grosset & Dunlap; © 1904 Fleming H. Revell).

Knight, Walter B. *3000 Illustrations for Christian Service.* (Grand Rapids: Wm. B. Eerdman Publishers, 1949).

————. *Knight's Masterbook of New Illustrations* (Grand Rapids: Wm. B. Eerdman Publishers, 1961).

Larson, Craig Brian, ed. *Illustrations for Preaching and Teaching* (Grand Rapids, MI: Baker Book House, 1993. Co-published by Christianity Today).

Matthews, David. *I Saw the Welsh Revival.* (Jasper, AR: Endtimes Hand-maidens Inc.).

Orr, Dr. J. Edwin. "The Role of Prayer in Spiritual Awakening." Address given at a 1976 Concert of Prayer in the United States. Printed form taken from transcript of video, "The Role of Prayer." Produced by Keynote Communications, copyright © Campus Crusade for Christ.*

Rice, Dr. John R. *We Can Have Revival Now.* (Wheaton, IL: Sword of the Lord Publishing, 1950.)

———. *The Holy Spirit.* (Wheaton, IL: Sword of the Lord Publishing.)

———. *The Power of Pentecost.* (Wheaton, IL: Sword of the Lord Publishing, 1949.)

Tozer, Dr. A.W. *The Pursuit Of God.* (City: Christian Publications, date of publication not known.)

Helen Wessel, ed., *An Autobiography of Charles Finney* (Minneapolis, MN: Bethany House Publishers, 1977).

---

*The Role of Prayer video featuring J. Edwin Orr is available from Campus Crusade for Christ. Retail price $19.95. Call 1-800-352-8273 or click on www.GOccc.com

For more information or
to order additional copies, please contact:

CANADIAN REVIVAL FELLOWSHIP
Box 584, Regina, SK, Canada S4P 3A3

DATE DUE

#47-0108 Peel Off Pressure Sensitive